# The Governor's Pawns

# INTERPRETING THE CIVIL WAR
*Texts and Contexts*



The **Interpreting the Civil War** series focuses on America's long Civil War era, from the rise of antebellum sectional tensions through Reconstruction.

These studies, which include both critical monographs and edited compilations, bring new social, political, economic, or cultural perspectives to our understanding of sectional tensions, the war years, Reconstruction, and memory. Studies reflect a broad, national perspective; the vantage point of local history; or the direct experiences of individuals through annotated primary source collections.

# The Governor's Pawns

## Hostages and Hostage-Taking in Civil War West Virginia

Randall S. Gooden

The Kent State University Press

*Kent, Ohio*

ISBN 978-1-60635-457-5
Published in the United States of America



Cataloging information for this title is available at the Library of Congress.

27 26 25 24 23 5 4 3 2 1

# Contents

# Acknowledgments

I first became aware of West Virginia's Civil War hostages many years ago as a doctoral student at West Virginia University. I haunted the West Virginia and Regional History Collection (now West Virginia and Regional History Center) at West Virginia University Libraries in those years. My preliminary research for my dissertation took me there, but I also worked summers there under the tutelage of Dr. George Parkinson, curator, and Dr. John Cuthbert, associate curator. These archivists both instructed and inspired me on the range of the archival continuum from initial appreciation and appraisal of materials to their use in research, and much of this work stems from the perspectives they taught.

My work often took me to the papers of West Virginia's first governor, Arthur I. Boreman, and there, among his semiprocessed letters, stood an aging envelope marked "Hostage Letters." One hundred and three pieces of correspondence and attachments told bits of the stories of ordinary West Virginians who were arrested and held by their own state government as hostages for the safe return of other West Virginians whom Confederate soldiers had seized. One case stood out because of the death of the hostage and his family's subsequent lawsuit against the governor. This was the case of Ohio County resident George Buchanon. The case led to a paper for the West Virginia Historical Association, and I thank my adviser and mentor, Dr. Ronald L. Lewis of West Virginia University, for his encouragement to explore the subject and Dr. Charles Bias of Marshall University for publishing the paper in the association's proceedings for 1988.

Other academic pursuits and an eventual career in public history diverted me from research in the hostage letters, but my work as assistant curator/manuscripts curator at the West Virginia and Regional History Collection continued to bring me into contact with the letters and kept my interest in the hostages alive. Archival work there and at Ohio Historical Society and the Georgia Archives heightened my appreciation of the letters as original materials and primary sources, and when I returned to the academic world, my initial interest lay in editing the letters into a documentary edition. As a professor at Clayton State University in Morrow, Georgia, I received support and encouragement from department chairs Dr. R. B. Rosenburg, Dr. E. Joseph Johnson (although he was a professor of French, not a historian), and Dr. Adam Tate and colleague Dr. David Gilbert as I explored the possibilities and introduced the topic at academic conferences. I discussed aspects of the hostage experience at meetings of the Appalachian Studies Association, Georgia Association of Historians, Virginia Forum, Southern Studies Association, and Society of Appalachian Historians and received important guidance and encouragement from Dr. Richard P. Mulcahy of University of Pittsburgh-Titusville and Lou Martin of Chatham University. Clayton State student Susan Smith of Fayetteville, Georgia, gave invaluable preliminary research assistance. Once again, John Cuthbert, provided enthusiastic support as he offered research services and duplication services from the West Virginia and Regional History Center, where he then was director, in coproduction of the edited work. After consultation with the National Historical Publications and Records Commission, however, I became convinced that a narrative book was a better medium for the history of West Virginia's Civil War hostages.

As I embarked on a narrative history of the hostages, Dr. Daniel B. Thorp of Virginia Tech assisted greatly in suggesting an article on the topic and recommending me to the *Smithfield Review*. I appreciate the help of editors Clara B. Cox and Sharon B. Watkins in this opportunity to put a short, general history of hostages and hostage-taking into print.

Shortly afterward, I approached Kent State University Press with a proposal for this book. Acquiring editor William Underwood and then press director Susan Wadsworth-Booth, series editor Dr. Angela M. Zombek, and assistant editor Kat Saunders and the entire staff at Kent State University Press have been very supportive, encouraging, and patient.

As I have researched and written this book, I have drawn extensively on not only my knowledge and skills of Civil War, West Virginia, and Appalachian history and my appreciation of archival media, but I have realized the value of my background in family history and genealogy, a topic any regional archivist encounters but one that I have taught at Clayton State University. Many of the sources that family historians and genealogists use on a regular basis proved useful in researching the very personal history of the hostages and others caught up in the hostage-taking saga. In this realization, I must acknowledge that my formative love of the Civil War, West Virginia, and Appalachia came from my father, Ronald L. Gooden, in the context of family history and community. This fact became very poignant when I discovered in my research that two of my West Virginia great-grandfathers spent time as civilian prisoners of the Confederates. Elza Haddock of Upshur County was held in Staunton, Virginia, for three months after he and two neighbors tried to bring a wounded Union soldier home from captivity in Franklin. Killis Herron of Randolph County was a Union scout who was arrested by the Confederates early in the war for spying. Gen. George B. McClellan tried to gain his release, but misspelled his first name as Quillers. Killis Herron and a young soldier made their escape over the mountains from Staunton five months later in the middle of winter. Their legacy guided my writing about the stark nature of captivity in the Civil War.

Finally, I owe much to my wife and fellow historian, Prof. Stacy A. Gooden of Georgia Military College. All that can be said of family and friends who support historical writing can be said of her. Continuing moral and academic support has been her gift to me, and I hope that I reciprocate.

With this view of its beginnings and progress, I give you *The Governor's Pawns: Hostages and Hostage-Taking in Civil War West Virginia,* and most of all I give you my thanks.

Randall S. Gooden
Griffin, Georgia

# Introduction

On the morning of April 12, 1864, the passage of the Thirteenth Amendment in the Senate dominated the front page of the *Daily Intelligencer* in Wheeling, West Virginia. Deeper in the newspaper, past a commemoration of the third anniversary of Fort Sumter, readers might have seen, toward the bottom of the third page, notice of the death of George Buchanon. The report of Buchanon's death two days earlier seemed offhand, tucked as it was between an announcement of the arrest of a group of "abandoned women" by city police and an advertisement for a merchant in candles, soaps, and lard. After all, death commonly darkened the pages of the newspapers. Just on the page where the *Intelligencer* noted Buchanon's fate, it reported the death of a young servant boy who fell through a passageway on a steamship docked on the Ohio River and the suicide of a young mother who drowned herself in Wheeling Creek.[1] The day before Buchanon died, over thirteen hundred men perished in the Battle of Pleasant Hill in Louisiana.[2] So, the newspaper might be excused for being offhand about Buchanon, but his death was different. Buchanon died as a hostage of the state of West Virginia.

The idea of hostages raises stark thoughts of terrorism, of individual vulnerability, and of uncertainty of friend and foe in gray areas between conventional and guerrilla warfare. Writing for the International Red Cross, Irene Herrmann and Daniel Palmieri described the "haunting figure" of the hostage. "In the annals of the victims of war, hostages occupy a special place," they wrote. "The interest aroused by them is in inverse proportion to their number, for even a single hostage becomes the focus of attention and mobilizes public opinion." The hostage is a haunting figure who draws disproportionate attention because the person could be any one of us. The idea of hostage-taking pulls deep fears from the minds of defenseless people, of people who lack power. The hostage could simply be in the wrong place at the wrong time, have the wrong views—real or perceived—or have the wrong family or friends. Hostage-taking suggests uncontrolled war with a chaos and randomness that could envelop us.

In many ways, the hostage resembled others in captivity, especially during the American Civil War. Soldiers and sailors became prisoners of war. Civilians languished as political prisoners—arrested outright for their beliefs and practices. Then, there were those in the era whose captivity was not a consequence of the war but whose fate hinged on the war. These were the millions of African American slaves, a handful of indentured servants, and the apprentices—mostly orphans and abandoned children—who lived and labored under coercion. These, too, were haunting figures, but there existed an otherness to them. They lived on the fringes of free society, and except for political prisoners, less randomness existed to their captivity. Hostages were unique to war and symbols of its close and inescapable nature.

Herrmann and Palmieri further analyzed hostage-taking and gave four specific reasons for its fascination to society: first, hostage-taking, by its very brutality, holds a strange fascination. Second, a high degree of innocence of the victim—often accentuated by factors such as age, nationality, or profession—underscores the noninvolvement of hostages in the events that brought about their capture. Third, the injustice done to the individual weighs upon the collective subconscious like a latent threat to one and all. Finally, a specter of death hangs over hostages, like George Buchanon. Although he languished in a military prison with hundreds of others, Buchanon's case pointed to the very personal nature of hostage-taking, but as Herrmann and Palmieri noted, the hostage, as an individual, remains a little-known figure.[3]

This book tells the stories of individuals—not only those of hostages but those of their families, their neighbors, military figures, and political players. Each of these people in his or her own way became a hostage to a situation that had been created by secession, the Civil War, and the creation of the new state of West Virginia in a border region of conflicting state political forces as well as national political and military forces. The secession of the South set off a domino effect. The forces of secession caused Virginia to wrestle with its status in the Union and to decide in favor of secession following the attack on Fort Sumter. This decision left pro-Union residents overshadowed by a coalition that joined the issues of the right to own slaves, states' rights, and opposition to calls upon Virginia to support US measures against the Confederacy. In turn, the pro-Union citizenry, concentrated in the western part of the state and fueled by longtime sectionalist feelings, came together over fears of economic disruption from the North and West, opposition to slavery, loyalty to the United States, and resentment of the moves in Richmond that took from them their US citizenship and their rights under its constitution. Military forces of the Confederate States moved into western Virginia in an attempt to protect the region against Union invasion, secure the Baltimore and Ohio Railroad, and quell the pro-Union movement just as that movement formally organized. The much-anticipated Union invasion came, and with its protection, pro-Union Virginians "restored" the state government by declaring the government in Richmond in rebellion and, therefore, illegal. The creation of West Virginia, out of a western portion of the state, exasperated the situation as even some Unionists opposed the splitting of Virginia. Afterward, three governments claimed jurisdiction where one state had existed at the beginning of 1861—the pro-Confederate government in Richmond, which still professed legal control over the entire state; the pro-Union government, which insisted that it was the rightful government for the state outside of West Virginia; and the new government of West Virginia.

While many people firmly favored either the United States or Confederate States or one state government over the other, many others did not hold strong beliefs. So, as a practical matter, they adhered to whichever government held military power in their area at any given time. Even loyalists to the respective sides became subject to the powers in control. This led to extraordinary political and legal measures to capitalize upon military control while it existed and to clandestine reactions to that control. This included the capture of political prisoners, including the arrest of residents for disloyal or suspicious acts, and the taking of hostages to force their release.

Military forces had practiced hostage-taking as far back as the eighth century BCE. During that century the Chinese exchanged hostages to guarantee friendly relations between antagonists. Sometimes, Chinese armies unilaterally took hostages to ensure pacification during negotiations for an armistice or surrender. Dominant powers also held hostages to guarantee the allegiance of a vassal country. Governments also kept hostages from their own military forces or diplomatic delegations when they were sent to the country's borders or beyond to ensure that the main body did not defect.[4]

Western powers also practiced hostage-taking in ancient times. In an exaggeration that pointed to the prevalence of the practice, it was said that Caesar had more hostages than soldiers. Throughout their history, the Romans seized hostages to guarantee good faith during negotiations and adherence to the terms of peace agreements once they were concluded. The Romans learned early that the keeping of hostages caused logistical problems and proved ineffective in preventing opposition.[5]

The Roman practice continued beyond the time of the empire and became a staple in the war powers of the nation-states of Europe. "Ever since antiquity such action has constituted a permissible expedient, as frequent in peacetime as during war," Ellen Hammer and Marina Salvin observed as they reflected upon the history of hostage-taking as European powers battled one another in World War II. In Europe, hostages were taken historically to secure treaties, force the payment of requisitions, to protect or gain the return of people held by the enemy, for reprisals, and to maintain order in occupied territories. The British ended the use of hostages in treaty-making in the eighteenth century, but they were used for the other purposes into the twentieth century.[6]

The European practice spilled over into the American colonies and was used by colonial forces against one another and against Native Americans, who had their own customs regarding hostages. Commenting on hostage-taking between the English and the Powhatan Confederacy soon after the settlement of Jamestown, Owen Stanwood made observations that applied to conflicts among peoples throughout colonial North America. Stanwood wrote in the *Virginia Magazine of History and Biography* that "both peoples commonly took captives in war, and this practice soon became one of the primary ways that colonists and natives built relationships." These relationships involved hostages as guarantors of peace and trade and as emissaries of diplomatic and intercultural communication and understanding. Hostage-taking in the North American colonies affected civilians as often as soldiers and sailors. Often, belligerents prized civilians as hostages. They carried a trace of detachment, if not actual impartiality, from the issues of state and made better intermediaries and subjects of sympathy. Civilians also were less subject to the ever-evolving rules and customs regarding actual prisoners of war as the eighteenth century progressed.

Mostly, authority over the taking of hostages rested with military officers as part of their inherent command authority and with company officials in the case of trade interactions. Nevertheless, colonial governments did recognize hostage-taking. As early as 1655, Virginia's General Assembly set rules for the treatment of children provided as hostages by Native American tribes.[7] Eight years later, the legislature took a more direct role and ordered three Native American tribes in northern Virginia to provide hostages to ensure peace or face full-scale war, but hostage-taking by colonial legislative fiat receded after the seventeenth century.[8]

With the outbreak of the American Revolution, Continental armed forces followed European customs of warfare. George Washington, as commander-in-chief of Continental armed forces, controlled hostage policy. Washington used hostages from among the British and their Native allies for retaliation and to prevent attacks by Native Americans. The Confederation Congress stepped into the arena of hostage-taking policy at war's end. It negotiated the Treaty of Fort Stanwix with the Six Nations in 1784 and required the Native peoples to deliver six hostages to the treaty commissioners to guarantee that the Iroquois released all prisoners taken during the war.[9]

Hostage-taking remained a practice between European Americans and Native Americans in both military and trading relations during the early US national period. David Igler addressed this period in a study of hostage-taking in the American fur trade in the Pacific Northwest. In a comment that applies generally to the practice in nineteenth-century North America, Igler concluded that "taking a hostage was ultimately about resolving a dispute when neither side trusted the other."[10]

The practice of holding hostages became more weaponized in the nineteenth century and was less of a diplomatic measure. The instances of Americans held for ransom in the Barbary States accelerated this, and the War of 1812 brought it to a head. During the war, it rose to the level of national governments. The most infamous case was in the aftermath of the Battle of Queenston Heights in 1812 when James Madison, with congressional approval, engaged in an escalating game of hostage-taking over the disposition of prisoners of war. Such instances of government involvement remained rare, however, and individual commanders continued to wield authority in hostage-taking during the conflicts with Native Americans and in the Mexican War.

Except for occasional legislative action, the custom of hostage-taking had been largely perfunctory since the beginning of US history. The nation adopted Articles of War in 1775, 1776, and 1806, but these made no mention of hostages. The Civil War began with this situation in place, but the Civil War was different. It involved a total mobilization of military and civilian effort. No one was immune from the war. It also pitted two sections of the same country against one another, and the relationships between these similar peoples became complicated as family, social, and economic ties remained intact in spite of political divides. This was particularly the case in the border regions. The lessons learned from the complications of civil war and the advent of total war with its mass mobilization and fast-moving events forced a new codification of war, including the practice of hostage-taking.

The War Department embodied its concept of hostages into General Order No. 100 in 1863. Article 54 stipulated that a "hostage is a person accepted as a pledge for the fulfillment of an agreement concluded between belligerents during the war, or in consequence of a war." It added that "hostages are rare in the present age." Article 55 followed with the admonition that "if a hostage is accepted, he is treated like a prisoner of war, according to rank and condition, as circumstances may admit."[11] Rather than emphasize the right of the US Army to take hostages, the order put written rules in place for hostages for the first time. The earlier US Articles of War in 1775, 1776, and 1806 made no mention of hostages, though the custom informally existed. General Order No. 100 recognized that the Civil War was different. It was a total war, an impersonalized war, which affected the military and civilians alike in very personal ways. Mark E. Neely Jr., in *The Fate of Liberty,* noted that "the practice of taking hostages never seems to have lived up even to the rough standard of justice in General Order No. 100."[12] While Neely observed that the practice of hostage-taking declined after the Lincoln Administration issued General Order No. 100, Webb Garrison maintained in *Civil War Hostages* that the "use of hostages continued throughout the conflict." He suggested that the number of hostages taken is sketchy because of the lack of records.[13]

In regard to West Virginia's hostage experience, it took place on the borders of history, much as the state itself was born in the borders between North and South and East and West in the midst of the Civil War. There, the nineteenth-century hostage practices of conventional armies—imbued with both honor and legal sanction—blended with the shadowy aspects of hostage-taking that became familiar in the twentieth century when it became a starkly unconventional weapon of terror. On the borders between state and federal interests, West Virginia took hostages on its own authority, based on its own laws, ostensibly to gain the return of its captured citizens from Confederate custody, but in practice, hostage-taking became a system of revenge, policing, and even social control. West Virginia's governor, Arthur I. Boreman, with a keen awareness of political as well as security issues, possessed sole authority to execute the state's vaguely written hostage law. Gubernatorial orders for the arrests of hostages came after emotional appeals from residents for action to get family and friends out of Confederate hands. These appeals called for the taking of specific people into state custody as hostages, and the governor, not intimately familiar with every community, depended upon the word of local residents who supported West Virginia and the Union in recommending hostages. Someone needed only to swear an affidavit that a personal enemy or economic or social rival was disloyal in order for that person to be taken away. Communities could band together to rid themselves of criminals, vagrants, the mentally ill, or others who taxed their legal and social tolerance. The law required no other evidence of disloyalty beyond a person's word before a justice of the peace or notary public.

In a sense, the governor himself was a hostage between the very real security concerns and the politics of personal interest that often accompany war in the shady peripheries of place and loyalties. The governor feared the demise of his state. Not only did the Confederate military and the Virginia government in Richmond challenge its right to exist, residents within its own borders and even politicians in Washington, who questioned the constitutionality of its creation, challenged its status. Governor Boreman also feared for his people. For better or worse, the law that allowed for the taking of hostages provided a means for protection. As ill-conceived and poorly written as it was, it was a tool at the governor's disposal for discouraging sedition, for deterring the Confederates from taking West Virginians as political prisoners, and for trying to gain the release of those who were taken.

In the borders of history, Boreman also found himself between his state and the federal government when it came to the hostage issue. While state authority initiated the arrest of hostages, West Virginia depended upon the US military to seize and confine men and women. While the state did not consider federal or military law in authorizing hostages, once they were in custody, General Order No. 100 and the military customs regarding hostages and prisoners of war came into play. This reality plagued Boreman and caused embarrassment for the US government and tensions between West Virginia and the federal government. Not only did a contradiction in laws, rules, and customs exist, West Virginia and the US military differed on the goals of military action in the state. The United States sought to defeat the rebellion and to protect US citizens, their rights, and their property, and West Virginia wanted these things as a part of the United States, but West Virginia's existence and the protection of its pro–West Virginia citizens was of paramount importance to the leaders of the state. These goals mattered to the military only secondarily insofar as they supported the ambitions of the federal government and its army.

The day after the *Wheeling Daily Intelligencer* reported the death of George Buchanon among West Virginia's hostages, its counterpart, the *Wheeling Daily Register*, printed his death notice and added "that the complete history of the case is enough to cause any man to shudder." It promised that it would "endeavor to trace it up."[14] This book endeavors to trace not only the history of Buchanon's case but the story of West Virginia's hostages and their captors together. It examines the pressures and tensions that led to the hostage situation. This includes the political and legal tumult that brought about West Virginia's existence and the security concerns in the months leading up to statehood and afterward, and the hostage law, which these concerns prompted. It portrays the place of Arthur I. Boreman as the first governor, commander in chief of the state's military forces, head of the pro-Union political coalition during the war, and executioner of the hostage law. It explores the place of the hostages themselves in the war, in West Virginia's struggle for existence, and in their communities. It touches upon the lives of the people, in Confederate captivity, for whom the hostages were held. Finally, it takes a look at the family, friends, neighbors, and enemies of the hostages.

To accomplish this, the book opens with a perspective of the state as a whole and takes the reader to a more local and personal point of view. It points to the practice of hostage-taking in West Virginia as more than an isolated occurrence in the conflict between North and South by tracing the antebellum sectional conflicts between eastern and western Virginia which ultimately led to the separation of the two parts of the state in the midst of the Civil War. The book explores geographical differences within the state that caused social and economic rivalries, which later played a part in political arrests and the taking of hostages in retaliation. With secession and the outbreak of the Civil War, the book takes a specific look at western Virginia's breakaway from the rest of the state at the time of secession and the organization of the pro-Union Virginia government in Wheeling. It looks at the security issues spawned by these events, the frustrations of the Wheeling government in trying to protect its leaders and citizens, and how those frustrations led to circumstantial hostage-taking and the eventual codification of hostage-taking into state law early in 1863.

The passage of the hostage law in pro-Union Virginia coincided with the final months in the steps toward the creation of West Virginia, and a paranoia set in among both supporters and opponents of the movement.

Political arrests and retaliatory hostage-taking took place, and as it did, a prominent case involving former congressman, US attorney, and state judge George W. Thompson brought the state at odds with the US War Department and federal court as issues of state versus federal rights surfaced because of the new law.

As the chapters of the book unfold, they explore these events along with the ways in which the new state—West Virginia—made use of the hostage law, which it inherited from Virginia. The modern reader benefits from the papers kept by West Virginia's governor, Arthur I. Boreman, after he assumed office in June 1863. The governor, or his secretary, filed documents related to the state's hostages as "Hostage Letters" and arranged them by county. This arrangement gives a glimpse inside the governor's mind as he dealt with the worries and frustrations of the hostage issue in the middle of all his other concerns about the war and the new state. It shows a regard for the hostages as a separate, pressing matter but also tells us that Boreman viewed each case separately as part of the varied politics and society of the different counties that comprised the state. With the archivist's eye toward value of provenance and original order in the understanding of history, this book proceeds with West Virginia's hostage experience from the governor's perspective as preserved in his papers at West Virginia University. Chronology is regarded in a general sense, but the story of the hostages and their relationship with the governor is told county by county, that is to say, region by region, just as the governor approached it. A timeline in the appendix helps to correlate events in the hostage saga in relation to one another and events in the Civil War and West Virginia statehood.

As Governor Boreman began his dealings with the hostage law, he danced around the issues of state and federal authority and adroitly used the law to enforce his state's existence and power, particularly in the aftermath of the Confederates' Jones-Imboden Raid into the territory of the state just before its birth. The hostage law allowed the governor to use Confederate sympathizers within the state to coerce the release of civilians taken by the Confederate troops. The governor's papers furnish material that leads the reader across the state—beyond the halls of government—to Randolph and Braxton County, from where the Confederates seized Union sympathizers during the raid and from where West Virginia took hostages.

With the governor's papers as a continuing framework, the book progresses to Barbour County in the aftermath of a raid into the Tygarts Valley by Gen. William L. Jackson in the summer of 1863. Governor Boreman viewed his response as an important sign of his new state's power, and the use of hostages for taken Unionists reveals the politics involved in the selection and retention of hostages. This includes the use of prominent and influential people as hostages in order for the state to gain more leverage. But the taking of important people had repercussions upon their communities, and the exclusion of some people as hostages showed race and class prejudices.

Following West Virginia statehood and the consolidation of Union Army efforts in the state in 1863, much of the Confederate effort was confined to guerrilla warfare, and the hostage story goes into the Little Kanawha and Middle Island Creek regions, where partisan fighting frequently included the seizure of pro-Union citizens, which resulted in hostage-taking. Social and regional divisions among the people in these regions determined their sides in the war, and the chapter devoted to this period and this section of the state explores the use of the hostage law for personal revenge. It also examines the practice of local women in pitting the government against its residents, through hostage-taking, for personal and family gain.

The book next highlights unrelenting guerrilla activity and political arrests and resulting hostage situations in peripheral areas of the state from 1863 into 1864. In the region of the South Branch of the Potomac River, east of Allegheny Mountain, pro-Union Virginia and West Virginia legislator Abijah Dolly and other mountain Unionists fell into Confederate hands, and efforts to free them took place not only through hostage-taking but by families who exerted local influence to free loved ones. One result was the intervention of Robert E. Lee himself to free a young Unionist. On the other end of the state, in the lower Kanawha, Guyandotte, and Big Sandy River region, guerrilla raids climaxed in 1864 with the capture of the sheriff of Putnam County, and various hostage cases resulted.

The year 1864 also brought an incident in Morgan County along the Potomac River. In March, Confederate raiders captured men who attended a meeting of the Union League at the county seat Berkeley Springs. These included the county prosecuting attorney and two leading legislators in West Virginia. The book follows the governor's swift response in ordering the taking of hostages, the zealous cooperation of Union commanders in the area—including the taking of hostages from within Virginia, pleas from other Union officers for the kind treatment of specific hostages, and the intercession of the Confederate War Department in ordering the release of the Unionist captives and its order against future arrests of civilians.

The book wraps up with the full story of George Buchanon and his death in the Atheneum. This includes a discussion of the prison and its conditions, the end of hostage-taking, the release of the last hostages, and the closing of the prison. But, the end of the war and of the Atheneum did not close the Buchanon case. His family brought suit, first in state court, then in federal court, for his death. The target was none other than Gov. Arthur I. Boreman.

The court case brought no redress for Buchanon's family, but it did bring finality. It showed the reality of hostage-taking by the state of West Virginia in the Civil War. It made clear the political and social verdict of short-term history. Still, there is a long-term historical verdict to be rendered. That is the purpose of this book. By its end, the reader will know the "haunting figure" but will also know of a state and its people who were held hostage by the events and circumstances of their time.

CHAPTER 1

# The Roots of Division and Animosity in Virginia and West Virginia, 1787–1861

West Virginia shared many experiences with other states in the turmoil of the Civil War. This was particularly true of states where divided populations not only fought opposing military forces but strived with one another for political control. States that bordered the North and the South fit into these categories.

In Kentucky, efforts toward mediation before the outbreak of war turned to precarious neutrality once the war began. Gov. Beriah Magoffin favored the South, but Unionists dominated the legislature and generally held sway in the state. The legislature refused to call a convention on secession, but a grassroots convention in November 1861 declared that Kentucky had seceded. It created a provisional state government with allegiance to the Confederate States, but that government was a mere shadow. Governor Magoffin's power waned, and he resigned in August 1862.[1]

On the opposite border of the future state of West Virginia, Maryland's pro-Union Gov. Thomas Hicks staved off secession early in 1861 by refusing to call the Southern-leaning state legislature into special session, thus keeping a convention from being called. Pressures eventually compelled the governor to call for a legislative session, but the heat of secession had cooled. Legislators declined to call for a convention or to sanction secession; they also voiced opposition to the federal government's use of force against the seceded states. In June, Unionists took all six of Maryland's congressional seats, and the election of a hardline Unionist governor in the fall all but ended Confederate activism in the state.[2]

Far to the west, Missouri experienced bitter strife from the beginning of the secession crisis through the Civil War. Pro-Confederate elements—including the lieutenant governor and the majority of the state legislature—rallied behind Gov. Claiborne Fox Jackson. Congressman Francis P. Blair Jr. led Missouri's Unionists, and Unionists dominated a convention called to consider secession. With the outbreak of warfare, Jackson refused Abraham Lincoln's calls for troops, brought the St. Louis Police under his control, and called out pro-Confederate units of the militia. Union forces went on the offensive and took conventional control of most of the state. Pro-Confederate Missourians resorted to a prolonged guerrilla warfare. The governor and legislature fled Jefferson City and met elsewhere. They eventually approved secession, but could not effectively exercise it, left the state entirely, and weakly attempted to govern in exile. The state convention—originally convened to consider secession—reassembled and authorized a pro-Union, provisional government.[3]

These states, and those where occupying Union forces established government over civilians, struggled with sedition and other security problems and took extraordinary measures to limit the freedom of civilian adversaries, even resorting to imprisonment. This included the taking of hostages. As early as May 1862, Andrew Johnson, as military governor of Tennessee, authorized the taking of hostages "in every instance in which a Union man is arrested and maltreated by the marauding bands."[4]

The experiences of the people of these states were similar to those of the people of West Virginia (both before and after its creation as a state) in the conflicts over secession and loyalties to the United States and Confederate States and even in loyalties to rival state governments. West Virginia's history differed from other states, however. First, much of its animosity had roots reaching beyond the secession crisis into Virginia's past. Second, its very existence as a state came about because of the Civil War. Its legitimacy and permanence—not just the outcome of the conflict between North and South—depended upon its government's ability to assert authority and provide security.

The roots of Virginia's internal animosity during the secession crisis and the Civil War clung to sectionalism. The classic historian of Virginia sectionalism, Charles H. Ambler, wrote, "The history of Virginia has been characterized by sectional antagonism."[5] Virginia was not unique in experiencing sectional tumult during the late eighteenth and early nineteenth centuries. Throughout the country, increasing populations in newly settled areas challenged the status quo, which favored the long-settled regions of states. Yet, Virginia's geography and its interplay with politics, culture, and economics were unique. Situated on the borders of the North and straddling the East and West, Virginia experienced tensions within its borders between North and South and East and West and compressions in reaction to them.

Dr. Ambler referred to the East-West tensions when he wrote, "The natural features of her territory and the different elements of her population made such conflicts inevitable."[6] Going east to west, the state had four primary regions before the Civil War—the Tidewater, the Piedmont, the Shenandoah Valley, and the Trans-Allegheny region, which eventually comprised most of West Virginia. A frontier nature and comparative isolation from the rest of the state characterized the Trans-Allegheny counties through much of their early history. The Allegheny and Blue Ridge Mountains largely determined this East-West sectionalism. The Blue Ridge defined the Shenandoah Valley, and the Alleghenies set apart the Trans-Allegheny section farther to the west. The mountain ranges formed walls, which slowed westward migration and development, and once areas west of the mountains became populated, the mountains separated the people in the eastern and western sections. Those people developed shared social and cultural traits with others in their sections as they experienced common challenges from the environment and geography and at the same time had limited cultural interactions from other sections.

The mountains not only created cultural separations, but they created geographic separations that gave the different sections of Virginia diverse economic resources, leading to differences in economic development. New agricultural pursuits and industrial interests in the West contrasted with and even rivaled the tobacco-centric economy of the Piedmont and Tidewater. Western farmers produced livestock, hay, and grain, and natural resources gave birth to flourishing, iron, salt, timber and lumber, charcoal, and coal industries. The mountain barriers directed much of western commerce toward the Ohio and Potomac transportation corridors—and Maryland, Ohio, and Pennsylvania—rather than the James, Rappahannock, and York rivers. Sectional social and economic differences led to different political demands from state government and inevitably to political differences and rivalries.

In modern terms, the Shenandoah Valley (along with the Blue Ridge Mountains) and Trans-Allegheny regions are in the area known as Appalachia. Jonathan Dean Sarris, in *A Separate Civil War: Communities in Conflict in the Mountain South,* captured the sectionalism that separated mountain regions from others in the same states and the nation as a whole. "Perhaps no region of the United States has been so misunderstood and misrepresented as the Southern mountain lands known collectively as Appalachia," he wrote.[7] Misunderstanding and misrepresentation characterized the relationship between Appalachian Virginia and the more mainstream, eastern parts of the state throughout the antebellum period and fractured the relationship between the eastern and western counties during the Civil War. Importantly, though, they also affected affairs within West Virginia, once it was created, between the relatively cosmopolitan Ohio River cities and towns and the more mountainous areas of the state.

Differences and rivalries between the Tidewater and Piedmont and the Shenandoah Valley and Trans-Allegheny regions arose almost as soon as settlement occurred on the western frontiers. As early as Virginia's convention to ratify the Constitution in 1787, debates indicate sectional divides as delegates from the West tended to favor a strong central government to protect the frontier, land rights, and trade rights in the interior. The tumult of the Whiskey Rebellion also drew attention to stark differences between the eastern counties and those west of the mountains.

As the nineteenth century dawned, sectional rhetoric between the East and West increased as differences over banking policy, legislative apportionment, funding of internal improvements, land policy, taxation, and suffrage rights expanded. Western newspaper editors, lawyers, clergy, and educators increasingly joined in calls for political and economic reform in Virginia. Westerners generally felt that the dominant political leaders in the East wanted to stifle the industrialization and agricultural diversification that distinguished their section from most of the East and its lingering focus on a plantation economy and its social and political institutions. Westerners believed that the deliberate goal was to curb the growth of western political power, but the economic nature of the divide also brought class into play. This came about as the planter-dominated upper classes opposed the extension of political rights to those who did not own property and as they discouraged the upward mobility that accompanied economic diversity.[8] Unrest—sectional and class—led to the organization of reform conventions following the War of 1812. In 1816, local meetings in Harrisonburg and Winchester in the Shenandoah Valley gave the momentum for a general convention in Staunton—farther up the valley. There, delegates—largely from the valley and the Trans-Allegheny counties—met and petitioned the legislature to call a constitutional convention, but compromises in the legislature over legislative apportionment tempered the call for a convention.

William C. Davis and James I. Robertson Jr. prefaced *Virginia at War, 1861* with the observation that Virginia's sectional crisis "grew in intensity after 1820" but added that the state's leaders "increasingly sought ways to mediate between the antagonistic sections."[9] The intensity led to a second convention in Staunton—again dominated by delegates from western counties—and a new call for a constitutional convention. In the democratic atmosphere that swept the nation during the era, the Staunton Convention echoed complaints about lack of direct representation in state and local government, which it specifically applied to Virginia. It expressed its "opinion" that disproportional representation in the lower house of the state legislature was "gross" enough by itself to warrant revision of the constitution; that the cloistered, unrepresentative, and authoritative executive council should be abolished; that an independent judiciary should be created; and that suffrage should be extended to all free, white males over the age of twenty-one who could prove that they had "common interest with and attachment to the community."[10]

The legislature eventually answered the calls for constitutional reform by calling a convention in 1829. Attended by such luminaries as James Madison, James Monroe, John Marshall, and John Tyler, the convention started out with strong prospects for significant reforms in legislative apportionment as moderates seriously studied change. In efforts to "mediate," however, the moderates disappointed the West in supporting only mild changes. Westerners had sought reapportionment based on the white population, but the convention adopted a slightly revised formula based on both the white and African American population instead. This formula benefited areas of the state with large slave populations. In the matter of suffrage, westerners were not alone in advocating universal, white, male suffrage. Proponents of direct democracy from throughout the state supported it. The convention instead adopted a compromise that broadened suffrage from freeholders to all white, male, heads of households. Westerners, and to some extent delegates from along the Potomac River, pushed back against compromise and hinted at an East-West split of the state. Moderates decried such talk, and the new constitution passed the convention by fourteen votes. Delegates from the Piedmont and Tidewater nearly all voted in favor of it. Notable exceptions came from Campbell, Fairfax, Loudoun, and Spotsylvania Counties. Almost every delegate from the Shenandoah Valley and

The ninety-six delegates to Virginia's constitutional convention in 1829 and 1830 included former presidents James Madison and James Monroe, as well as future president John Tyler and Chief Justice John Marshall. (George Catlin, *Painting of the Virginia Constitutional Convention,* West Virginia and Regional History Center, West Virginia University Libraries, Morgantown, WV)

every one from the upper James and Potomac River regions and the Trans-Allegheny and southwestern Virginia voted against the constitution. When presented to the voters, the constitution won approval with the Piedmont and Tidewater united in favor of it (with the interesting exception of Lancaster County at the mouth of the Rappahannock River). The Shenandoah Valley and upper James swung their support toward the Constitution, and the upper Potomac and Southwestern Virginia split. The Trans-Allegheny region stood solidly against the new constitution.[11]

The results of the vote in the ratification of the 1830 constitution indicate a sectional realignment in western Virginia. During the eighteenth and early nineteenth centuries, the Shenandoah Valley and the Trans-Allegheny regions shared a political and cultural affinity with one another. As the nineteenth century progressed, however, the far western counties formed increasing economic ties with the Ohio Valley states. Meanwhile, the Shenandoah Valley became more aligned politically and commercially with the Piedmont and Tidewater. The new constitution enhanced this realignment as it gave greater legislative representation to the Shenandoah Valley and nearby areas of the Piedmont.[12]

Many observers noted that the 1830 constitution fostered East-West sectionalism rather than alleviated it. Even newspapers in the East expressed concern about this situation. "The State is laid off into four great divisions, each supposed to have distinctive features, with different interests," acknowledged the *Richmond Enquirer*. "Each is to have a fixed representation, and thereby to be kept separate and distinct by imaginary or geographical boundaries, through all time."[13]

"The trans-Alleghenny region refused to be reconciled to the constitution of 1829," wrote the historian James Morton Callahan. In a haunting allusion to the extremes of the sectional controversy, he added that the people of the region "continued to talk dismemberment."[14] Indeed, popular agitation continued through local protests and newspaper editorials and included calls for secession of the western counties from Virginia.

The issue of slavery increasingly contributed to the East-West divide. Before the adoption of the 1830 constitution, the matter involved differences in the appraisal of slaves for property taxation compared to other property and the use of slaves in determining population for legislative apportionment. During the constitutional convention, the subject of ending slavery emerged from debates over taxation and representation on the basis of white population; easterners inferred that the end of the consideration of the slave population in legislative apportionment and the end of tax breaks for slave property would lead to the end of slavery in the state. These inferences led to abstract discussions of emancipation. In writing about the subject in this era, Charles H. Ambler explained that "discussions in the constitutional convention of 1829–30 and the abolition agitation caused the question of negro slavery to assume an alarming sectional aspect in this period," and that portions of the East began to defend slavery as a "divinely sanctioned institution and the only practical means of dealing with an inferior race." By contrast, Ambler wrote that westerners "became more grounded in the conviction that slavery was an economic evil, and consequently continued to favor gradual emancipation and deportation." Ambler contended that few immediate abolitionists existed among the people of western Virginia.[15]

Right on the heels of the constitutional convention, two events further expanded the discussions of slavery. These were the end of slavery in the British Empire in 1830 and, closer to home, the Nat Turner insurrection in 1831. Both heightened fears of increased efforts to force abolition and of slave uprisings and brought questions of the wisdom and practicality

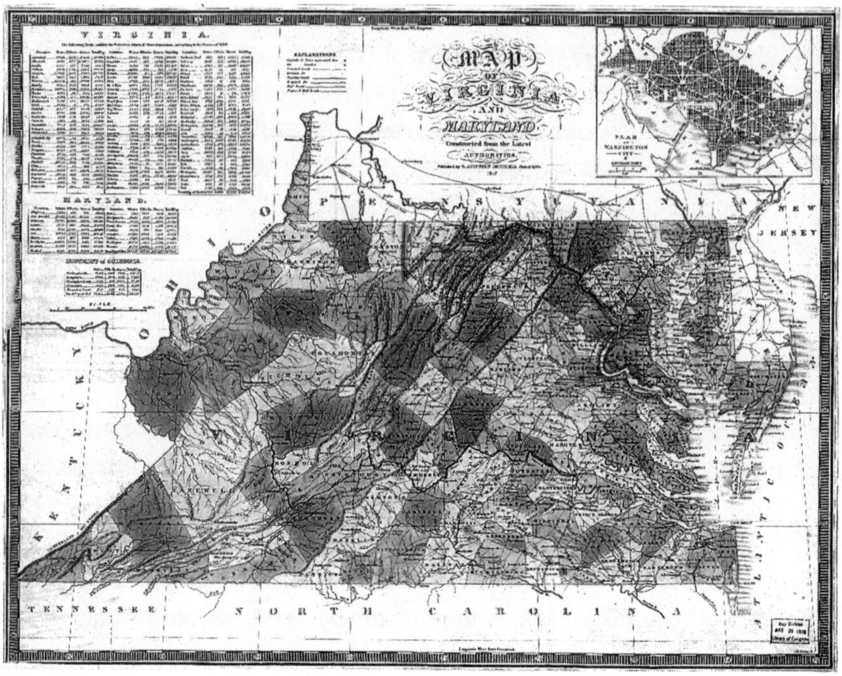


Virginia as it appeared just after the Constitutional Convention of 1829–30. (S. Augustus Mitchell, and J. H. Young. Map of Virginia and Maryland, constructed from the latest authorities. Philadelphia: Published by S. Augustus Mitchell, 1832. Map. https://www.loc.gov/item/2012593331/)

of slavery in Virginia. Citizen petitions in support of slavery and against it flooded the Virginia General Assembly in 1831 and 1832. In addressing legislators, the governor denounced abolitionism, favored stricter slave codes, and called for the removal of free African Americans from Virginia while withholding his personal views in support of gradual emancipation or a ban on slavery west of the Blue Ridge Mountains. Lively debate followed in the lower chamber of the legislature, the House of Delegates.[16]

"The general tone in the argument of the western delegates in 1831–32 was quite different from what it had been in the constitutional convention of 1829–30," reflected Dr. Ambler. "Now they looked upon negro slavery as the greatest evil which could befall them."[17] In a lengthy editorial widely circulated during the 1831–32 legislative session, the *Rockbridge Intelligencer* in Lexington, on the western waters of the James River, joined calls for the separation of eastern and western Virginia and pointed to slavery as the major reason for it. "So long as that connexion lasts, the enormous evil of SLAVERY, with all its direful consequences, must continue to exist among us," the editor wrote.[18] When the House of Delegates voted on a proposal to end slavery in Virginia, every delegate west of the Allegheny Mountains voted in favor of it. Yet, the measure failed. Instead, the legislature adopted the governor's recommendations.[19]

The state government eased sectional tensions for a time with new internal improvements and the creation of new counties in the West. In the 1840s, however, residents of the Trans-Allegheny region once again pushed for a new constitutional convention after the legislature failed to reach a compromise on reapportionment based on the 1840 Census. The West pointed to population shifts that gave their section the majority of the white population and to new economic clout, much of it based on industry. Even on the mixed basis for representation, the West was catching up by 1850. It lagged behind the East in property value by only $15 million in valuation. The lack of legislative reapportionment sparked protest meetings and a general convention in Lewisburg in Greenbrier County in 1842 where residents formalized calls for a constitutional convention.[20]

In the middle of the growing movement for a new constitutional convention, slavery once again arose as a major issue in Virginia. Henry Ruffner, president of Washington College in Lexington, wrote and delivered an *Address to the People of West Virginia Shewing That Slavery Is Injurious to the Public Welfare, and That It May Be Gradually Abolished, without Detriment to the Rights and Interests of Slaveholders,* which was published and widely distributed. Ruffner called for the gradual end of slavery west of the Blue Ridge Mountains and advocated colonization for largely economic and racist reasons. The speech criticized the abolitionist movement as extremist and, although the issue held the attention of the entire country as the country considered the status of slavery in areas acquired through the Mexican War, it did not tackle slavery as a national issue but as a state issue. It professed a formal tone of cooperation with leaders of eastern Virginia but lapsed into sectional criticism of the East. "You have submitted patiently, heretofore, to the refusal of the East to let West Virginia to grow in political power as she has grown in population and wealth," Ruffner told western Virginians. As he concluded, Ruffner advised, "It is for you to determine whether the slavery question shall be considered, discussed and decided, at this critical, this turning point of your country's history: or whether it shall lie dormant until the doom of West Virginia is sealed."[21]

Differences over whether delegates should be elected according to the white population or not delayed the authorization of a convention. Eventually, however, the legislature called a convention in 1849 with representation based on a combination of the white population and the property tax valuation in each of the "four great divisions" of the state. Easterners wanted reform in suffrage, taxation, and the judiciary and direct election of the governor and county courts; ironically, residents west of the Alleghenies opposed the convention without representation on a strictly white basis. Yet, voters approved the convention and elected delegates at a separate election, and the convention met in October 1850.[22]

Eastern Virginians were divided at that convention, and westerners succeeded in obtaining expanded voting rights, apportionment of the lower house of the legislature on the basis of the white population (the majority of whom lived in the western counties), and direct election of state and local officials. Nevertheless, eastern factions gained new constitutional provisions that favored their section of the state as well. One limited the property taxes paid for slaves. Another reduced the ability of the state to fund internal improvements, which were blamed for a burgeoning state debt. Both of these measures rankled people in the West.[23]

Western Virginians received significant gains under the new constitution in spite of continued representation on the mixed basis in the state senate. Not only did they enjoy increased constitutional power in the 1850s, but they wielded increased political power. In the same year that Virginia ratified its new constitution, both gubernatorial candidates came from the Trans-Allegheny region. The Democratic candidate, Joseph Johnson, lived in Harrison County; the Whig contender, George W. Summers, resided in Kanawha County. Johnson won the election and entered office praising the new constitution. "Our beloved commonwealth has just passed through a revolution, instantaneous and radical in its character, operating upon and affecting every class and condition of society, and yet all is peaceful and quiet within her borders," the governor told the legislature hopefully. In regard to sectionalism, he added:

> Those arbitrary lines by which the state has been heretofore laid off into political divisions and districts, were unnecessary and unwise in their conception and only productive of pernicious results. These lines are now obliterated. And though our magnificent mountains traverse the state from one extremity to the other, they no longer are assumed to divide a people having conflicting interest and a separate destiny. Henceforth, the Blue Ridge will not form a dividing line between the East and the West; Tide Water and Piedmont, the Valley and Trans-Alleghany are united by

indisoluble [*sic*] bonds, and with a common interest and a common destiny we shall know no East, no West, but all shall be VIRGINIA.[24]

Virginians generally echoed the governor's hopes for the demise of East-West sectionalism as the decade progressed. These included author, literary magazine editor, and future New Jersey congressman Thomas Dunn English, who was sojourning in the Trans-Allegheny county of Logan while speculating in coal lands. While attending the state Democratic convention in Staunton in 1854, he expressed his sentiments, which the *Richmond Daily Dispatch* paraphrased. "In the matter of sectional jealousy, he spoke what he knew—If there were any jealousy. . . . It was not in his [section]," the newspaper reported. "After a bold and positive disclaimer of such feeling . . . he said that when the time came to show her hand, the West would be found as loyal to our institutions, and as resolute in their defence as any other portion of the Old Dominion."[25]

Virginians clung to the hope of the unity of its sections through the 1850s. An unwritten rule provided for rotation of the governor's office between the East and West, and many legislators advocated a balance between the two sections in Virginia's US Senate delegation. Party loyalties and common issues occupied the state's politicians. Much of the work of the legislature involved banking, railroads, and other internal improvements. Slavery smoldered in the background as an issue, but most of the state's leaders worked very hard at professing unity in supporting slavery and castigating abolitionism. Historian William Shade noted, "Although both political parties played the politics of slavery, attacking their opponents for being soft on slavery, the Democrats were more vociferous in their defense of the peculiar institution."[26]

When the Virginia General Assembly formed a joint committee on escaped slaves in 1855, Augusta County delegate and future Confederate general John D. Imboden objected to the exclusion of delegates from the northwestern counties from the committee as their region was "especially exposed to the inroads of the abolitionists." The speaker of the house conceded and named six northwesterners to the committee, including Wood County delegate Arthur I. Boreman. The future Civil War governor of West Virginia "spoke earnestly of the deep interest the Ohio River counties took in the matter, from their exposure to the operations of the fanatics."[27]

In the 1859 gubernatorial race, the Democrats and the "Opposition," as the Whigs were called, each championed slavery. Congressman John

Letcher of Rockbridge County, the Democratic candidate, staved off attacks for his support of the Ruffner Pamphlet in 1847. Letcher contended that he had repudiated his support of emancipation, and indeed his political record in the 1850s had been one of loyalty to the peculiar institution. In writing about the race, historian W. G. Bean observed that "sectional attitudes were sometimes more prominent than party loyalty" as western Whigs defended the nomination of Letcher, if not his election. The *Lexington Gazette* crowed, "We have the power in the West to elect whomever we please and our eastern Hot-spurs may as well be careful."[28] Sectionalism still lay beneath the parties' efforts at maintaining a unified Virginia.

National events aggravated the situation, and the fallout from the Compromise of 1850, the Kansas-Nebraska Act, and the rise of the Republican Party stirred North-South sectionalism. People in western and eastern Virginia took sides. Eastern Virginia especially became more involved with Southern nationalism, if not politically, at least economically. John Brown's raid on Harpers Ferry in October 1859 further polarized the country and the state.

Most Virginians decried the violence of Brown's raid, but they became more divided on the issue of slavery. A reader of the *Pruntytown Family Visitor* in Taylor County remarked about his own region, "The people of Northwestern Virginia are all a set of abolitionists."[29] Indeed, antislavery sentiment had become more evident in the West—not so much in criticism of the morality of the practice but because of the inequities it caused between the East and West in taxation and legislative apportionment. The future pro-Union governor of Virginia, Francis H. Pierpont, spoke and wrote extensively on the issue in 1860 but focused much of his opposition to slavery on a new state tax on income from labor, which he claimed unduly burdened western Virginia and benefited eastern Virginia. "It was designed and is part and parcel of their plan to drive the whole horde (as they call it) of the free laborers from the State," he told industrial workers in Wheeling.[30]

In his activism throughout 1860, Pierpont supported the views of the Republican Party, if not the election of its candidate. Abraham Lincoln performed well along the upper Ohio River, but he failed to win a single county in Virginia (see appendix for a timeline of events of the secession crisis, the Civil War, and statehood, as well as hostage-taking in West Virginia). By contrast, the Constitutional Union candidate, John Bell, whom Pierpont actually supported, won the state. Bell's victory in Virginia undoubtedly came with support from old Whigs, but more likely because many Virginians feared that disunion would place them in the middle of the conflict many dreaded with a Lincoln victory.[31]

Pierpont's future fellow governor, Arthur I. Boreman, after flirting with the Know-Nothings four years earlier, threw his support behind Bell and attended the Constitutional Union convention in Baltimore. Like Pierpont, Boreman emerged as a leading voice in 1860—not for the antislavery movement but for preservation of the Union. He and twenty-six other legislators had sought the counsel and endorsed the views of Virginia's Whig luminary, former congressman John M. Botts, as they tried to ease emotions and quash North-South sectionalism in the aftermath of the Harpers Ferry raid. Boreman joined with the majority of the legislature in March to oppose a Southern conference.[32]

When Lincoln's election and the first departures of states from the Union forced the secession question on Virginia, Boreman tried to throw early stumbling blocks in the path of Virginia's exit from the United States. He was one of only five members of the House of Delegates who, in early January 1861, opposed a resolution stating that the Union should not be maintained by force, and that the federal government had no power to coerce states. At the same time, Boreman voted against the creation of a house committee to draft a call for a state convention. A few days later, he submitted Unionist petitions from his home county and opposed a call for an open-subject state convention. When the Joint Committee on State and Federal Relations issued a report calling for compromise between the North and South, Boreman joined the majority in staving off efforts to insert a preamble in support of secession.[33]

A convention did follow. It convened on February 13 with even numbers of unconditional unionists and unconditional secessionists. The majority of delegates stood somewhere in between. They understood the seriousness of their work. As William W. Freehling and Craig M. Simpson put it, "If divided Virginia could agree unanimously on an alternative to civil war, so could the whole South." Likewise, they wrote, "If all seven Upper South states followed Virginia out of the Union, Abraham Lincoln's truncated nation would have little chance of triumph (as Lincoln admitted)." Still, Freehling and Simpson concluded, "If Virginia and the entire Upper South stayed in the Union, Jefferson Davis's constricted Confederacy, containing but a third of the South's people, would have scant possibility of survival."[34]

Seemingly endless debates consumed Virginia's convention in February and March 1861. Rather than posturing and pontificating for self-promotion, however, most delegates rhetorically wondered and questioned and feared as they waited for the results of the new president's inauguration, the Peace Conference in Washington, and the siege at Fort Sumter. They either hosted or fended off lobbying by representatives from the Confederacy. Then the storm broke when Fort Sumter was bombarded and fell, and President Lincoln proclaimed an insurrection and called for soldiers from the states. Virginia was driven over the edge, and the convention voted for secession. Trans-Allegheny delegates at the convention hurried home and consulted with citizens at mass meetings in their home counties. West Virginia historian John Alexander Williams reflected, "Even after the fall of Fort Sumter and President Lincoln's call for troops had shattered the hope for peace, a new period of uncertainty settled over Virginia."[35]

That uncertainty involved the sequence of events that followed. The state government in Richmond and its overeager supporters almost immediately started military action after the secession vote, most notably against the federal armory and arsenal at Harpers Ferry and the naval yard at Norfolk and the Baltimore and Ohio Railroad in western Virginia. This occurred in spite of the requirement for a formal referendum on secession in late May. Meanwhile, a full-scale Unionist convention took place in Wheeling in May and adjourned to wait for the results of the referendum. When the vote favored secession, a second convention, consisting of pro-Union state legislators and other elected delegates, met in Wheeling in June and "restored" the government of Virginia to the United States. It and the pro-Union legislature soon put in motion the movement toward the creation of a new state, which became West Virginia two years later. Sectionalism between eastern and western Virginia exploded with the flame of secession and led to the creation of the rival state government and the new state, which challenged Confederate Virginia.

These interstate conflicts, in the context of the North-South war, led to the taking of hostages by the Virginia and West Virginia governments at Wheeling. These governments provided the political and legal structures that justified the practice as a security measure to protect themselves and their adherents.

East-West sectionalism in Virginia was more than political. It was social and economic as well, and the emergence of dual Virginia governments in 1861—one in the East and one in the West—embodied these social and economic differences and helped to define the allegiances and alliances of the people. Thus, the dynamics of hostage-taking were more than just governmental or military, they were social and economic.

Williams hastened "to point out that most of the leaders who fought those sectional battles also fought the creation of West Virginia, either as Confederates or Union supporters who refused to go along with the division of the state."[36] Indeed, residents of western Virginia were not united in opinion on the questions of slavery, secession, the organization of a pro-Union Virginia government, or the formation of West Virginia. This obviously meant that more than North-South sectionalism in the nation or even East-West sectionalism in Virginia was at play. Sectionalism existed between various regions in Virginia on smaller scales and influenced politics, culture, and the economy and differences among the people from one region to another.

John Majewski, in an article in the *Journal of Interdisciplinary History,* illustrated this small-scale sectionalism through a discussion of rivalry in antebellum times between small Virginia cities for commerce and trade. Battles between these communities found their way to the legislature as representatives competed for the funding and location of internal improvements. Majewski wrote, "Internal improvements led to incessant bickering in every state, but the political battles in Virginia are noteworthy for their protracted strife and conflict."[37]

Intense rivalry existed, particularly between Alexandria, Lynchburg, Norfolk, Petersburg, and Richmond, according to Majewski, and the areas surrounding these cities coalesced around their economic ambitions, and common political and social ties formed as a result.[38] While the rivalry centered on the cities, it drew its strength from the cities' positions in key transportation corridors, and these positions, and the geography that separated them, created sectionalism. These rivalries and coalitions that arose from them complicated East-West sectionalism and made it less clear-cut.

Of course, the communities that Majewski emphasized were not the only ones engaged in competition. The geography of Appalachian Virginia narrowed and starkly defined the transportation corridors in that region and created intense sectionalism, sometimes between areas that were short distances apart. This gave rise to many rivalries in western Virginia. In one of many examples, Grafton, situated on the Baltimore and Ohio Railroad, on the Tygarts Valley River, competed with Morgantown, twenty-five miles away, farther down the same river basin on the navigable reaches of the Monongahela River. "Morgantown is one of the wealthiest towns in Western Virginia," commented a Grafton resident, visiting Morgantown for a temperance lecture in 1860. "Upon a very moderate calculation

Older river towns in western Virginia, such as Morgantown, faced new economic and political competition from upstart towns along the Baltimore and Ohio and Northwestern Railroads on the eve of the Civil War. (Suspension Bridge Between Morgantown and Westover, WV, West Virginia and Regional History Center, West Virginia University Libraries, Morgantown, WV)

Morgantown is worth about five times as much as the 'city of Grafton,' in our own county; and from the very nature of thing[s] must always keep greatly ahead of that 'city.'"[39]

The same geography that separated communities and encapsulated political, social, and economic development also provided avenues of ingress and egress from communities, often through the transportation corridors, which defined the communities. In studying similar effects of geography upon western North Carolina in the same era, Martin Crawford, in *Ashe County's Civil War,* wrote, "As historians abandon the traditional conception of preindustrial Appalachia as an isolated, static, largely undifferentiated society, the diverse, competitive, and potentially conflictual nature of communities such as Ashe County—of communities within communities—becomes more apparent."[40] Bruce E. Stewart, in *Blood in the Hills,* concurred that "mountain culture was . . . dynamic and diverse, the product of neither geographical isolation nor ethnicity, but of the same historical forces that influenced the development of regions elsewhere in the United States."[41] Crawford and Stewart were correct that mountainous areas such as western Virginia were dynamic and diverse, but it would be a mistake to dismiss the importance of ethnicity and geographic isolation in the development of the Trans-Allegheny and the Potomac and Shenandoah regions of Virginia. Often migration through mountain passes and valleys and along rivers brought diverse ethnic groups and people from particular localities to one community while people of different backgrounds came to another. Available natural resources, also determined by geography, further enhanced differences between communities. The peoples and resources in communities added to and sometimes prompted rivalries.

At the start of the Civil War, community rivalries turned into open conflicts where differences between communities and their histories of animosity were especially rancorous. In May 1861, a situation erupted in Buckhannon, the county seat of Upshur County, which points to such a case. Maj. Albert Reger, who had put aside his law practice in Philippi, county seat of neighboring Barbour County, led a Confederate force into Buckhannon with the express purpose of tearing down the US flag at the courthouse. Upshur County supported the Union by a ratio of approximately three to one. This was largely the case because of the heavy influx of settlers from New England onto lands along the Buckhannon River in the second and third decades of the nineteenth century. New England land speculators had gained control of the lands and sold them to farmers who escaped Massachusetts and Connecticut in the aftermath of "the year without a summer"—1816. They and their descendants opposed slavery, and many became early Republicans. Meanwhile, Philippi, on the Tygarts Valley River, was heavily pro-Confederate, and many there resented the nearby Unionist enclave.[42]

"Nothing, though, could have prepared the community for the explosive energies unleashed by the sectional conflict," Martin Crawford explained. "As historians have now begun to insist, the war that erupted in April 1861 was more than a contest between rival social or economic systems: it was a domestic struggle in which local loyalties—to household, family, church, and neighborhood—would help forge the patterns of individual and community response."[43]

Geography separated communities, and the mountains of Virginia made these separations especially pronounced. Twentieth-century political writer Neal R. Peirce referred to the results of such separation on the people in West Virginia as "afghanistanism" and labeled the separation as "fierce sectionalism."[44] Peirce studied the state as it experienced the consequences of history, including the Civil War. The war exasperated antebellum sectionalism, and in its "fierce" form it became quite personal.

The rugged terrain of Virginia's mountain counties compartmentalized day-to-day life and accentuated personal animosities. Within the larger war, these animosities often played out openly. Old grudges involving property lines and titles, water rights, timber and mineral rights, trade and business transactions, the location of roads, taxation, debts, and family problems folded into the war between North and South and the battle between the state government at Richmond and the shadow one at Wheeling and later between Confederate Virginia and West Virginia. Families and even communities sided together in these animosities based on boundaries set by mountaintops, ridgelines, and streams, and personal aspects contributed to the local aspects of war in western Virginia and West Virginia.

Much of the animosity that burst forth during the war involved money and property and the sense that one party had been wronged by another. Families, towns, and mountain and valley communities coalesced in these conflicts based on the belief that they were included in the offense, or that the same party or parties had offended them at some point as well. Divisions between perceived advantage and disadvantage existed, and economic classes formed. Parties to these divisions began looking for signs of new offenses and exaggerated them. Sometimes all that was needed was the belief that the other side had all the advantages in location along transportation routes, fertile land, or natural resources. In his groundbreaking book, *Victims,* Phillip Shaw Paludan confirmed that when the Civil War came, the Appalachian South was "bitterly divided, and the division was not just ideological, not just over the theory of union and disunion." Rather, Paludan wrote, "The line was often drawn between rich and poor." In peacetime, such divisions decided political alignments. Paludan pointed out that wealth and social position translated into political power, and that the wealthy were better organized, often because the wealthier people of Appalachia tended to concentrate in towns.[45] So, an aspect of countryside versus town existed. In war, these divisions determined which government and which army one supported. In predominantly pro-Confederate counties, people who felt disadvantaged generally sided with the Union. The opposite was the case in counties with majority pro-Union populations. W. Todd Groce identified this phenomenon in similarly situated eastern Tennessee, where economically powerful Confederates in the towns were unable to gain complete control over counties early in the war. "Outside of a few counties, they were unable to control most of the rural voters of the region and were incapable of translating their growing economic power into any real political muscle," he noted.[46]

On an even more localized level, families took opposite sides from old antagonists in the same neighborhood, often with the same "haves" and "have-nots" resentments coming into play.

These local and regional conflicts helped to kindle the flames of the Civil War, and the nationwide conflict fueled the fire into which provincial issues merged. Crawford pointed out that "when the sectional cauldron boiled over," families, communities, and regions "could not act independently of the larger society, however divorced or differentiated their interests might appear from those of Americans elsewhere."[47]

In the fluid situation near the front lines of combat and political division, people did not limit their fighting to enlisting in conventional armies or attending mass meetings or conventions but engaged in irregular warfare. This included participation in home guards and quasi-legal or extralegal guerrilla bands. It also included pitting government against their adversaries by labeling them as suspicious or disloyal. Sometimes antagonists did not care about the sides in the war but used the competing armies and governments to their advantage against their old foes. The war created new fuel for ongoing animosities.

The saga of hostage-taking in Virginia and West Virginia is not only a story of government versus government, of nation versus nation, and state versus state, it is a story of individuals, families, and communities and their engagement with government and armies and with each other. Unionist leaders in Wheeling conceived of the hostage law and implemented it to protect the Union and particularly their state governments, but in carrying out the law, state leaders depended upon local residents to identify Confederate sympathizers in their areas for capture. This provided the opportunity for Unionists to trap old adversaries who supported the Confederacy. It also allowed for the false designation of personal enemies as Confederates. On the other hand, antebellum friendships and political, social, and economic relationships came into play at times to spare or rescue people from being hostages.

The story of West Virginia's hostages is a tale of people—leaders, soldiers, and ordinary citizens—caught up in war in the context of place. This involved many places—East, West, city, town, county, mountain, valley, and home. Then, of course, it involved North and South. The unfolding of this story begins with particular people—those who set Virginia's pro-Union government in motion—at a particular place—Wheeling.

CHAPTER 2

# Pro-Union Virginia and the Move toward Hostage-Taking, 1861–63

Wheeling, Virginia, exhibited a mixture of exuberance, trepidation, and monotony in June 1861 (see appendix for a timeline of events in chronological context). The Second Wheeling Convention opened in the US Custom House, a follow-up to the first convention, which had occurred a month before in response to the secession vote by the state convention in Richmond in April. The First Wheeling Convention had been precipitous and unwieldy but had adjourned to wait for the results of the election on secession. The second convention responded to that vote and went about the serious work of addressing the finality of Virginia's departure from the Union and of calls for the separation of the western counties into a new state.

A host of reporters from across the North descended upon Wheeling for the second convention in a week of sultry weather and saw an industrial city that hugged the banks of the placid but mighty Ohio River and which nested between hills that stretched eastward toward Pennsylvania and westward to Ohio, looming across the river above Wheeling Island. "The city of Wheeling might be a beautiful as well as a thriving place but for the coal smoke, which gives it a dingy appearance," remarked the correspondent from the *New York Herald* in words that evoked scenes from the recent *Atlantic Monthly* short story, "Life in the Iron-Mills" by Wheeling's Rebecca Harding Davis.[1] Further describing the setting for the convention, the *Wheeling Daily Intelligencer* observed, "All the dust that has been collecting in our streets for a week was swept up on Saturday by various gusts of wind and dashed into the faces of the people, or into open

A crowd outside the US Custom House in Wheeling in June 1861 while the Second Wheeling Convention met inside. (Custom House, Wheeling, Virginia [West Virginia], West Virginia and Regional History Center, West Virginia University Libraries, Morgantown, WV)

windows and doors." The newspaper added dolefully, "Everybody looked gray and dirty, and so did everything else animate and inanimate."[2]

The smoke and dust bespoke the monotony in which industrial workers trudged to and from their shifts in plants ranging from breweries to vinegar distilleries and necessarily labored and lived in spite of looming war. The gray and dirt reminded visitors not only of the many ironworks and glass factories but brought to mind the trepidation that had occupied Wheeling in the weeks after secession. Rumors of approaching troops from Richmond, of pending arrests of Unionists, and confiscations of property and supplies for the use of the Confederacy had circulated. At one point, fears of the seizure of the US Custom House at the order of Virginia Governor John Letcher prompted a citizen guard to surround the building.

Still, from beneath the smoke and dust and the gray and dirt rose exuberance. The *New York Herald* correspondent noted countless US flags hanging from posts and martial music and strawberry festivals. Residents eagerly welcomed US troops whose presence helped allay the trepidation.

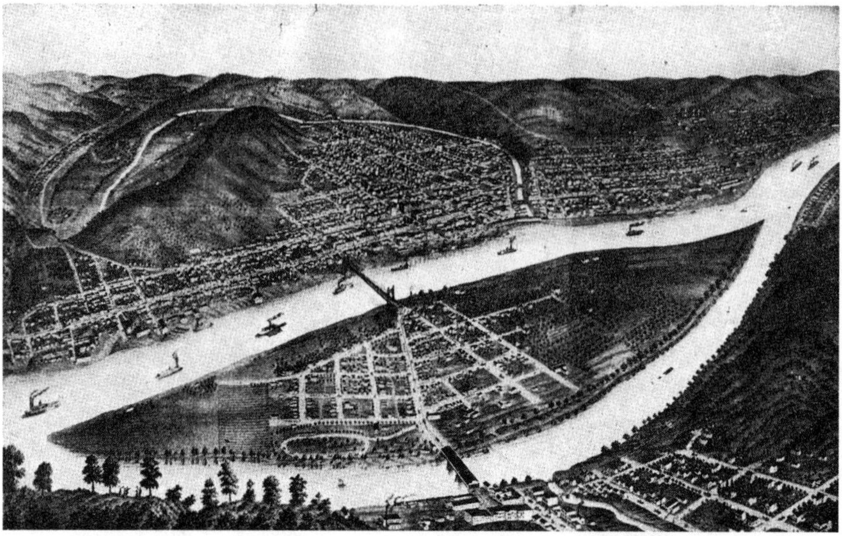

A sketch of Wheeling, Virginia, in 1861, from the Ohio side of Ohio River. (Bird's Eye View of Wheeling, WV, West Virginia and Regional History Center, West Virginia University Libraries, Morgantown, WV)

That same exuberance filled the delegates at the convention, 105 men from 38 counties, five of which lay east of the Allegheny Mountains. Virginia legislator Arthur I. Boreman presided over the convention, and in its exciting first days it thanked the federal government for sending troops into western Virginia in reaction to the Confederate military presence there and specifically praised Maj. Gen. George B. McClellan for leading them. The convention dampened some of the exuberance by hushing calls for the immediate creation of a new pro-Union state from within Virginia. Uncertainty about responsibility for and the funding of Virginia's antebellum debt greatly helped to postpone that action.[3]

Aside from perfunctory and ceremonial measures, the convention soon took up the business the reporters had anticipated in coming to the city. *Harper's Weekly* announced that the convention "very properly assumed control of the destinies of Virginia, and deposed the present rebel State Government."[4] In doing so, delegates declared the state government in Richmond illegal because of secession, proclaimed that state and local offices held by Confederate sympathizers were vacant, and called for the members of the Virginia General Assembly who remained loyal to the Union to convene as a legislature. It also chose a provisional governor and executive officers.[5]

On June 20, 1861, the Second Wheeling Convention elected one of its members, Fairmont attorney and industrialist Francis H. Pierpont, as governor of Virginia. Upon nominating him, Daniel Lamb, a delegate from Ohio County, said, "He is known throughout this country as having been one of the ablest, the most decided and indefatigable advocates of our cause from the very start." Lamb added, "We all know heart and soul he is with us."[6]

Pierpont's record as a "decided and indefatigable advocate" had begun in the early weeks of the secession crisis. Under normal circumstances, as pointed out by his biographer, Charles H. Ambler, Pierpont was "too aggressive and independent to appeal to orthodox and conventional politicians."[7] Yet, the *Wheeling Daily Intelligencer* from the start had expressed confidence in Pierpont as a leading opponent to secession. He had gained much of that confidence as a result of a debate during those early weeks against former state legislator and congressman Zedekiah Kidwell, a Fairmont physician and attorney, during a court session in Marion County. His name had surfaced during the early spring as a possible Unionist congressional candidate, and in April, he had attended a Unionist congressional district convention and served as an official spokesperson for the pro-Union stance of that convention.[8] As keynote speaker at a rally in Morgantown on April 22, Pierpont had "handled the secessionists without gloves," according to the *Morgantown Star,* and had prompted a minor walkout at the rally.[9] At another rally in the Harrison County Courthouse on May 3, Pierpont had spoken for two and half hours while pouring rain outside had turned to snow and back to rain.[10] On the following day, in spite of a hoarse voice, he had delivered an address in the courthouse in Ohio County, after which the *Wheeling Daily Intelligencer* had described Pierpont as "one of those men well-fitted for the stormy and revolutionary times upon us."[11]

When Pierpont had arrived at Wheeling for the First Wheeling Convention, a crowd—including an honor guard and bands—had gathered in front of McLure House, where he and other delegates were staying, and called for Pierpont and John S. Carlile of Clarksburg, a noteworthy opponent to secession in his own right, to speak. Before the convention ended, Pierpont, along with Carlile and seven others, had been named as a member of the Central Committee, which had represented the interests of the convention until the second one took place in June. In that capacity, Pierpont had been among the leaders who requested the presence of US troops in Virginia. His role as a Central Committee member had also thrust him into the limelight as not just a speaker against secession but as a face of the

Francis H. Pierpont, governor of the pro-Union Restored Government of Virginia. (Francis H. Pierpont, Loyal Governor of Virginia, 1861–1868, West Virginia and Regional History Center, West Virginia University Libraries, Morgantown, WV)

emerging opposition government. Just after the close of the convention, Pierpont had toured the military training camp on Wheeling Island, and soldiers had eagerly persuaded him to give an impromptu speech.[12]

So, when Pierpont had arrived at the Second Wheeling Convention, he was a well-known and popular figure, and all seventy-seven delegates present voted for him as governor. Like many revolutionary figures, however, Pierpont's reputation depended more on rhetoric than real government experience, and rhetoric filled his acceptance speech. Yet, a portion of his speech presaged the style of governance that eventually led to hostage-taking: "It will be for us by firmness, and by prudence, by wisdom, by discretion, in all our acts, to inaugurate every step we take for the purpose of restoring law and order to this ancient Commonwealth."[13]

While it was still in session, the Second Wheeling Convention took definite action in "restoring law and order." It passed an ordinance "to authorize the apprehending of suspicious persons in time of war" and placed the enforcement of the ordinance in the governor's hands. The measure allowed for the imprisonment or exile of "suspicious persons," public officials who supported the Confederacy, people who assembled in support of the Confederacy, and men who participated in Confederate military units.

It also authorized the governor to use force to prevent pro-Confederate public gatherings and military assemblies. The convention rejected efforts to expand the reach of the ordinance, including to those who opposed the Second Wheeling Convention. John S. Carlile succeeded in amending

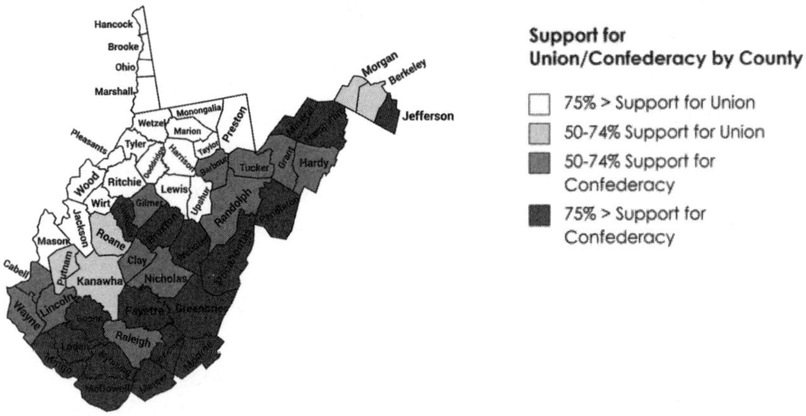


Votes by county delegates on secession at the Richmond Convention, votes in the referendum on secession, and participation in the presidential election of 1864 provide a snapshot of support for the Union and Confederacy within the present county borders of West Virginia, which are shown for perspective. Geography and transportation connections influenced the national leanings of the counties.

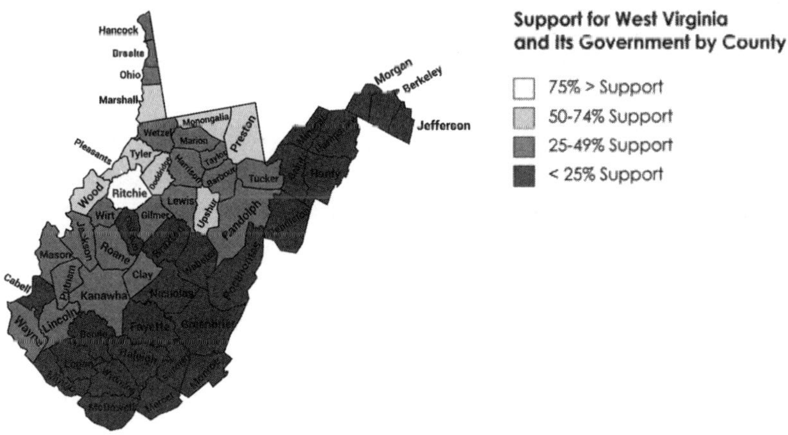


Support for the Union did not necessarily translate to support for the pro-Union government of Virginia or for the State of West Virginia, which explains why many Unionists found themselves classed as "suspicious" or as people with "known disloyal sentiments" under the state hostage law. For the sake of perspective, Grant, Lincoln, Mineral, and Mingo Counties, which did not yet exist during the Civil War, are included.

the act to require satisfactory evidence for apprehension and concurrence from a majority of the governor's council. The ordinance passed with only three votes against it. John C. Vance, a member of the House of Delegates from Harrison County, was among them. Vance questioned the authority of the convention to legislate and warned against the convention becoming a "star chamber" as he said the Richmond Convention had become.[14] Boreman, the president of the convention, also opposed the ordinance. Still, on the last day of the session, Boreman left the door open for future security measures in his concluding remarks. "And if gentlemen who are opposed to us in politics on this great question of secession see fit to attempt again to oppose the free execution of the laws, it will be necessary for us, by the strong arm of the law, to put our purpose into execution," he warned.[15]

Boreman's remarks not only alluded to law enforcement but to political opposition. During the same period in divided eastern Tennessee, similar issues played out as Confederates tried to assert power. W. Todd Groce, in his book on the subject, *Mountain Rebels,* questioned whether efforts to "suppress dissension" were really attempts to bolster loyalty or whether the enforcers really intended to "cement their advantage over their old political rivals by completely destroying them as a potential threat to their domination of the region."[16] The same might be said of western Virginia and later West Virginia. Security measures, including the eventual hostage law, struck fear into opponents of the reorganization of Virginia's government and the later creation of West Virginia, as well as personal political rivals of those who held power.

The provisional government went about the work of a state at war. During the weeks that followed Pierpont's election, the US government sanctioned the pro-Union government of Virginia out of military and political necessity. The War Department sent more troops into western Virginia at Pierpont's request. Congressmen were elected, and the House of Representatives seated them. The state legislature convened on July 1 and soon afterward elected US senators, and these too were seated.[17]

Beyond the expected business of a state during wartime, the legislature considered the matter of creating a new state. It, like the Second Wheeling Convention a month earlier, decided against action because its members felt that the people were unprepared for it. That did not stop the Second Wheeling Convention from acting on its own when it reconvened in August. Despite reservations about the intentions of the legislature, the convention decided to call an election in October to gain approval for creation of a new state and choose delegates for a constitutional convention. The voters chose sixty-one delegates to the constitutional convention, which convened in November.[18]

For his part, the governor embarked in office with little time to learn. He fulfilled the duties of chief executive with all the administrative and political tasks and the extra responsibilities of implementing a new government in time of civil war. In this, Virginia's existing laws applied as well as a set of interim ordinances passed by the Second Wheeling Convention to provide for the transition of government. Pierpont appointed executive officials; called the legislature into session; formally removed state and local officials who sided with the Richmond government; reorganized county governments in areas overrun by McClellan's forces; delegated routine and mundane tasks; and directed citizens, soldiers, and vendors—most of whom wanted personal preferences—to the right person or ignored them entirely.

Pierpont's most pressing responsibility came from his role as commander in chief of the state's armed forces. Besides commanding the state militia, he had charge of raising Virginia's quota for the US Army and had charge of volunteer regiments until their acceptance into federal service. He commissioned field officers and authorized the election of company officers for the regiments. When news of threats or rumors of threats from Confederate conventional and guerrilla forces to civilian populations reached the governor, he requested Union commanders to respond. He purchased and otherwise acquired weapons and supplies for state forces. Then there was the never-ending parade of people seeking military appointments, release from military service, or furloughs from service.

Pierpont, who had never held a public office beyond county school commissioner and presidential elector, faced a rapid transition from cheerleading to actual governing. As he uneasily but necessarily settled into his new role, the *Richmond Enquirer* poked fun at "the obscure person who is playing Governor at Wheeling, as a boy plays captain on a school play ground."[19]

A significant part of Governor Pierpont's "play" involved the law and order of which he spoke in his inaugural address. Civilian and military officials began dealing with security problems involving alleged spies, suspicious characters, and people who resisted the pro-Union Virginia government and US authority. Just three days after taking office, Brig. Gen. Thomas A. Morris, who had commanded Union forces in their first engagements in western Virginia, apprised the governor of the arrest of a civilian, Louis Stephens, by Col. Benjamin F. Kelley. Stephens had been taken to Wheeling and confined at Camp Carlile, but no specific charges had been filed against him. A. F. Ritchie, a member of the House of Delegates, vouched for Stephens, and Morris asked for Pierpont's instructions. Over the next few weeks, military leaders, respectful of the jurisdiction of civil authorities, sought Pierpont's direction concerning the arrest of a number of other citizens. The commanders sent detainees to Wheeling and asked the governor to take custody. When the number of prisoners became unmanageable and evidence against them stopped at suspicion, army commanders counseled release of the suspects as long as they took an oath of loyalty to the United States.[20]

During the legislative session in July, Governor Pierpont talked to the delegates and senators about the Second Wheeling Convention's ordinance against suspicious persons and called for consideration of additional security measures. "When a civil war is raging in the midst of us, an efficient system to protect the loyal people of the Commonwealth against the intrigues, conspiracies and hostile acts of those who adhere to our enemies, is necessary for the safety and good order of the community," the governor told them.[21] The legislature considered a number of punitive measures, but confined itself to endorsing the removal of Confederates and those who would not swear loyalty to the Wheeling government from public office.[22]

Security issues for the pro-Union government became more pressing and hit home when a member of the Second Wheeling Convention fell into Confederate hands. While Thomas A. Roberts represented Roane County in Wheeling, the residents of the county, according to the *History of Roane County*, "recognized the dangerous dilemmas of the situation; they whispered, they conferred; family conferences, neighborhood conferences; finally, a county mass meeting was called to meet at the court house on Saturday evening, June 22, 1861." The meeting turned into a pro-Confederate forum, and when Roberts returned from the convention to his home on Reedy Creek and began recruiting for the Union Army, he soon faced a dangerous situation. County resident Albert G. Ingraham received a commission in the Confederate Army under Brig. Gen. Henry A. Wise's command and stationed a company at the town of Reedyville, near Roberts's residence.[23] Ingraham's mission included the capture of Roberts, who did not stay in his own house for weeks while "his footsteps were continually dogged by his secession neighbors," according to his own account, published in the *Wheeling Daily Intelligencer*. Then, on July 29, "he was pounced upon by twelve men at the house of a neighbor." His captors tied Roberts to a horse and rode him through the night to Charleston, sixty miles away. There, he appeared before General Wise, who insisted that Roberts swear loyalty to the Confederacy. When he refused and argued with Wise, who was a former governor of Virginia and an early supporter of secession, the general sent Roberts to Richmond. Confederate authorities in that city kept him manacled in solitary confinement in an eight-by-ten-foot cell.[24] Roberts's situation was not unique in many ways. Many civilians in Virginia on both sides found themselves in custody because of their political activity, even their political expressions. Others, like Roberts, were arrested for their support of one of the warring armies. Most of these cases passed with little notice, with informal, sometimes secretive resolutions.

Still, Roberts's case draws historic attention, which others do not. While Roberts was in custody, Andrew Parks, an elderly Charleston attorney, fell into the hands of the Virginia government at Wheeling. Authorities technically arrested Parks under the suspicious persons ordinance, which the Second Wheeling Convention had passed. Parks had replaced Unionist George W. Summers as a delegate to the Richmond Convention after the approval of secession and was considered a leading supporter of the state government at Richmond. After his capture, Parks spent most of his time in a Wheeling hospital, but that did not deter Governor Pierpont from negotiating the exchange of Parks for Roberts, with the assistance of US authorities. Parks was an unofficial hostage.[25]

For Pierpont, a thin line lay between holding people as suspicious and exchanging them for prisoners held by the Confederacy, especially when state leaders were involved. After all, the US government often took hostages in Virginia. One sensational case unfolded in the summer of 1862. Confederate soldiers captured Dr. William P. Rucker, a US Army doctor, in Nicholas County, and state authorities in Richmond insisted that he be turned over to the sheriff of Allegany County for trial on charges of murder, horse stealing, and treason, which arose from his resistance to arrest for refusing to swear an oath of loyalty to the Richmond government and his service as a guide for Union troops in the Greenbrier Valley. While Jefferson Davis drew a line against the treason charge against his government, Confederate authorities delivered Rucker to state officials. When the US Army sought Rucker's release, the Confederates refused on the basis that Rucker's captivity was a civilian issue. Union commanders in the area responded by taking civilians in Greenbrier County as hostages, and, when the case reached the attention of the War Department in Washington, several Confederate Army doctors in US custody were held as hostages. After a series of delays in his trial and changes of venue, Rucker managed to escape the Pittsylvania County Jail and make his way home in October 1863.[26]

Still, while Pierpont worked for the exchange of Parks for Roberts, the term *hostage* appeared only in press reports. The governor's inclinations as a lawyer apparently kept him from actively taking hostages under state authority, and the Roberts case appears to be the only one in which someone taken under the suspicious persons law was used as a hostage. Even if Pierpont had been inclined to use the suspicious persons ordinance again to force exchanges, he could not. A sunset provision on the existence of the governor's council made the ordinance invalid since it required the approval of the council for arrests. Meanwhile, arrests of civilians on both sides became common through 1862, and pressure increased for action by the pro-Union government of Virginia to aid in the release of prisoners held by the Confederates and to thwart further captures.[27]

A letter from Eliza A. Leavens of the Paint Creek area of Kanawha County to Governor Pierpont exerts such pressure. Leaven's husband, Charles, a justice of the peace, and her son, Charles Henry, a draftee in the Confederate Army who had deserted, had been taken by men under Col. John N. Clarkson of the Third Virginia State Line, a pro-Confederate state guard unit. "Oh! Sir, is not your arm of power long enough, and strong enough, to rescue and protect those who are suffering for their steady adherence to the right, at the hands of these traitors and robbers?" Leavens pleaded. "Oh, as you love your Country and your own dear ones, I pray you listen to the cry of my anguish and make yet another effort to restore to me my poor crippled husband, and my dear and only child, ere it be too late to save their lives from the power of their enemies."[28]

Both Governor Pierpont and the state legislature—through the governor—asserted themselves with federal authorities on behalf of specific individuals in Confederate hands, including Charles Leavens. Legislators boldly asked the secretary of war to choose hostages "of like standing and condition" from among prisoners in Union custody "with the assurance that whatever afflictions, punishments or penalties have been or may be imposed upon the persons thus demanded be inflicted upon the persons so held." Pierpont stopped short of calling for hostages but rather asked the secretary to include captive Unionists in prisoner exchanges. An assistant secretary replied simply that the matter would "receive careful attention."[29]

Pierpont, meanwhile, turned his efforts toward Union commanders in his state and began speaking of hostages. He first approached Brig. Gen. William S. Rosecrans, then commanding the Mountain Department, about taking hostages upon the state's request; Rosecrans referred the matter to Brig. Gen. Lorenzo Thomas, US Army adjutant general and chair of the War Board.[30] Soon thereafter, Maj. Gen. John C. Fremont relieved Rosecrans, and prominent western Virginians petitioned him to take two or three hundred prominent Confederate sympathizers as hostages for pro-Union citizens in Confederate prisons. Fremont proved very supportive of the Wheeling government's security concerns, but he did not remain in command for long, and no mass hostage-taking occurred.[31]

The frequent reorganization of military departments and changes in command hindered policymaking, but other factors caused Union Army officers to take a long look at civilian arrests in western Virginia. The focus in this regard fell mainly on Maj. Joseph Darr Jr., the department provost marshal in Wheeling. William A. Blair, author of *With Malice toward Some: Treason and Loyalty in the Civil War Era,* pointed out that provost marshals "were the men who pounded on a door in the middle of the night to roust a traitor out of bed and into military prison," who "disrupted worship services, removed judges from the bench during judicial proceedings, seized mail, and closed newspaper offices," who "shut down taverns, closed brothels, . . . restricted the travel of citizens," and "issued countless oaths of loyalty to people who had little choice but to sign their pledge of fidelity to the nation or remain confined under military jurisdiction without a hearing in civil court." Blair explained that department provost marshals held jurisdiction over a specific geographic area and "established a longer-term posture [than front-line provost marshals] in communities" and "walked a fine line between imposing army discipline and respecting civil law."[32]

Darr, a former Democratic city council member in Cincinnati and a bookkeeper by profession, had come to the city as part of Rosecrans's staff in 1861 and had charge of the military prison at the Atheneum, the converted theater in Wheeling.[33] He had quickly formed a good relationship with Governor Pierpont and had been quite obliging in responding to the governor's requests.[34] In 1862, a series of questionable arrests and Darr's practice of sending prisoners from the overcrowded Atheneum to Camp Chase brought him under the scrutiny of the War Department. His superiors required Darr to report to Washington and bring complete lists of civilian prisoners and justifications for their confinement.[35] Military prison inspector Capt. H. M. Lazelle described Darr as "very zealous; perhaps too hasty and arbitrary." When told by the governor's aide that a major in the army judge advocate corps thought that the number of arrests in western Virginia was excessive, Darr lashed back. "The fact is we ought to have a variety in the shape of a little hanging," Darr wrote. "We have a nest of traitors all around us to deal with."[36]

While authorities in Washington focused attention on Darr, he was not alone in the limelight. Union commanders struggled throughout 1862 to curb excessive arrests. "Time and again commanders of departments and armies complained to officers within their jurisdiction to exercise vigilance against treason but to make arrests only when clear violations existed," Blair noted in his book.[37] Still, Darr's practices drew enough attention to make his position very tenuous by mid-year, but he managed to retain his post through concerted appeals.[38]

The time was not right for a blanket policy for hostage-taking. Even when western Virginians called upon Union commanders on a case-by-case basis to take hostages, their requests went unfulfilled. When James H. Trout, a member of the pro-Union Virginia House of Delegates from Hampshire County, was arrested by the Confederates in August, Brig. Gen. Benjamin F. Kelley, who had charge of protecting the Baltimore and Ohio Railroad, refused appeals from Trout's family to take hostages on his behalf. Instead, Governor Pierpont lobbied Washington for assistance in negotiating Trout's release.[39]

In spite of these disappointments, the drive for action continued. Editorials, letters to the editor, and resolutions in mass meetings added to the call for the army to seize hostages. One letter acknowledged "that this policy is objected to by some of our loyal men," but the writer maintained that "if there could be any other means suggested by which Union citizens could be protected, I would cheerfully acquiesce."[40]

As the city of Wheeling was "creeping along in the month of December and rapidly nearing the holidays" in 1862, the state legislature convened there for an extraordinary session.[41] Pierpont addressed the delegates and senators and dramatically reviewed the security situation. "In the mountain districts the guerrillas are carrying on a system of wholesale, indiscriminate robbery and murder," the governor said. "Not only do they strip our Union fellow-citizens of horses, cattle, and every other species of property, but they seize and carry away captive, their persons." Pierpont referred to the captivity of "numbers of our most worthy and respectable citizens." He appealed to the legislators, "I have felt the want of sufficient legislation on this subject, and respectfully suggest that a law be passed, authorizing the Executive, or appointing a commission, to designate influential secessionists in the loyal portion of the State, to be arrested and confined until their friends procure the release of an equal number of loyal men."[42] The governor, without using the word *hostage*, called for a hostage law that would place authority in the hands of the state to act in lieu of the federal government.

The legislature busied itself with routine matters before the holidays—paying government officials, amending Wheeling's municipal charter, adjusting the municipal boundaries of Buckhannon, incorporating an insurance company, appropriating money for an academy in Brooke County, staying the collection of debts, and changing a polling place in Preston County. Events pushed the hostage issue in front of legislators after the start of the new year, however. A Confederate detail, under orders from Brig. Gen. John D. Imboden, robbed the home and store of Barbour County sheriff James Trahern (Trayhorn) on the evening of January 4, 1863, and took Trahern captive. Union soldiers stationed about ten miles away at Philippi, the county seat, swiftly responded and took eight men in the vicinity hostage, apparently under the orders of Col. Nathan Wilkinson, who commanded the Sixth Virginia Infantry. Wilkinson sent the hostages to Wheeling, where Darr took responsibility for them.[43]

The rapidly unfolding events stirred action in the legislature. The debates that followed showcased the diverse people and politics represented in Wheeling, and it is worthwhile to profile the key legislators in the hostage issue.

As soon as reports of Trahern's capture and the army's reaction reached the legislature, William B. Zinn, delegate from Preston County, referred to the governor's request for action in his December address and presented a resolution to put the hostage question in the hands of the Committee on Courts of Justice. Zinn, a prominent farmer and miller, had presided over the First Wheeling Convention, served in the Second Wheeling Convention, and was a Union Party candidate for Congress in 1863. His county, tucked up against Maryland and Pennsylvania, was a bulwark of Unionism.[44]

On the same day, Owen D. Downey shared in the dismay over Trahern's capture, but the Hampshire County Democrat immediately questioned why the army had taken no hostages for Delegate Trout. Downey, a former state legislator in Maryland and former member of the First and Second Wheeling Conventions, represented the same county as Trout and published the "conservative" *Wheeling Press* while serving in the legislature. He owned a mercantile store and hotel in Piedmont on the B&O Railroad at the Maryland border and had a keen interest in keeping the railroad secure from the Confederates.[45]

On the heels of Downey's speech, New York native Daniel D. T. Farnsworth, an Upshur County merchant and former member of the Second Wheeling Convention, proposed a rapid-fire resolution calling for passage of a hostage law. The speaker of the house, George McC Porter, ruled the motion out of order. Farnsworth's impulsive action was typical. In May 1861, he had gone to Philippi from his own Unionist-dominated county and delivered a speech, which had prompted threats on his life. Soon afterward, when a Confederate patrol had entered Buckhannon, the county seat of Upshur, from Philippi, Farnsworth had locked his store and paced back and forth in front it, twirled the key on his finger, and successfully warned the Confederates to leave the town or risk their lives. Later, he was a key leader in the West Virginia statehood movement, served briefly as governor of West Virginia in 1869 in his capacity as state senate president, and was a diehard Radical Republican during Reconstruction.[46]

The next day, January 13, Governor Pierpont sent a message to the legislature, ostensibly as an update about state mental institutions, but the message broke new ground. For the first time, Pierpont used the word *hostages*. Pierpont introduced the subject, not so much for the benefit of the legislators, who knew the situation well, but for the historical record. "A large number of unoffending men, and in some instances women, have been seized by the rebels, for no other reason than that they are loyal to the government of the United States, and have been carried to distant prisons and there confined and ignominiously treated, and in some cases put to death," he wrote. In the last statement, the governor varied from his address a month earlier, in which he stated that the Confederates had not executed civilians. No knowledge exists of such executions in the intervening month, and Pierpont may have been exaggerating deaths from other causes inherent to Civil War prison life. The governor also specifically included the state government in Richmond, as well as the Confederate government, as responsible for some of "these oppressive arrests."[47]

Pierpont then closed in on his purpose. "Whenever the State demands allegiance, it should not only give protection, but should give the most ample assurances by those having the authority, that it would protect to the uttermost," he argued. "My opinion is, that there should be some law passed authorizing the arrest of distinguished secessionists to be held as hostages for the release of union citizens that have been, or may hereafter be arrested."

In setting forth his intention of using hostages in negotiating exchanges, the governor explained that those "who openly avow their attachment to the Southern Confederacy, and are living under the protection of the State and Federal government, should be made to use their influence with their secession friends to procure the safety of the persons and property of loyal men who are non-combatants, at least within the Federal lines."[48]

Pierpont shared with the legislators that he received pleas about imprisoned residents on almost a daily basis and placed upon the lawmakers part of the responsibility for remedying the problem. "I am powerless under the law as it now stands," he told them. "If you will enact a law providing for the establishment of a system by which loyal men can be protected by retaliation, I am confident it will have a most beneficial effect." He concluded with the request that a new suspicious persons act also be passed to replace the 1861 ordinance, which had become useless. Pierpont added a caution that applied to hostage legislation as well: "It should be carefully guarded to avoid oppression by abuse of power: but because the power may be abused, is no argument for [not] taking steps to protect the loyal citizens."[49]

Delegate Fontaine Smith, chair of the Committee on Courts of Justice, brought a hostage bill to the floor the day after Pierpont's message. Smith, an active Democrat, came from Marion, the same county as the governor, where he practiced law and taught school at Mannington on the B&O Railroad.[50]

On January 31, Spicer Patrick, representing Kanawha County, moved to take up the hostage bill in the House of Delegates. The seventy-two-year-old Patrick, a medical doctor originally from New York, began a hot debate over the bill.[51] Lewis Ruffner, of the same county and the same generation as Patrick, hastened to call for modification of the bill. The venerable Ruffner, leading salt manufacturer and veteran of Virginia's antebellum legislature, believed that the bill was too broad in allowing the arrest of people just for their sympathies. He thought that hostages should be limited to those who had committed overt acts of disloyalty against the United States and the Wheeling government. Patrick, who had spent time in Confederate custody during Maj. Gen. W. W. Loring's incursion into the Kanawha Valley in 1862, countered that the legislation was "not as broad as the raids made every few days by the rebel brigands into the different counties." He said that the legislature must "fight the devil with fire." Patrick admitted that the proposal was harsh but insisted that "if loyal citizens could not be protected by modes consistent with the character of civilized people," he was "prepared to resort to uncivilized, barbarous, or savage modes, if that was the only way it could be done." Ruffner stood his ground and moved to strike out the phrase "persons sympathizing with the rebellion" from the portion of the bill that defined potential hostages and to substitute the wording "persons of known disloyal sentiments." The house adopted Ruffner's amendment with thirty members voting in favor and four against.[52]

John J. Davis, Democratic delegate from Harrison County, entered the fray. The bill troubled Davis, future congressman and father of 1924 presidential candidate John W. Davis. The Clarksburg attorney wanted to limit hostages to people in Confederate territory. Patrick claimed that Davis's proposal would make the measure impotent. Farnsworth said that such an amendment would "forbid arresting the traitors amongst us." He insisted that "there is no danger that the Government would arrest a loyal man for the redemption of a loyal man."[53]

Solomon Parsons of Tucker County, located in the mountainous edges between Union and Confederate forces, stormily reacted to Davis. The medical doctor and merchant from St. George had dodged Confederate raiders who had sought him the previous year because of his service in the legislature and in the Second Wheeling Convention. "Why the sympathizers around us are the very men most to blame," Parsons argued from firsthand experience. "They point out the Union men when the guerillas come in." He slurred Davis for his relative safety in Clarksburg by saying that the attorney did "not know what danger is."[54]

Davis reasoned that he "had no disposition to screen from just punishment any party who may be guilty of committing these depredations." He said that he abhorred "the practices of the guerillas as much as anyone," but he considered "similar practices on the part of the Federal army just as wrong." Davis regretted that "gentlemen should let their prejudices and passions so mislead their judgments as to give their endorsement to a measure which I conceive to be fraught with immense evil." He added, "No man's liberty is safe when such laws as this are in force." Davis rested his argument for limiting hostages to those beyond Union lines on a fatal flaw. He claimed that the Confederates only arrested people past their own lines. To that, Patrick asked, "Where are John Minor Botts and a thousand others in the Southern states? Arrested and in dungeons." He continued, "Every man who dares to express a sentiment in favor of the Union is seized and carried off, not only themselves but their property." Davis's amendment failed.[55]

The bill moved toward approval after the intense debate. G. S. Miner, an attorney from Alexandria, moved that, in each case, hostages be limited to the same county from which a citizen was taken by the Confederates. The house quickly moved past his proposal, and the bill passed to engrossment. On the afternoon of January 31, Patrick wanted to take the bill up again, but the delegates were not in *that* big of a hurry.[56]

Three days later, LeeRoy Kramer of Monongalia County moved that the hostage bill be taken up again. The vote was called and it passed, 24–7. Richard Fast of Marion County, George W. Henderson of Wood County, John M. Powell of Harrison County, and James A. Williamson of Wirt County joined Davis, Downey, and Smith in voting against the measure.[57]

The bill went to the state senate on the same day, but less excitement surrounded it than in the house. It underwent first and second readings, and it was referred to the Committee on Courts of Justice and General Laws. The committee reported the bill favorably the following day. The committee chair, Chapman J. Stuart, former prosecuting attorney of Doddridge County, suggested amending the bill so that it allowed hostages to be taken only in future instances of the seizure of people by the Confederates. Stuart was a well-regarded attorney and politician who had served in the Richmond Convention and the Second Wheeling Convention and was doing double duty in 1863 as a member of the constitutional convention for the proposed state of West Virginia. The senate refused to include the provision, however, and the bill passed on its third reading on February 4, 1863. The governor signed it the same day.[58]

The legislature justified the new measure because "evil disposed persons and others under the influence and orders of the assumed rebel government, have made it a practice (and recently, too,) entered West Virginia and seized and carried away citizens" and imprisoned them without justification. It contended that "unless this system of kidnapping be promptly checked, such conduct will continue and increase." The act authorized and requested the governor "in all cases of the seizure of persons of loyal citizens of this state by any parties acting under the authority of the so-called southern confederacy, the pretended state government at Richmond or other military organizations acting in sympathy or concert with them, or either of them" to take hostages. The law allowed the governor to take as many hostages from among people "of known disloyal sentiments" as he thought necessary to ensure the "safe rendition" of Unionists in Confederate custody.[59]

The legislature also passed a pair of companion measures. It granted Pierpont's request to reauthorize him to arrest "suspicious persons." The new law required evidence of suspicious activity upon oath or affirmation.

In addition, the legislature passed a joint resolution calling for the president to order army commanders to take federal hostages to compel the release of Unionist citizens from Confederate captivity. That measure had originated in the senate.[60]

Governor Pierpont had what he wanted. He had tools at his direct disposal to deal with security. He also had the prospect of clearer cooperation from Union Army commanders. Not only had the legislature sent a political signal to the president to encourage a consistent policy of federal hostage-taking, but the organization of the army brought hope. The War Department had designated a provost marshal general the previous fall, and Congress created the Provost Marshal General's Bureau in March 1863. Those moves gave Major Darr a more definite chain of command that concerned itself more with law enforcement than prison administration.[61]

Speaking to the delegates at West Virginia's constitutional convention shortly after the passage of the hostage law, Pierpont touted his new authority. The *Alexandria Gazette* reported, "One thing he wished to impress upon the minds of the members of the Convention from the Border Counties, was, that if the rebels did not cease molesting and capturing West Virginians they must abide by the consequences; he would take hostages not only from the other but this side of the lines, and, by the eternal God, they should be taken and subject to like treatment as those taken from us received; he would not take any but the most prominent and influential enemies of our Government; he hoped the work would not be commenced, but if it was he would make them suffer severely."[62]

In Wheeling, and throughout western Virginia in the late winter of 1863, such words gave Unionists some hope that their lives would be safer, if not more comfortable. For those in the region who supported the Confederacy and those whose loyalties were unclear, the prospects seemed somewhat dimmer. Everyone knew that nothing was certain. In her memoir, wartime Wheeling resident Rebecca Harding Davis recorded that the "histories which we have of the great tragedy give no idea of the general wretchedness, the squalid misery, which entered into every individual life in the region given up to the war." The writer specifically pointed to the chances of captivity while detailing day-to-day life:

> Even on the border, your farm was a waste, all your horses or cows were seized by one army or the other, or your shop or manufactory was closed, your trade ruined. You had no money; you drank coffee made of roasted parsnips for breakfast, and ate only potatoes for dinner. Your nearest kins-

> folk and friends passed you on the street silent and scowling; if you said what you thought you were liable to be dragged to the county jail and left there for months. The subject of the war was never broached in your home, where opinions differed; but, one morning, the boys were missing. No one said a word, but one gray head was bent, and the happy light died out of the old eyes and never came to them again. Below all the squalor and discomfort was the agony of suspense or the certainty of death. But the parsnip coffee and the empty purse certainly did give a sting to the great overwhelming misery, like gnats tormenting a wounded man.[63]

Still, the state tried, and the hostage law was one of the ways that it tried. Its efforts did not take place without challenges, however, and some of the strongest challenges took place in the very first hostage case in 1863. That case pitted Governor Pierpont against an eminent state politician and jurist—George W. Thompson of Ohio County.

CHAPTER 3

# Judge George W. Thompson, Governor Pierpont, and the First Hostage Case

Just after Christmas in 1860, Judge George W. Thompson spoke at the county courthouse in Wheeling and expressed hope that the border states would take a moderate stand in the face of the secession crisis (see appendix for a timeline of events in West Virginia from the secession crisis through Reconstruction).[1] Thompson enjoyed high esteem in the community. Not only had he served as circuit court judge for nearly a decade, he had been a congressman, US district attorney, and candidate for governor and for state auditor general. Voters had reelected him by a large majority in November. So, residents of Wheeling considered Thompson a solid, deliberate, and experienced jurist and politician. In December 1860, his views reflected many of their own.

After the first of the year, however, the secession crisis escalated quickly. Politicians, newspaper editors, and even ministers fanned the flames, and people heard and read what they wanted. Unionists in Wheeling embraced Judge Thompson as an opponent of secession and advocate for the Union. They circulated Thompson's speech as a pamphlet. They overlooked his broader cautions against radicalism and did not consider that the judge's criticisms might apply to them.

On the afternoon of Saturday, January 5, 1861, activists in Wheeling began circulating handbills announcing a rally of the pro-Union industrial workers of the city. That evening people crowded into the Atheneum, the theater on the third and fourth floors of the Crescent Manufacturing Company's building at Sixteenth (John) and Market Streets. Patriotic music filled the air, and organizers drafted resolutions. Then, only two people

Judge George W. Thompson (George Wesley Atkinson and Alvaro Franklin Gibbens, *Prominent Men of West Virginia* [W.L. Callin, 1890])

spoke; George W. Thompson was one of them. Newspaper accounts reported that the crowd made "deafening calls" for the judge to speak. He hesitated because he was unwell, but Thompson made a short speech. He laid blame for the secession crisis on extremists in both the North and the South and said that officials in both regions had violated the Constitution. Thompson blamed "designing and ambitious politicians," and then spoke in apparent anticipation of a split between his views and those that would eventually prevail in the community. "The Constitution had always been his guide in politics and he stood by it now" read the account in the *Wheeling Daily Intelligencer.* "He warned the working men (the last time, perhaps, he should ever address them on a public occasion), to look well to themselves." Thompson took his seat "amid loud applause," and at the end of the meeting the audience gave three cheers each for Fort Sumter's commander Maj. Robert Anderson, the Union, the American flag, and Judge Thompson.[2]

Over the next weeks and months, Thompson's positions remained unchanged. Virginians prepared for the state convention in Richmond, which considered the secession crisis. In choosing a candidate for the convention, residents at a pro-Union meeting in Hancock County endorsed the judge's views. After the convention voted for secession on April 17 and most delegates from western Virginia returned home in exasperation before the convention ended, local government continued to operate even though the future of the state became unclear. Judge Thompson continued to hold court in the counties in his circuit—Hancock, Brooke, Ohio, Marshall, Wetzel, Tyler, and Monongalia. As Thompson presided over the court in Tyler County, William I. Boreman, an attorney in Middlebourne and candidate for the Virginia House of Delegates—and brother of the future governor of West Virginia—described for Francis H. Pierpont the frenzy over secession among the people gathered for court days. Boreman noted that county residents had previously opposed suggestions of separating western Virginia from eastern Virginia but had gravitated toward the idea. He also discussed several local leaders who had endorsed secession, but he emphasized that Judge Thompson was an "out and out Union man."[3]

The situation intensified in May. Gov. John Letcher called out the state militia in support of the Richmond government on the first of the month and asked for additional volunteers for Virginia's pro-Confederate forces two days later. Robert E. Lee, commander of Virginia forces, assigned Col. George A. Porterfield of Jefferson County to command the state's forces in northwestern Virginia on May 4, and Porterfield arrived in Taylor County on May 14. There, he found Capt. William P. Thompson and his Marion Guards from Fairmont ready to support him. The captain was Judge Thompson's oldest son. Eight days earlier, Thompson and his men had paraded at a pro-Union rally in Fairmont.[4]

The tide began to turn against George W. Thompson. Not only did he have a son in command of a pro-Confederate company, but his conservatism ran counter to the growing mood in Wheeling toward separation from Virginia. On May 10, three days before the First Wheeling Convention convened, Thompson issued instructions to the grand jury in Ohio County. He discussed the oaths that he and the jurors took and their obligation to the US Constitution and the state as a dual obligation. The judge spoke of the mutual commitments of the federal and state governments to one another. In this light, he said, the federal government had the constitutional duty to suppress insurrections but also the responsibility to guarantee that no state was formed from another without the consent of the older state.[5]

The Unionist activists, especially those taking the opportunity to advocate splitting the western counties from Virginia, bridled at Thompson's words. Granville Davisson Hall, who served as recorder at the First and Second Wheeling Conventions, wrote about the judge's instructions years later. He called Thompson "a judicial crank." Hall, ignoring the full context of Thompson's charge, remarked that instead of being aimed at the

Confederacy as it should have been, "it was directed at the much smaller game, the persons who were talking about the division of the State." With an ironic hint of disingenuity, Hall insisted that Thompson's opinion had minor effect. "All realized that however else the fundamental questions at issue might be solved, they were not to be solved by the interpretation of small-bore courts," he wrote.[6]

After the First Wheeling Convention and the statewide referendum on secession the following week, Virginians separated into more definite camps. Colonel Porterfield recruited soldiers in Taylor and nearby counties, and the Confederacy sent additional troops from eastern Virginia. Porterfield consolidated his forces around the junction of the Baltimore and Ohio and the Northwestern Railroads at Grafton. Union forces from Indiana, Ohio, and Virginia gathered at Parkersburg and Wheeling, and Maj. Gen. George B. McClellan ordered them toward Grafton. Judge Thompson rendered another fiat in this intensifying atmosphere. "I hereby, in the names of those Constituencies and the laws made in pursuance thereof, in times of peace and prosperity, and with the consent of all the good people of the Commonwealth, as necessary for the protection of life, liberty, property and the lawful pursuit of happiness, do call on all the good citizens to obey these wise and salutary laws; and to aid me in their firm and salutary enforcement by obedience themselves, and for the punishment of the lawless," Thompson said in a written statement. "To those citizens of West Virginia, whose large majority against secession show a firm determination to maintain and defend their Constitutional obligations, I appeal to maintain the law and order which both of these instruments guarantee and enforce," Thompson wrote to Unionists. To pro-Confederate residents, which included his two oldest sons, he pleaded, "To those citizens of Western Virginia who claim the right of secession, in like manner I appeal to lay down their arms against their brethren and fathers, and to submit to the judgment and wish of their own people, in as large a portion of the State as West Virginia."[7]

Archibald W. Campbell, the Republican editor and copublisher of the *Wheeling Daily Intelligencer*, commented on Judge Thompson's "sort of extra-judicial proclamation, or rather exhortation, to the malefactors in arms against the Government." He believed that Thompson's statement was "well meant" and hoped that "so far as it has any effect at all it will be a good one," but he did "not see that it bids fair to accomplish much." Campbell referred to the spiraling events and concluded, "This is not the time to address malefactors with the 'logic of the law.'"[8]

Unionists might no longer have paid heed to Thompson's words, but leaders of the pro-Confederate state government in Richmond did. The state convention in Richmond, after the vote on secession, continued in session and labored as a legislative body while the actual legislature was not in session. By July 1, George W. Thompson remained as the sole circuit court judge in the state who had not openly sided with the governments in Richmond, and the convention moved to suspend his salary. Leonard S. Hall, a Wetzel County attorney, was among the few western Virginians still serving in the convention. He told the convention that he knew Thompson as a fellow lawyer and had practiced in his court as a prosecutor. Hall called Thompson "an enemy of the State of Virginia" and said that "instead of wearing the judicial ermine, he ought to wear a halter around his neck." The delegate described Thompson as "a very weak man, too" and evoked laughter when he remarked, "I do not attribute his disloyalty to the State of Virginia to any malignity, but to an utter want of sense." In supporting the measure against the judge, Hall referred to Thompson's charge to the grand jury in Ohio County, to his statements against secession, and to an order that he issued to open polls for pro-Union elections for the Wheeling Conventions. He added, "We [Confederate loyalists] cannot even obtain the benefit of habeas corpus in his circuit, and we are unable to obtain release from prison whenever we are incarcerated, as many of us are at this time."[9]

George W. Berlin of Upshur County gave Thompson the benefit of the doubt. "Knowing Judge Thompson as long as I have to be a patriotic gentleman, I have no doubt that if he is at this moment guilty of any impropriety towards the State of Virginia, it is owing more to the pressure of circumstances and the influence of affairs around him, than to any lack of sense of patriotism," Berlin said in the judge's defense. "He is in the situation of hundreds and thousands of other Virginians in that country who are peculiarly surrounded and controlled by circumstances that prevent him from uttering his sentiments in safety, or acting, as I have no doubt he would, if his hands were free." In the end, however, the convention suspended Thompson.[10]

Meanwhile, the pro-Union government of Frances H. Pierpont began enforcing the extraordinary legislation of the Second Wheeling Convention. That included a new oath for public officials that required allegiance to the government at Wheeling as well as to the United States. Another ordinance required public officials to certify to the secretary of the commonwealth that they had taken the oath. Thompson refused to take the oath. In a rambling letter addressed to the US Senate, the Supreme Court, and the "People of North West Virginia" on the Fourth of July, he explained his refusal and anticipated his removal from the bench. Thompson insisted that the ordinance, which required the oath, was ex post facto, and, referring to the state leaders at Wheeling, contended that "this faction cannot place their touch on a single expression of sentiment nor a single act of unkindness, or hostility to the Union or to the movement of the Union so far as the Union has taken ground for the defence of the Union sentiment in Virginia or elsewhere" or "to a single expression which connects me in principle or sentiment with the Secession movement." In direct disdain of Pierpont, he wrote, "I believe that the [federal] government is strong enough to protect them [the people]; and is pledged by constitutional principles, in the enforcement of the laws of the Union, and not on the idle fallacy of the demand of an unconstitutional and in no legitimate sense of the phrase, a *de facto* Governor to protect them against domestic violence."[11]

Reaction to Thompson's letter was swift and withering. "His gun scatters well, but he has loaded it too heavily," quipped a fellow member of the Ohio County bar. "It shoots stronger backwards than forwards." The lawyer suggested, "I would recommend the Judge, by all means, to get into the Southern Confederacy, or the Asylum at Staunton; I do not know . . . which would be best."[12]

Thompson's letter suggested a personal animosity between Thompson and Governor Pierpont, and no one seemed surprised that a strained history existed between the men. One editor called the two "life-long opponents."[13] In an account written at the end of the Civil War, Thompson attributed his difficulty with Pierpont to a disparaging remark that he had once made in chambers about Pierpont's sole appearance as an attorney before Thompson's court.[14]

Four days after Thompson wrote his letter, Governor Pierpont declared his seat on the circuit court vacant and arranged for a special election to fill it. The governor cited the fact that Thompson had refused to take the oath established by the Second Wheeling Convention.[15]

Following his removal from the bench, Thompson became the butt of jokes, and went from being viewed as one of the most intelligent men of western Virginia early in 1861 to being labeled as a fool and from being seen as a patriot to being branded as a rebel. "We wouldn't stop much to be very severe on the Judge for his turn-coat disposition which has characterized him all the days of his life, but it would be disgraceful to strike at so successful a suicide," the editor of the *Tyler County Plaindealer* wrote in response to the ridicule that was heaped upon Thompson. "Poor man, let him go—he is now reaping the reward which he so richly merits."[16] The public scorn against Thompson died down, but he lived under suspicion.

The light of suspicion became bright when the former judge stepped forward to post the $10,000 bail for a fellow Wheeling Democrat. In September 1861, a federal grand jury indicted Thomas Hughes for treason because he had "lent aid and comfort to the enemy." The federal prosecutor based the charge on the fact that Hughes had provided clothing to men who had signed up for the Confederate Army. Wheeling attorney Nathaniel Richardson, while waiting for his own client's hearing on another charge, watched the proceedings against Hughes and made an observation that might have easily applied to Thompson. Richardson remarked that "it is a very convenient thing to find an indictment for treason against a man," that "nearly every man you meet on the street has his own law of treason, in the present condition of the country," and that "nearly every member of the Grand Jury has his own law of treason."[17]

The light of suspicion continued to follow Thompson. In the same month as Hughes's hearing, a correspondent, styling himself as "Northwest," wrote to the *Richmond Daily Dispatch* from Camp Bartow, a Confederate outpost on the headwaters of Greenbrier River in Pocahontas County: "Judge Thompson, long bitterly against secession, now writes that he 'sees no hope for constitutional liberty save in the success of the arms of the Southern Confederacy.'" The anonymous report might seem insignificant except that the Thirty-First Virginia Infantry, the regiment in which Thompson's sons, William and Lewis, served, was then posted at Camp Bartow.[18]

As Christmas drew near in 1861, Thompson and his family received reports that their sons, William and Lewis, had been severely wounded in a Union attack on the Confederate position on the Parkersburg-Staunton Turnpike at the summit of Allegheny Mountain on the Highland and Pocahontas County line.[19] Judge Thompson remained on his farm east of Wheeling, and his wife, Elizabeth, hastened to Richmond in company with Dr. N. W. White, a lawyer from Wellsburg in Thompson's old circuit. She learned that William was all right, but Lewis had been killed in the battle.[20]

Elizabeth Thompson returned to Wheeling, and her visit behind the lines, along with the death of their son in Confederate service, only added to the qualms about her husband. The provost marshal at Wheeling, Joseph Darr, shared in the suppositions about Thompson. On May 30, 1862, Darr ordered two squads of Union soldiers to arrest a group of men, ostensibly because of their public "joy" at Nathaniel P. Banks's setbacks in the Shenandoah Valley. Darr had, in fact, expressed his intention of arresting all who had voted for secession (known because of Virginia's viva voce voting system) at the least excuse. The squads swept down upon Thompson and seven others.[21]

Soldiers apparently apprehended Thompson away from his home, and Major Darr allowed him to go home and to notify his family of his arrest. Thompson reported back to Darr the next day, and the provost marshal offered to release him if he swore the loyalty oath to the federal government and the state government. Five others had taken the oath and were released. Thompson, William S. Goshorn, and Dr. Alfred Hughes refused to take the oath. Goshorn, a retail merchant, was a brother-in-law of Union general Benjamin F. Kelley. Hughes, a homeopathic physician, was a brother of Thomas Hughes. Major Darr held the three in the county jail and sent them to Camp Chase five days later.[22]

The *Wellsburg Herald* reported Major Darr's "lively time recently in stirring up the secesh sympathizers" and noted that Darr's crusade had been effective in convincing "a number more of the same sort" to take the loyalty oath rather than risk arrest. In its report, the Brooke County newspaper could not resist mocking Thompson. "Poor Judge, wise logomachist, author of the Dialogue of Devils, profound delver in the Infinite Category, let us not be thought making light of thy captivity or doubting thy tenderness of conscience, but the day of humbuggery is past, Judge, and it is the very folly of the moon to be wasting time that might be otherwise better employed, and heaving sighs for history within the walls of the Ohio county jail, as yet unconsecrated except by very ordinary victims of the law," chided the editor. "We take the liberty of advising the Judge, by all means, to swear, lest posterity set him down something that he isn't."[23]

Thompson had fallen from political and social grace in dominant, wartime Wheeling circles, but he was not without friends. Some influential associates and family kept quiet contact when necessary. Among them was his son-in-law, Johnson N. Camden, a Parkersburg attorney and pioneer in the oil industry. In turn, Camden's associates included Judge John J. Jackson Jr., an early partner with Camden in the oil business. Camden's biographer Festus P. Summers emphasized another of Thompson's connections. Summers pointed to Thompson's friendship with Edwin M. Stanton, the US secretary of war. Summers does not make clear the basis for their friendship, but Thompson and Stanton likely crossed paths on a number of occasions. Both were active Democrats in the Upper Ohio Valley beginning in the 1830s and may have known one another when both practiced law in Ohio. Stanton certainly knew of Thompson while the latter served as US attorney. They also may have encountered one another during controversy over the Wheeling Suspension Bridge impeding river traffic to and from Pittsburgh. Thompson had represented Wheeling interests in the case, and Stanton had represented the interests of Pennsylvania. Regardless of how they met, Summers described Stanton as Thompson's "old friend," and wrote that Stanton intervened on Thompson's behalf in 1862 for his release from Camp Chase.[24]

Still others belonged to Thompson's network of friends. He himself attributed his release from Camp Chase to "the instrumentality of personal friends at Richmond," and the work of those friends may have met with success because of a receptive Stanton.[25] Moves toward Thompson's release began in Richmond in August 1862. The *Richmond Daily Dispatch* told its readers that the Confederate government had begun efforts to exchange Thompson for a Union Army sutler in its custody.[26] Efforts proceeded quietly. The US War Department exchanged Thompson on September 23 by order of the secretary of war. The US Army judge advocate Levi C. Turner executed the order, and by the end of September, Thompson was back home.[27] The War Department did not clue Major Darr in on the particulars of Thompson's release, and Darr seethed when he learned of the judge's return. The provost marshal wasted no time in summoning Thompson, and insisted that, unless he was officially told otherwise by his superiors, he would confine those who refused to take the loyalty oath. Thompson's family deflected and advised Darr that the judge was too ill to come to town.[28] Darr persisted and pressed the War Department with concerns about Thompson's disloyalty. Turner conceded to Thompson's detention "till further orders" and admonished Darr to "report proofs of his disloyalty since his exchange."[29]

According to Thompson's own account, "on my return home I was loudly threatened by Darr, the instrument of Peirpoint, when I appealed to the Sec. of War and the Judge Advocate and the latter made an express order that I would not be disturbed except upon instruction from Washington."[30] Thompson alluded to a letter sent to Darr by Turner on October 3, which referenced back-and-forth communication between the provost marshal and the judge advocate. In the letter, Turner made it clear that if Thompson "does nothing that is disloyal in word or deed since his return, he cannot be molested for anything that occurred before his exchange." He told Darr that if Thompson did anything disloyal to the Union after his return home that the major should "send the proofs."[31]

Public reaction to Thompson's return varied. His friends and supporters were heartened, even emboldened, by the fact that the War Department had not required him to take the loyalty oath to the federal and state governments. Unwavering Unionists reacted differently. "We need not say that we in the last degree condemn the false contrivance by which this bad man has been sent back among us unhumbled," expressed the editor of the *Wheeling Daily Intelligencer.* "And we feel it our duty now to loudly protest to the Government against the pernicious act by which he was let loose without compliance with the most stringent letter of the law."[32]

George W. Thompson remained a symbol of opposition as 1862 came to a close, and the movement for West Virginia statehood entered its final stages. Congress gave its approval for the new state, and Abraham Lincoln signed the statehood bill in December. As the new year dawned, the state constitutional convention took final actions to meet congressional demands to end slavery, and residents began to prepare for the new state. The politics surrounding these events proved divisive. The Republican *Wheeling Daily Intelligencer* and the *Wheeling Press,* its Democratic counterpart, quibbled over the inclusion of Democrats in the new state movement. The *Daily Intelligencer* insisted that Democrats had been well represented in the movement, while the *Press* contended that Democrats had been marginalized and persecuted.[33] The truth is that a number of prominent Democrats participated in the creation of West Virginia, but it also is true that Democrats who formed most of the loyal opposition to the formation of a new state had been equated with secessionists and Confederate sympathizers, and Thompson had been made their face.

Statehood supporters feared the least criticism of their efforts, but their concerns went beyond political ones. They had witnessed the pattern of arrests of officials of the Restored Government of Virginia, with the seizure of Sheriff James Trahern of Barbour County in January being the latest. Trahern's arrest had triggered retaliations, including the taking of hostages by the Union Army, and those actions had resulted in the deaths of two Barbour County civilians. Col. John D. Imboden, the Confederate commander who had ordered Trahern's capture, responded in turn with wording that interchanged the Restored Government of Virginia and the newly created state. Imboden promised the arrest "within the limit of the pretended State of West Virginia" of "every man I can lay my hands upon who holds an office under the usurped State Government at Wheeling."[34] The threat to the Wheeling government and the proposed state widened as Robert E. Lee endorsed Imboden's course. "The idea of capturing the municipal officers of the Peirpoint government is a very good one," Lee wrote to Imboden. "It would relieve the people of the northwest very much to capture them all, and render the office of sheriff as dangerous position as possible."[35]

Future West Virginia governor Arthur I. Boreman, serving as a circuit court judge in Parkersburg early in 1863, shared his sense of the political and physical dangers in the months leading up to the admission of the new state into the Union. "I feel more fearful for the future of West Virginia than ever heretofore," Boreman confided in a letter to Governor Pierpont. "Is it possible that the enemies of the country upon the pretext that their purpose is to discuss the 'new State proposition,' are to be permited [*sic*] to preach treason all over the new State territory?" Boreman complained that the opponents of the new state operated "under the guise of pretended loyalty" and claimed only to be warning the people "against usurpations and efforts to take away their liberties." Though not aware of the communications between Confederate leaders, Boreman saw a rise in military and paramilitary activity against Unionists and proponents of the new state in his circuit, which he believed to be inspired by the campaign against statehood and told Pierpont that "below the 'Panhandle' it is not safe for a loyal man to go into the interior."[36]

In March, the Confederates formulated a plan that added to the fears of Boreman and other supporters of the Union and the new state. Imboden, by then a brigadier general in command of the Northwestern Virginia Brigade, proposed a two-pronged attack into northwestern Virginia in conjunction with Brig. Gen. William E. Jones, commander of the Valley District. Imboden listed one of his goals as holding "that section of the country long enough to overthrow the local government."[37]

Imboden and Jones launched their raid in late April 1863, and, according to local historian Charles A. Wingerter, "the state of apprehension that existed throughout the country was shared by the people of Wheeling."[38] The provost marshal, Joseph Darr, instituted martial law in the city as Jones's men reached Morgantown and Fairmont (where they burned the governor's home library), and rumors swirled that they were approaching Wheeling. The major closed bars and saloons, banned the discharge of firearms in the city, put a 10 P.M. curfew in effect, and required passengers to obtain passes to travel on the B&O Railroad. He also made another roundup of suspected Confederate sympathizers.[39]

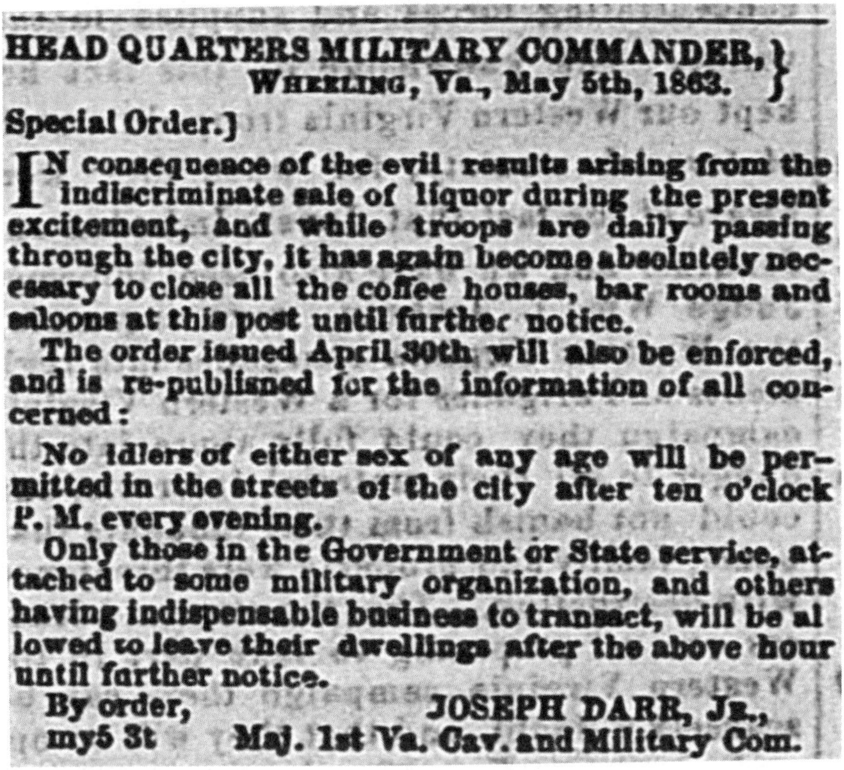

**HEAD QUARTERS MILITARY COMMANDER,**
**WHEELING, Va., May 5th, 1863.**

**Special Order.]**

**IN consequence of the evil results arising from the indiscriminate sale of liquor during the present excitement, and while troops are daily passing through the city, it has again become absolutely necessary to close all the coffee houses, bar rooms and saloons at this post until further notice.**

**The order issued April 30th will also be enforced, and is re-published for the information of all concerned:**

**No idlers of either sex of any age will be permitted in the streets of the city after ten o'clock P. M. every evening.**

**Only those in the Government or State service, attached to some military organization, and others having indispensable business to transact, will be allowed to leave their dwellings after the above hour until further notice.**

**By order, JOSEPH DARR, Jr.,**
**my5 3t Maj. 1st Va. Cav. and Military Com.**

Provost marshal Joseph Darr Jr. policed West Virginia, especially Wheeling, with a firm hand, and he imprisoned many residents for the least opposition to the Union and Virginia's pro-Union government. (*Wheeling Daily Intelligencer,* May 7, 1863)

Darr undertook his work with earnestness and relish. The English novelist, George A. Lawrence, provided some insight on Darr's approach to his work. Brought before the provost marshal as a suspicious person, Lawrence described Darr as a "functionary" and said that he "affects a Napoleonic curtness and decision of speech." Lawrence added, "Nevertheless, he was amenable to reason."[40] William A. Blair, in *With Malice toward Some: Treason and Loyalty in the Civil War Era,* explained, "Because of its strategic importance and volatile politics, the border region brought out the best and worst in the officials charged with monitoring internal security."[41]

In his earnestness, Darr included George W. Thompson in his roundup of Confederate sympathizers during the Jones-Imboden Raid. On April

28, a detail of soldiers took Thompson into custody under Darr's orders and placed him in the Atheneum.[42] The provost marshal was well aware of the judge advocate's admonition from the previous fall but used the ongoing Confederate raid to justify Thompson's arrest. He telegraphed the judge advocate, Levi C. Turner, and rationalized that the prisoner was being held "on account of suspicious movements of his for the past few days." Darr added that Thompson's "son is among the rebels now committing raids in West Virginia," and that Thompson was "an enemy of the Government whose surveillance for some days is requisite and demanded by the present state of affairs." Darr further revealed to the War Department that Thompson was being held as a hostage by order of Governor Pierpont. The provost marshal took a stand in closing that seemed to allude to Thompson's release from Camp Chase the previous year. "I trust no influence can be brought to bear upon the Government to release him from custody until the rebels are driven out of this part of the State," he wrote.[43]

Thompson's family appealed directly to Edwin M. Stanton the next day. John Thompson told the secretary of war that no charges had been filed against his brother and that the former judge simply was being held as a hostage.[44] With this and Darr's telegram in hand, the judge advocate replied two days later, "I am directed by the Sec'y of War to say—That, whenever the public safety is not endangered by rebel raids in your vicinity, you will discharge Judge Thompson, provided he be not guilty of treasonable and disloyal actings, since his exchange."[45]

Darr, however, had no intention of releasing Thompson once the Confederate raid subsided, and he used pro-Union Virginia's hostage law to keep the judge in custody. Based on the cooperative relationship that had grown between Governor Pierpont and Darr, the governor allowed Darr a great deal of discretion in situations where state and federal concerns intersected.

In his book, Blair observed that the "Union's internal security and mobilization systems consisted of federal, state, and local officials who sometimes pursued competing goals."[46] In the case of pro-Union Virginia in 1863, and perhaps in other states, a symbiotic relationship lessened competition for the sake of common interests. Thus, when Darr desired to confine Thompson once and for all, the Confederate raid provided the kindling, but the continuing imprisonment of Barbour County's sheriff by the Confederates furnished the fuel.

Thompson fit the bill for arrest under the hostage law. State and federal officials in Wheeling agreed that Thompson had expressed "known disloyal sentiments," and Trahern needed "safe rendition" from the hands of "the so-called southern confederacy, the pretended state government at Richmond or other military organizations acting in sympathy or concert with them, or either of them." In this way, George W. Thompson became the first hostage held under the hostage law passed in February 1863.

In further comments on security roles during the Civil War, William A. Blair noted that "state and local power remained in play and mitigated the reach of national agents in certain communities."[47] In the Thompson case, a federal official collaborated with state officials to keep state and local power in play. That collaboration mitigated the reach of national agents from Washington.

Thompson commented on that collaboration as he recounted his plight in a March 1865 letter to Col. James Washburn, Darr's successor as provost marshal in Wheeling. He recalled that "in the excitement of the times, and the fresh occasion furnishing a pretext under which to cover the indulgence of malignant passions I was again seized by these men and thrown into their common receptacle among lunatics, drunkards, deserters, common soldiers and prisoners of war." Thompson noted that he was confident "that Peirpoint's law could be of no validity except as ancillary to the war powers of the General Government." He explained that despite the existence of "not only the order of the Judge Advocate already alluded to in my behalf, but a subsequent order made after this last arrest that I should be discharged unless held under some proper state authority I was then in evasion of that order turned over from the government prison to the County Jail."[48]

Thompson's transfer from the government prison—the Atheneum—to Ohio County Jail took place because of events that had occurred shortly beforehand in federal court in the US Custom House in Wheeling. Nathaniel Richardson, Thompson's attorney, filed a petition on June 17 that alleged Pierpont, Darr, or Capt. Robert Hamilton, commander of an exempt company assigned to guard the Atheneum, illegally held Thompson. The US attorney, Benjamin H. Smith, responded with an affidavit from Darr in which he insisted that he had no control over Thompson because the prisoner was a hostage under state law.[49]

Judge John J. Jackson Jr. granted a writ of habeas corpus the next morning and ordered Darr to produce Thompson by 2 P.M. that day. Darr appeared in the afternoon and contended that he had not arrested Thompson but that the former judge had been arrested under the governor's authority. The major admitted that Thompson had been held in the Atheneum

Judge John J. Jackson Jr. pictured during the Thompson hearing. Jackson remained on the federal bench until Theodore Roosevelt was president. (Hon. John J. Jackson, Joseph H. Diss Debar Collection, West Virginia State Archives, Charleston, WV)

but said that when the federal court became involved, he, "fearing that the United States might become involved in a difficulty in which it had no interest, refused to keep him any longer in confinement." Jackson dismissed the case involving Darr, and Richardson requested a new writ naming Pierpont and James S. Wheat, the state attorney general.[50]

Judge Jackson began a hearing on the petition on June 19 but granted a two-day continuance. In the meantime, jurisdiction over Wheeling passed from the Restored Government of Virginia to West Virginia, and Wheeling was its capital. In addition, a new attorney general replaced Wheat, and the restored government moved to Alexandria.[51]

When the court reconvened, no one appeared from Virginia's pro-Union government—neither attorney general nor governor. With no argument against it, Jackson granted the writ and required the state to produce Thompson. The judge added that if the hearing on the writ ended in Thompson's favor, he would have to take an oath of allegiance to the United States.[52]

A Saturday hearing took place on the writ on June 27, but in the meantime the writ had expired. Pierpont used that as a reason not to appear, and neither did his attorney general. Instead, West Virginia's attorney general, Aquilla B. Caldwell, appeared. Judge Jackson pressed for an answer from Pierpont, and Caldwell left the court to confer with the governor. Still, Pierpont demurred, and the judge became frustrated that his patience with Pierpont had not been respected.[53]

The hearing proceeded with Caldwell moving for dismissal of the writ. He argued that the federal court had no jurisdiction since Thompson had been arrested under state authority, and he called Darr to the stand to reiterate the point. Richardson took the opportunity to cross-examine the provost marshal and showed him as resentful of Thompson's release from Camp Chase the previous year and of his protection by the War Department. In exasperation, Darr insisted that Thompson had been "a disloyal man and a traitor to the Government," but when Richardson pressed, Darr could not cite a specific instance.[54]

Following the provost marshal's testimony, Caldwell mysteriously produced a written response to the writ from Governor Pierpont. Richardson objected to the form of the response, and Jackson asked Caldwell if he thought it was "a respectable document and whether he was responsible for it." The West Virginia attorney general assured the court that Pierpont had prepared the document. The judge called it "a paper which no gentleman, having any respect for himself or the court, would have submitted."[55]

Richardson added his objections to the surreptitious nature of the response and Caldwell's acquisition of it. "It will be well for us to know whether we are to be slaves of midnight caucuses, or whether we shall have redress in the courts," he said. Richardson then asked that the judge refuse to admit the response, which essentially repeated Caldwell's and Darr's arguments. Jackson agreed to consider the request and added, "The court regrets that there should be any conflict of authority, but it [will] do what it conceive[s] to be its duty in spite of any man, no matter how high his official position."[56]

Richardson saw an opening to move for Thompson's discharge. He labeled his client's arrest and imprisonment as a "malignant and diabolical outrage," but Caldwell countered that such talk was inappropriate "when we are engaged in a constitutional effort to suppress a wicked and infamous rebellion." He pressed the point that Thompson's refusal to take the oath to the federal and state governments constituted disloyalty, Richardson called the oath unconstitutional and asked the judge to set it aside from consideration.[57]

The spatting between attorneys ended, and Judge Jackson had the final say. He stated "that it [the court] was clearly of the opinion that it had jurisdiction in the case, and that the prisoner was arrested by color of authority of the United States." The only question involved whether Thompson had been illegally detained. With that, the arguments had pushed into Saturday afternoon, and the court adjourned until Monday.[58]

Richardson fired the first volley when the hearing reopened on June 29. He took on the hostage law and insisted "the Governor who would demand such an act and the Legislature that would grant it were unworthy the confidence of a free people." He focused on the prosecution's inability to name a single act of disloyalty on Thompson's part. Caldwell held to the notion that refusal to take the allegiance oath constituted disloyalty.[59] Further quibbling between the lawyers and outbursts of personal animosity between Thompson and Caldwell punctuated the rest of the day. All that was left was the judge's decision.

The judge, John J. Jackson Jr., had come to the federal bench in 1861 when his predecessor resigned due to the secession of Virginia. Before that, Jackson had been an active Whig and doubtless had encountered Francis H. Pierpont when the two served as presidential electors on behalf of the party. He certainly had interacted with Pierpont when they both had served in the First and Second Wheeling Conventions in 1861. Jackson had served in the Virginia House of Delegates in the early 1850s and had been succeeded in his seat by fellow Whig Arthur I. Boreman. In his early political life, he had been prosecuting attorney of both Ritchie and Wirt Counties at the same time. Of interest in the Thompson case, Jackson's sister eventually married one of George W. Thompson's sons. Jackson bore criticism as a judge during the Civil War from some Republicans, who thought him too lenient toward Confederate sympathizers because of his strict interpretation of laws. A biographer, who practiced in his court, explained that Jackson "always openly denounced what he conceived to be wrong wherever it appeared, in friend or foe," and that the judge's "nature was above that mean level where men sometimes consent to serve a cause, they even conceive to be just, in the dark and devious ways of fraud and conspiracy."[60]

Given his reputation and his comments during the hearing, Jackson's opinion in the case came as little surprise. Jackson recognized the grave situation and shared his desire to avoid a clash with either military or state authorities. He rehearsed the facts of the case and concluded that Thompson had been under the jurisdiction and protection of the War Department in April 1863 because of his exchange in 1862, that Darr had acted as a US Army officer without input from Governor Pierpont at the time that he had taken Thompson as a hostage (though Pierpont had later endorsed Darr's actions), and that no state court had ordered Thompson's arrest in the due process of law. Jackson, therefore, denied the claims of the state that Thompson's case should be a state matter and that the federal court held no jurisdiction.[61]

The judge addressed the odd transfer of Thompson from the Atheneum on the day that the writ of habeas corpus was served. "The removal of the prisoner under such circumstances has the appearance of an attempt on the part of those who detained him in custody to avoid the jurisdiction of the court, though such may not have been in fact the intention of the parties," Jackson said. He made it clear that the transfer would not have had any effect because "once the jurisdiction of a court attaches to any subject of controversy it cannot be deprived of its jurisdiction by any effort of any character so long as the subject of controversy is under the process or within the power of the court." Jackson noted that after the transfer Darr, Pierpont, nor the attorney general had brought Thompson to court. Rather, the jailer of the Ohio County Jail had responded to the writ.[62]

Judge Jackson also discussed the hostage law. He mentioned hostages taken by the army, including ones requested by the governor before passage of the hostage law, and noted that the War Department reported the existence of such hostages to the federal court in compliance with the Habeas Corpus Act of 1863. Jackson made no distinction between those hostages and Thompson and at the same time in an apparent effort at diplomacy backed away from blaming Pierpont for Thompson's confinement despite the governor's insistence that Thompson was a state prisoner. Jackson referred to the War Department's control over hostages and said, "The Governor cannot and does not claim more in this case." The judge stated while the governor could ask for hostages to be taken that it "must be done under the power of the War Department, and subject to its confirmation." He observed that the power to make war and to make rules and regulations regarding war belonged to Congress. "It is true that a State possesses the inherent right of self-defence," Jackson went on. "But no State relies, under our Constitution, upon her own natural and inherent rights for defence." He pointed out that states had claim on the federal government for protection and that any action taken "towards suppressing the present rebellion, although it may be done by a State officer, is in pursuance of the Constitution of the United States and the laws enacted by Congress relating to the subject." Jackson cited federal jurisdiction over prisoners and hostages resulting from the war and affirmed that any "State law passed upon this subject is only a cumulative remedy in aid of the General Government, and would not deprive the prisoner of the rules and regulations of war, as laid down by the law of nations relating to this subject." In discharging Thompson, the judge concluded, "I am, therefore, of the opinion that all prisoners and hostages taken in this war, are in point of civil as well as military law, subject to the Federal authorities." Darr had denied claim of jurisdiction over Thompson. So, Judge Jackson determined that federal authorities had no further interest in holding Thompson.[63]

Jackson did not release Thompson without condition, however. He had earlier in the case mentioned the need for Thompson to take an oath of allegiance if he was released. At this point, the judge explained that he "could not ignore the fact that the loyal portion of the country are engaged at this time in a most patriotic effort to suppress a most wicked rebellion." He told Thompson that he must swear allegiance to the United States or post a $5,000 bond and leave the state until readmitted by the War Department. Thompson did not take the oath, posted the bond, and went to live across the Ohio River in Belmont County, Ohio, where he had once lived and practiced law.[64]

Francis H. Pierpont did not let the judge's ruling pass unanswered. Nine days after Jackson rendered his opinion, the governor sent a response to the *Wheeling Daily Intelligencer.* Pierpont began with a justification of the hostage law as a necessary protection for the people of the state. "Self preservation is the first law of our nature," Pierpont asserted. "It is the highest duty of a State to protect its loyal citizens." He revealed that both the president and the Confederate government had been informed of the passage of the law and affirmed the intention of his administration to enforce it. Pierpont claimed that the mere announcement of the law had resulted in the release of close to four hundred pro-Union citizens from captivity by the Confederates.[65]

The governor argued against the judge's opinion that the hostage law was unconstitutional. He cited the existence of dual federal and Virginia laws since the existence of the nation that allowed the chief executive to arrest, confine, or exile the citizen of a country at war with the United States. Pierpont wrote that the existence of Virginia's law had never been challenged by the federal government as interfering with its powers, and he compared it with the new hostage law. He based the legitimacy of both laws on the assumption that allegiance and protection were linked. Pierpont further reasoned that if a state's defense powers could be exercised only in subordination to the federal government, a state could not call out its militia or quell a riot without federal approval. The governor condescendingly asserted that "the Judge was bewildered and did not understand his subject."[66]

Pierpont contended that while hostages were seized without a court order, victims of the hostage law could seek relief in state courts and appeal to the state supreme court. He denied that Thompson had been anything but a state prisoner. In that regard, he noted that Jackson's assertion that Thompson was a federal prisoner contradicted the judge's early dismissal of Darr from the writ of habeas corpus. Pierpont then claimed in his own contradiction that the provost marshal was not a US Army officer but held his commission from the state and therefore could not have placed Thompson in federal custody. In fact, Darr, like most army officers, held a commission with a state regiment that had been mustered into federal service. Indeed, his commission in the First Virginia Cavalry was merely a formality, and he never served with the regiment in its operations. He served under the orders of the army and War Department, was responsible for the federal military draft, and regularly arrested prisoners on behalf of the federal government.[67]

Pierpont closed with an assault on Jackson's exile of Thompson. In this, the governor hurled insults at the judge. "He had the same authority to send him to Botany Bay, as to send where he did," Pierpont wrote. "I suppose there is not a lawyer in the country but sincerely regrets the humiliation of seeing a man on the bench first prescribing extra judicial oaths under solemn order—then backing down and entering up orders of banishment without authority of law." He ended, "The records of all courts for the trial of witches, in this country or in Europe, cannot furnish a parallel for absurdity and ridiculousness compared with this case."[68]

The troubles between Thompson and Pierpont did not end with Jackson's ruling. Thompson apparently still had important friends in Ohio. On August 3, while Pierpont waited for a train to Washington at the railroad station in Bridgeport, directly across the Ohio River from Wheeling, the Belmont County sheriff arrived and arrested Pierpont on a warrant for the false imprisonment of George W. Thompson. Pierpont posted a $10,000 bond and made his way to his new capital across the Potomac River from Washington. The sheriff also had a warrant waiting for Darr.[69]

The press reacted swiftly. The Republican *Wheeling Daily Intelligencer* predictably stood by Pierpont and Darr as Thompson sought to "gobble up and annoy" them.[70] Newspapers outside of Wheeling were not so supportive of the governor and provost marshal. The *Washington Examiner*, in Washington, Pennsylvania, just to the east of Wheeling, gleefully announced the arrest of Pierpont, "that paragon of loyalty," and the warrant against Darr. It commented that the "treatment of Judge T. by these two men has been of the most infamous character, and we sincerely hope he may be able to obtain reparation."[71] The *Ohio Statesman* in Columbus wrote, "It is hoped that the course of justice will not be impeded," and it added that "the defendant should have, what the plaintiff had not when arbitrarily seized and imprisoned, a speedy and public trial by an impartial jury of his countrymen, and a judgment upon their verdict."[72]

Pierpont returned for the next term of court in Belmont County in November 1863. The case against him was dropped in time for him to attend the Gettysburg Address. Thompson persisted, however, and instituted a civil suit against Pierpont. The suit dragged on until the War Department in 1864 consented to Thompson's return to West Virginia with the condition that he end the suit. Thompson did not actually return until near the end of the war.[73]

Pierpont's adversaries and detractors did not just include Thompson, Ohio courts, and opposition newspapers. The judge advocate general of the US Army, Joseph Holt, weighed in after Thompson's exile and concurred with Judge Jackson. He shared with Edwin M. Stanton his belief that the "seizing and holding of hostages in reprisal for captures made by the enemy is certainly an exercise of the war-making power, belonging exclusively to the General Government, and which cannot be shared by the Governor of the States without leading to deplorable complications."[74]

It seems that the outcomes of the Thompson case should have stymied the hostage law. The notorious nature of the case took it to the attention of the highest levels of the War Department and to federal district court. The agreement of the executive department and the judiciary in the matter gave weight to the opposition against the law. Their roles also pointed to two facts that are not readily realized. First, the War Department—generally through the US Army Judge Advocate Corps and the commissary general of prisoners—carefully monitored civil liberties and often intervened to safeguard them. A few prominent exceptions accentuate the extraordinary exercise of war powers by the Lincoln Administration. More often, however, abuses of civil rights took place not on the orders of officials in Washington but through the ignorance or zeal of lower-level military and government officials. Second, the federal judiciary was alive and well, even in border areas. Again, infamous cases make it seem otherwise, but judges such as John J. Jackson Jr. kept their courts open and active throughout the war.

Yet, the political and bureaucratic atmosphere of the nineteenth century and especially the Civil War kept the hostage law alive. War Department directives had a way of becoming misplaced or forgotten, especially in the flux of administrators and military commanders. Related to this, army officers tended to give higher regard to their line commanders, and as Pierpont alluded, to the state and local officials with whom they formed clientele relationships.

Additionally, elected officials—particularly governors—used their political relationships and the principle of states' rights to avoid and even ignore federal edicts. Abraham Lincoln was sensitive to the complaints and whims of the governors. He needed their cooperation in raising troops and their political support to keep the administration's war effort popular. The president keenly wanted to keep support in the border states, and Pierpont was key to this. Moreover, he firmly believed in states' rights.

The nineteenth century also remained unsettled about the role of the judiciary, and Jackson's ruling was not the final word on the hostage law. In spite of the growth in judicial power, which had begun in the John Marshall years, acts of Congress and extenuating circumstances such as war often pushed aside court actions. The effect of court opinions often depended upon the political clout of judges with state officials and members of Congress and the executive branch. Thus, it was that Pierpont tried to portray Jackson as inexperienced and over his head in order to dilute his influence.

Finally, the outcome of the Thompson case lost some of its meaning with the transition of state governments in Wheeling. The case arose because of the actions of Francis H. Pierpont and the Restored Government of Virginia, and Pierpont and Darr bore the brunt of criticism from the federal court and the War Department. Some of the wind of that criticism died out, however, as Arthur I. Boreman had taken over as governor of West Virginia by the time Thompson's case was concluded, and the area in which Thompson had been arrested and confined was then in Boreman's domain. Boreman, while undoubtedly interested in the outcome of the case, remained detached from it. He had his own set of problems stemming from the war. They included the seizure of Unionist citizens by the Confederates and the protection of state and local officials from overthrow by the Confederacy and the Virginia government at Richmond.

One remedy presented itself from among the code of laws that West Virginia inherited from Virginia—the hostage law.

Governor Boreman did not order the taking of hostages until September 1863, three months after he took office. The Jones-Imboden Raid figured in Boreman's first hostage cases, just as it did in the George W. Thompson case. Much happened between the capture of Unionist citizens in the spring raid and the early fall when the governor learned of the arrests. Statehood came to fruition, the Thompson case climaxed, and the new state government began its work. The full effects of the Jones-Imboden Raid came slowly to Boreman, but once they did, he responded with the full force of the hostage law.

CHAPTER 4

# The New State and Hostage-Taking after the Jones-Imboden Raid of 1863

A mixed group of men made their way to Parkersburg, downriver from Wheeling, during the first week of May 1863 (see appendix for a timeline of events in chronological context). Some came by steamboat from towns along the Ohio River or came down the Kanawha River to the Ohio. Others came overland from the east on the Northwestern Railroad, Northwestern Turnpike, or Parkersburg and Staunton Turnpike. Others, like Judge Arthur I. Boreman, lived in Parkersburg, but they, too, gathered at the Wood County Courthouse. This group of politicians came together as the Union Party to nominate candidates for the election of West Virginia's first government. For Boreman, the first week of May in 1863 was a monumental time. The Union Party convention launched a series of political events that led him to take fellow West Virginians as hostages four months later, but in the same week, military actions took place that made Boreman a hostage-taker.

Confederate general William E. Jones headed toward Parkersburg in his final advance of the Jones-Imboden Raid that week as well. While conventioneers listened to speeches in the crowded courthouse on May 6, the first day of the convention, word reached them that Jones had attacked West Union, the county seat of Doddridge County. That was just fifty-nine miles away, and "a visible nervousness" gripped many of the delegates. Many believed that the Confederates meant to disrupt or even capture the convention. "I suppose Libby [Prison] would get most of us," the correspondent for the *Wheeling Daily Intelligencer* wrote satirically. "But then we have two gunboats at the landing and a force whose numbers it would hardly be legitimate to speak of, and some of the delegates have revolvers and others have pen-knives, and we're all as valiant as lions, besides."[1]

Jones moved into neighboring Ritchie and Wirt Counties the next day, but the convention stayed on task. The party members included long-winded lawyers, preachers, and professional politicians, yes, but they also included practical men—railroad executives, oilmen, lay ministers, farmers, physicians, merchants, hotel keepers, salt manufacturers, and carpenters—who did not waste time. One of the sages of Appalachian history, Ron Lewis, described this coalition: "The founders of statehood constituted a new mélange of Whigs, Republicans, and Union Democrats who were more economically utilitarian than they were party faithful or political radicals."[2]

On that second day, the convention nominated Boreman for governor.[3] Boreman responded with modesty that he "had hoped that the honor would be conferred on someone else." He accepted, he said, because "no man has a right to withhold his services from the cause of his country" in the midst of the war and the creation of the new state. "Ours is the last hope of an enlightened and liberal Republic on the face of the earth," Boreman seriously maintained. "If it goes down all is lost."[4] The *Wheeling Daily Intelligencer* called Boreman "peculiarly fitted for the place at this time." The newspaper reminded its readers that Boreman had served as president of the Second Wheeling Convention, which had organized Virginia's pro-Union government in 1861. "His abilities as an executive officer—his fearlessness—intelligence and unconditional patriotism were conspicuously manifested in that position."[5]

As Boreman started on the road to becoming governor of West Virginia, the Confederate raiders started on the road home. They did not come into Parkersburg, let alone capture the delegates at the Union Party convention. They did leave a trail of dead, wounded, theft, destruction, and captivity. Over the course of three weeks in April and May 1863, Brig. Gen. John D. Imboden, in his leg of the raid, had advanced up the Parkersburg and Staunton Turnpike, captured Beverly, Buckhannon, and Weston and moved into Barbour County. A roving cavalry force under Imboden had destroyed B&O Railroad bridges west of Fairmont. Imboden's troops had caused Union forces to retreat and burn abandoned supplies and bridges on the turnpike. General Jones had crossed the Potomac region into Maryland and then fanned his forces across Preston County. He had attempted to destroy the strategic B&O Railroad bridge at Rowlesburg but had to satisfy himself with tearing up track, demolishing small bridges, and burning an enginehouse farther west on the railroad and cutting down a suspension bridge over the Cheat River at Albrightsville. Jones's forces had sprinted into Morgantown, thrown the previously secure population into a panic, and nearly burned the suspension bridge over the Monongahela River. Townspeople had convinced the officer in charge, Lt. William L. Wilson, to order the fire doused. In an interesting twist of history, Wilson returned to Morgantown nineteen years later as president of West Virginia University.[6]

Jones next had gone to Fairmont, where the Confederates had blown up the B&O Railroad bridge and burned the books from Francis H. Pierpont's home library. His forces then had moved through Harrison County, avoiding Clarksburg, where Union forces had consolidated, and had destroyed property of the Northwestern Railroad at Bridgeport. Jones and Imboden had rendezvoused at Buckhannon and briefly positioned themselves to move against Clarksburg. The generals had thought better of the plan, and Imboden had started east while Jones had embarked on his foray into Doddridge, Ritchie, and Wirt Counties during the time of the Union Party convention. In the process, Jones had caused minor damage to the Northwestern Railroad and burned oil production and storage facilities on the Little Kanawha River.[7]

The Jones-Imboden Raid had a bracing effect on the Union Army in northwestern Virginia. Union commanders temporarily pulled back from a number of outposts. They lost large amounts of military stores and equipment, and the raiders captured over five hundred Union soldiers. Civilians bore the brunt of the raid, however. Jones and Imboden's men seized over thirty-one hundred head of cattle; substantial numbers of horses, mules, and wagons; and corn, whiskey, and sundry items from stores. Confederate soldiers burned homes of local militia leaders and killed at least two civilians and wounded others who resisted them.[8] Some found themselves held by the Confederates, and while the raiders released most captives before they left their communities, officers sent a handful to prison. The cases of these captives gave Arthur I. Boreman some of his first experiences in using the hostage law.

These cases unfolded in Randolph County, which took the tip of the spear in Imboden's thrust into western Virginia. Randolph County lay sprawled across a series of mountains and valleys that stretched north and south along the length of the county. The Tygarts Valley dominated the county. Resembling the Shenandoah Valley with its rich farmland and northward flowing river, this valley became the center of Randolph County's population. The Parkersburg and Staunton Turnpike entered the valley from the

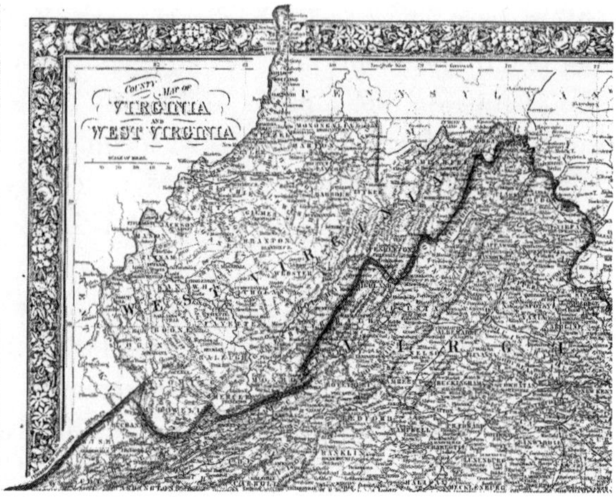


West Virginia and part of Virginia in the aftermath of the Jones-Imboden Raid in 1863. (S. Augustus Mitchell and W. H. Gamble, *County Map of Virginia and West Virginia* [Philadelphia?: S. A. Mitchell, 1863] Map. https://www.loc.gov/item/lva0000095/)

southeast and linked the two most prominent towns—Huttonsville and Beverly, the county seat—with Rich Mountain guiding the traveler on the west side of the valley and the darker, higher Cheat Mountain looming to the east. Scattered settlements lined the turnpike before it turned west at Beverly and passed over Rich Mountain and its battlefield, which figured prominently in the opening months of the Civil War. The villages of Mingo Flats and Valley Head sat south of Huttonsville, where Point Mountain and Valley Mountain hemmed in the southern reaches of the valley. To the north of Beverly, along the road that led to Philippi and eventually to the B&O Railroad, Leadsville thrived near the foot of Laurel Mountain, the scene of another early battle of the war.

Tygarts Valley, with fertile and relatively level farmland, hosted the most prosperous residents of Randolph County. To the west, across Rich Mountain, and to the east across Cheat, Shavers, Middle, and another Rich Mountain, more remote, sparsely populated communities and isolated farms existed. The people in these areas practiced subsistence agriculture more than market agriculture and were less advantaged than those in the Tygarts Valley. Economic divides led to social and political divides. In the Tygarts Valley, with the exception of Leadsville—which competed with Beverly and was more northward oriented—Confederate sympathy was high. In the Middle Fork and Roaring Creek areas to the west and the Glady and Gandy Creek and Dry Fork areas to the east, Union sympathy was more pronounced. Overall, Randolph County favored the Confederacy by a ratio of about three to one. This dynamic caused significant conflict over territory, resources, and power, and the presence or lack of presence of the respective military forces in the county meant that one faction or the other controlled the county at various times between 1861 and 1865.

When General Imboden launched his raid in the spring of 1863, Union forces occupied the Tygarts Valley. Open conflict occurred sporadically, mostly in the mountainous areas to the west and east, between guerrilla units. Imboden's appearance in the valley made conflict more general and threatened the status quo, and individual residents jockeyed to take or maintain position in favor of their side. The war became personal in these instances when the status quo was challenged. The fact that many of Imboden's men came from Randolph County intensified the personal nature of his raid.

A particularly stark event illustrates this personal warfare and points to intertwined relationships as the eventual hostage drama unfolded. Near the opening of the raid, Jesse F. Phares, sheriff of Randolph County and deputy US marshal, encountered a Confederate cavalry detachment at the bridge over Mill Creek on the turnpike as he made his rounds to collect taxes. Phares evaded the horsemen and hurried toward Beverly to warn the Union troops there of the approaching raiders. About seven miles farther down the valley, a scouting party intercepted him. Capt. J. French Harding of the Thirty-First Virginia Infantry, the leader of the party, grew up at Leadsville next door to one of Phares's cousins and had entered the Confederate Army in 1861 along with several of his classmates and their teacher from the academy at Huttonsville. As his party came upon the sheriff, Harding himself fired a shot that wounded Phares in the lungs. In spite of this, Phares stayed on his horse until he reached a Union outpost at the bridge over the Tygarts Valley River, two miles down the road. The Union Army withdrew from Beverly, Imboden occupied the town, and the personal drama continued. Harding visited Phares twice during his recovery in Beverly. "Finding no soldiers there, I again called at the jail to see the wounded sheriff," Harding wrote about the second meeting. "I was armed and suppose my appearance was somewhat brigandish, for certainly Mrs. Phares was badly frightened at it, and it took the assurance of both her husband and myself to quiet her."[9]

As it turned out, Harding participated in the first of the civilian captures of the raid shortly after shooting the sheriff. "Keeping to the pike we now proceeded on our return, meeting and arresting on our way George Bradley and James McCall, both citizens, mounted, armed and hastening to Beverly to report our coming," Harding recalled. "We met our advancing cavalry near the present Valley Bend station, and leaving my comrades and our prisoners with them, I crossed the river to the back road on Bradley's horse."[10] Twenty-five-year-old George Bradley (also known as John G. or J. George) served as a lieutenant in the pro-Union militia and operated a hotel at Beverly. McCall, an Irish immigrant, was a forty-nine-year-old farmer. During the course of the raid, troopers from the Nineteenth Virginia Cavalry took another lieutenant in the state militia prisoner. Lt. William S. Phares, age twenty-two, happened to be a brother of Sheriff Phares.[11]

The prisoners caused some consternation during a meeting among Imboden's officers. Harding described the scene upon his return from a brief leave to his home. "Returning to Beverly early next morning, I found the General still there with most of his command, and, in the conversation which followed learned that we differed materially as to what should be done with our citizen prisoners and their horses," Harding remembered. "I contended that the men should be released and their property returned to them, but the General was of the opinion to, and did, send the prisoners to the Richmond prison and turned the horses over to the cavalry." Harding wrote that he worried about Union reprisals upon local Confederate sympathizers.[12]

Thirty-five miles southwest of Beverly—as the crow flies—Braxton County experienced the same sort of personal warfare. The county lay in the Allegheny Plateau, where rivers carved narrow valleys and high ridges and knobs from a once level area between the Allegheny Mountains and the Ohio River. In Braxton County, the Birch and Holly Rivers came down out of the mountains and fed the Elk River, itself originating in the mountains. The Elk made its way to Charleston and the Kanawha River to the south. The county seat, Sutton—also called Suttonsville and Braxton Courthouse—and the smaller communities of Newville and Frametown sat on the banks of the Elk in the middle of the county. To the north, Little Kanawha River likewise flowed out of the mountains, but it ran northwest toward Parkersburg and the Ohio River. Bulltown, Burnsville, Falls Mill, and Flatwoods dotted the Little Kanawha and its tributary creeks. The rugged country between the Elk and Little Kanawha accentuated the different geographic orientations of the two streams, and a harsh sectionalism existed between the two watersheds. Only the Weston and Gauley Bridge Turnpike, which bisected the county and linked the Kanawha River basin with the Monongahela River basin, somewhat ameliorated the sectionalism.

The sectionalism and isolation inherent to the county's geography promoted conflict, which exploded at the start of the Civil War. Rutherford B. Hayes, stationed at Weston as part of the Twenty-Third Ohio Volunteer

Infantry, recorded the observations of patrols into Braxton County early in the war. Hayes noted in his diary that "a few good Union men" lived in the county but jotted that the majority of the people were "most ignorant" and "timid but cunning." He described the Confederate sympathizers as "the wealthy and educated, who do nothing openly, and the vagabonds, criminals, and ignorant barbarians of the country." The Union sympathizers, Hayes wrote, comprised "the middle classes—the law-and-order, well-behaved folks," and he observed that the overwhelming pro-Confederate majority harassed them "for opinion's sake." On the other hand, the pro-Union population took advantage of the presence of the Union Army and often leveled charges of subversion "merely to gratify personal animosity, knowing that in the nature of things a full investigation is impossible," according to Hayes. He added that in Braxton County "persecutions are common, killings not rare, robberies an every-day occurrence."[13]

By 1863, the situation had not changed in spite of a more or less constant presence of Union companies at Bulltown and Sutton. "Into this neighborhood, robbers, thieves and small bands of Confederate troops have recently made repeated raids," reported a pro-Union citizen two months before the Jones-Imboden Raid.[14] When the raid reached Braxton County in the second week of May, the activity of Confederate partisans increased, as did Union reaction. Imboden's main force moved swiftly through Bulltown and Sutton, and Jones's troops followed shortly behind before the two commands reunited at Summersville in neighboring Nicholas County. Nevertheless, screening forces and patrols—some consisting of irregular units—lingered in the area.[15]

Andrew J. "Jack" Tuning, a twenty-seven-year-old tenant farmer from the Salt Lick Creek area of Braxton County, led one of those units. Officially, he was part of the Nineteenth Virginia Cavalry under William L. Jackson, but Tuning associated loosely with the regiment, and his company, recently of the Virginia State Line, conducted itself in extramilitary fashion. Tuning was not the actual company commander but often acted independently of the captain, John S. Spriggs. Local tradition tells of Tuning's reputation for ruthlessness. Amateur historian B. Marie Mollohan remarked that written histories were "kind to Jack Tuning, much kinder than the oral tradition was toward him." She added that he "was the worst of the worst, according to the frowns that greeted his name."[16]

During the Jones-Imboden Raid, Tuning rode with Jackson's regiment, which was attached to Imboden's command. In Braxton County, he and his men trailed after the main force and took the opportunity to exact revenge.

They targeted Capt. Nimrod H. Hyer of Company F of the Tenth West Virginia Infantry. Hyer's company, based at Sutton, had been active against Confederate insurgency and its supporters in Braxton County. In the words of one of its sergeants, "there are other bad characters not necessary to name who have been sent to that bourne from whence they will not return, for stealing horses and shooting at our men while passing along the highway, and if we are not called away too soon from this Post, Capt. Hyer and his men will take the last man of them yet remaining in the woods of Braxton."[17] In that vein, a squad from the company had captured and destroyed property belonging to Tuning and his compatriots while they were away at war. So, when Hyer visited his home on Salt Lick Creek while on a scouting mission, Tuning's band struck in the last days of the Jones-Imboden Raid. The Confederates found Hyer, his wife, Elizabeth, and their son and two daughters having dinner with four men from Company F—Orderly Sgt. John D. Baxter, Sgt. S. E. Knicely, Pvt. E. B. Wheeler, and Pvt. William M. Barnett. Three neighbors—M. L. Barnett (brother of the private), the captain's brother, Harvey Hyer, and George D. Mollohan joined them.[18]

Braxton County historian John D. Sutton described the events when Tuning and his men came on the scene. "After several shots had been fired and a demand for surrender had been made, Captain Hyer thinking that the house would be fired and his family exposed and further resistance would be useless against the protest of Orderly Baxter and perhaps others, surrendered to a party, part of whom at least were thirsting for the blood of some of the inmates of that house," Sutton recounted. The captors tied their prisoners in pairs and headed on an arduous journey across the mountainous terrain of Webster and Pocahontas Counties toward the camp of William L. Jackson on the headwaters of Greenbrier River. Not far from the point of their capture, William Barnett, Baxter, Knicely, and Wheeler managed to loosen their ropes and escaped. Barnett was recaptured, but the others got away. The Confederates released all the civilians but Mollohan before leaving Braxton County. They tied Private Barnett and Mollohan together. Sutton recorded that Tuning refused to allow Mollohan to have water and as a whole, "the cruel treatment he received came near ending his life."[19]

Apparently, Tuning held a special grudge against Mollohan, but whether it originated before or during the war is unclear. The two certainly knew each other before the war since they both lived in the same area. Mollohan, at fifty-one, was a generation older than Tuning. He was a widower with two teenaged daughters and a son at home. Another son, Harrison, served in Captain Hyer's company in the Union Army. An older son, William, fought in the Confederate Army. George D. Mollohan recognized and cooperated with the pro-Union government of Virginia. In peacetime, Mollohan had been one of the most prosperous farmers in the area.[20] "Before the war his house stood in the valley on the farm in Braxton County," wrote B. Marie Mollohan. "The robbers burned that house." The captive himself explained, "Before I was arrested all of my personal private property had been destroyed or carried off, reducing me to the necessity of supporting my children as a daily laborer." His capture "left them without any means of subsistence and also motherless and without any natural protection."[21]

As the effects of the Jones-Imboden Raid still gripped the region, the voters within the designated boundaries of West Virginia elected Arthur I. Boreman as governor—without opposition—on May 28, 1863. Military matters began to occupy Boreman.[22] Less than a month remained before West Virginia statehood, and Boreman prepared for his duties as commander in chief of the state.

A great deal of fanfare accompanied the day of statehood and Boreman's inauguration as governor. Early on June 20, a brigade of the West Virginia Militia escorted the governor-elect and other elected state officers and members of the state legislature from their lodgings at the McLure House on Market and Monroe (Twelfth) Streets in Wheeling to Linsley Institute, the military school on Eoff Street, which had been leased for the state capitol.[23] There, Francis H. Pierpont bade farewell as he prepared to move the Restored Government of Virginia to Alexandria and formally introduced the new governor. "Boreman is a man worthy of your confidence," he assured the audience. "I have known him from his boyhood." Pierpont told his listeners that Boreman was "in this cause as steel."[24]

Boreman spoke and not surprisingly turned to the war. "Our State is the child of the rebellion," the governor reminded the onlookers. He was keenly aware that the stability of the state was linked with "the speedy suppression of this attempt to overthrow the Government of our fathers." Boreman declared his "duty, as soon as these ceremonies are closed, to proceed at once to aid the Federal authorities in their efforts to stay its destructive hand." He apprised the crowd, "While the war continues I must necessarily be engaged in military matters, and to the defence of the State, and it may not, therefore, be expected that I shall give much time at present to the internal civil policy of the State."[25]

In *Seceding from Secession,* a book that might be called a lawyer's history of West Virginia statehood, the authors summed up the course of

Arthur I. Boreman was thirty-nine years old when he became West Virginia's first governor. He was reelected in 1864 and 1866 and became a US senator in 1869. (Illustration, Arthur I. Boreman drawing by Joseph H. Diss Debar of the first governor of West Virginia, inaugurating the new state at Wheeling, June 20, 1863. Joseph H. Diss Debar Collection, West Virginia State Archives, Charleston, WV)

Governor Boreman and those who created and nurtured the new state. "West Virginia's tortured road to statehood took twists and turns, and only ended successfully because the determined leaders of the new state persevered and overcame opposition from both within and from outside their borders, all while a brutal civil war raged," they concluded.[26] Boreman's inaugural address acknowledged that West Virginia had not come to the end of the road. The new state was not yet secure, and the governor steered it through many more twists and turns.

Boreman kept to his word and went to work after his speech and the fanfare of the statehood ceremony ended. He prepared a message to the legislature that reviewed the situation in the state and outlined his goals and recommendations. The Jones-Imboden Raid and the vulnerability of the state to further raids weighed heavily on his mind.

"Our State has recently been invaded by large bodies of rebel soldiery," the governor wrote as he revisited the raid. Boreman praised the response of the people to the Confederate attack and gloated over the inability of the Confederates to build support and disrupt statehood. He continued, "Although disappointed in failing to accomplish the main purpose in their last raid, it is, no doubt, their intention to return upon us, if not prevented." Boreman noted that the state was "overrun at times by these large bodies of rebel soldiery, but, as many of you know from bitter experience, bands of guerrillas—many of them believed to have been detached from the larger armies for the purpose—continue to infest portions of the State." He pointed to robbery, murder, "and carrying off others of the Union men of the country" at the hands of the guerrillas.[27]

The governor made recommendations to tighten the state's security. He designed some to meet the military and extramilitary threat. They included a reorganization and revitalization of the state militia. During the Pierpont years, authorities had collected state arms from militia members to keep guerrillas from seizing them from homes and using them against the state. Boreman called for the rearming of the militia and the activation of militia members on a rotating basis. This would allow squads of militia to patrol for Confederate insurgents and outlaws on a continual basis.[28]

Boreman aimed some measures at Confederate sympathizers and opponents to the new state, whom he accused of providing tangible and intangible support to Confederate forces. He called for legislative measures to punish treason against the state. In a more far-reaching move, Boreman called for the disenfranchisement of opponents of the United States and West Virginia.[29]

The governor acknowledged West Virginia's dependence upon the federal government for its protection, and both the state and federal government quickly moved to cooperate. Within four days of Boreman's inauguration, the War Department consolidated regional military authority in a single department—the Department of West Virginia. It placed Brig. Gen. Benjamin F. Kelley, a resident of Wheeling before the war, in command of the department with his headquarters in Clarksburg. Kelley had previously had charge of defending the B&O Railroad. The Department of West Virginia encompassed the area of West Virginia and Maryland west of Hancock, Maryland, and the Ohio counties along the Ohio River as far south as Big Sandy River. Technically, it did not include the northern panhandle, but Kelley had operational control there.[30]

The creation of the department demonstrated the federal government's support for the new state and recognition of its permanency, and the appointment of Kelley—who was familiar with the state and its leaders and vice versa—showed political astuteness in promoting continuing cooperation between the military and state leaders. The existence of the Department of West Virginia eliminated the problem of working with overlapping and often contradictory army bureaucracies, which had plagued Pierpont's government.

Still, in the wake of the Jones-Imboden Raid, the organization of the new department served more than political purposes. During the raid, an uncoordinated command structure had diluted the response of the Union Army, and the creation of the new department fixed that problem. Further, Kelley had shown himself as an intuitive and aggressive leader, and under that leadership in the new department, a number of infantry regiments became cavalry regiments to better counter Confederate raids and to allow the Union to make its own raids into Confederate territory.[31]

It did not take long for Kelley to work with Governor Boreman. The general traveled to Wheeling to confer with the new governor just days after he assumed command. For his part, Boreman campaigned to Kelley and Secretary of War Stanton for increased federal support, and in spite of some prickliness on Stanton's part, the federal government generally acceded to West Virginia's requests. These included handing over muskets no longer needed by the converted infantry regiments to the reorganized state militia.[32]

As Boreman took action to strengthen the state militia and coordinate Union Army commitments to the state, he also looked to the hostage law. Except for a few modifications, especially those needed to conform to the new state's constitution, West Virginia adopted Virginia's code, which included the laws that the Restored Government of Virginia had passed. When it came to the hostage law, Boreman executed it differently than Governor Pierpont. Boreman had served as a judge and was more experienced in government. Plus, he needed to consider the implications of the George W. Thompson case, which concluded just days after he took office. While Pierpont had not seen the need for a formal paper trail in the taking of a hostage, Boreman implemented a consistent, written process. He required an affidavit, sworn before a justice of the peace or notary public by loyal citizens, attesting to the capture of a person by the Confederates and suggesting disloyal people from the same area of the state as potential hostages. The governor then issued a written order for the arrest of the hostage.

Boreman's precautions came just as new threats of Confederate raids pressed upon West Virginia. William L. Jackson sprinted across Cheat Mountain on a minor raid into the Tygarts Valley early in July 1863, and later in the month Brig. Gen. John H. Morgan skirted the western borders of the state on his more famous raid into Indiana and Ohio. These expeditions greatly alarmed the people of the state, and the state government and Union Army rallied to defend the state. The governor centered his attention not only on immediate dangers but on preparations for the future and in dealing with the consequences of past Confederate attacks. Much of his focus rested on the effects of the Jones Imboden Raid, which continued to emerge.

In September 1863, Governor Boreman took his first hostages, and these included hostages for George Bradley and William S. Phares, who had been taken by Imboden's men in the raid. Boreman ordered that Andrew M. Wamsley and Adam See be held for Bradley and designated Alfred Hutton and Samuel L. Wamsley as hostages for Phares. Boreman referred to his orders as warrants issued under the authority of the state hostage law, but he could not rely upon state authorities to execute them. State militia commanders and county sheriffs generally did not have sufficient forces to seize hostages. Neither did he rely upon Joseph Darr Jr., the department provost marshal, to carry out his bidding as Pierpont had. Instead, the governor called upon Union Army field commanders to enforce the hostage law. He addressed the warrants to Col. Augustus Moor, whom he believed commanded the Union post at Beverly, but rather than direct the colonel to execute the warrants, the governor "requested" him to do so.[33]

It turned out that Brig. Gen. William W. Averell, new commander of the Fourth Separate Brigade, had established his headquarters at Beverly, and Boreman's warrants came to him. Averell believed Boreman's course to be irregular and sought the guidance of his superior, General Kelley. The assistant adjutant general for the Department of West Virginia, Capt. Thayer Melvin, responded on behalf of Kelley.[34] Melvin had an intimate knowledge of state politics and the law. Before the war, he had been elected at age twenty as prosecuting attorney of Hancock County, at the top of the northern panhandle. He joined the Union Army early in the war, and he, in fact, performed double duty for a time as county prosecutor and as a lieutenant in the First West Virginia Infantry. Following the war, Melvin served as attorney general of West Virginia during Boreman's second term and then as a circuit court judge.[35] So, it is no surprise that he approached Averell's question with legal precision and political finesse. "The General Com'd'g cannot regard this document as a military order, and hence commends the course pursued in forwarding it to these Hd=qrs," Melvin wrote on the back of both warrants. "But it may properly be regarded and treated as a request from the Chief Executive of the State of West Virginia." The captain called "the object sought to be accomplished proper and advisable" and told Averell that "desiring to act in concert and harmony with the State authorities in all matters relating to the public good, the General Commanding directs, that the arrests be made and the parties turned over, as indicated within."[36] In a few sentences, Melvin, under General Kelley's direction, asserted the chain of command in the Union Army and the principle of federal and state cooperation—with the subtle point of federal supremacy. Melvin, Kelley, and the Union officers in the Department of West Virginia respected the role of the governor. After all, Melvin, Kelley, and many other officers were West Virginians. Yet, they were federal officers first. They doubtless knew about Judge John J. Jackson Jr.'s ruling in federal court that delineated between federal and state prisoners, and they may have been aware of the War Department's criticisms of the Pierpont administration for confining hostages and other political prisoners. They had to take these into account and view the governor's warrants as requests rather than orders. Only the US government could order federal officers. Thus, a precedent was set for carrying out West Virginia's hostage law.

General Averell turned the warrants over to his provost marshal, Capt. Louis A. Myers, and within five days the hostages were on their way to Wheeling. "Four citizens of Randolph County were brought to the city last evening and confined in the Athenaeum," reported the *Wheeling Daily Register* on October 10. "These four men have been arrested as hostages."[37]

The newspaper made a mistake in the blur and confusion of war, however. It told its readers that the hostages were held for James Faris rather than William S. Phares or George Bradley.

Ironically, news reports could be impersonal as the effects of the Civil War cascaded day after day. To those who experienced it, of course, the Civil War was quite personal, and that included Bradley and Phares and their families. It also included the hostages and their families. The hostages from Randolph County were family men. They were not among the obvious Confederate supporters—those either had entered the Confederate Army or gone beyond Confederate lines. Yet, the hostages had ties to Confederates and shared at least some sympathies with them. They were prominent enough that their captivity would affect their communities and would make effective bargaining chips to pressure the Confederates to release their captives.

The first on the list, Andrew M. Wamsley, turned fifty-one years old in 1863. He was a substantial farmer from the same neighborhood as Bradley and Phares and had served as a justice of the peace and a constable. Wamsley and his wife, Mary, had five sons ranging in age from eleven to twenty-five and two daughters, aged four and ten.[38] Their three oldest sons served in the Nineteenth Virginia Cavalry under William L. Jackson and had accompanied Imboden on his raid into Randolph County in the spring.[39]

Little is known about Adam See during the Civil War. He was thirty-seven years old in 1863. His father had been a prominent attorney in pioneer Randolph County and had served in Virginia's 1829 constitutional convention. Adam See lived for a time in Barbour County before the war and lived in Mingo Township in extreme southern Randolph County after the war.[40]

Alfred Hutton had an active role in the war. At thirty years old, he had just inherited his father's large farm.[41] Alfred never joined the Confederate Army, but two of his younger brothers did. Elihu Hutton had answered a militia call in 1861 to defend Randolph County against George B. McClellan's forces and served as a Confederate scout until 1863. He had then joined the Thirty-First Virginia Infantry and had been with Imboden on his raid. By the end of the war, he rose to the rank of lieutenant colonel in the Twentieth Virginia Cavalry. Eugenius Hutton also had joined the Thirty-First Virginia Infantry and later the Twentieth Virginia Cavalry. He was killed in 1864 and was a second lieutenant at the time of his death.[42]

Alfred Hutton pretended neutrality. Early in the war, he had supplied the Union Army with hay and oats, but Brig. Gen. J. J. Reynolds had not trusted him. The general had sent Hutton to Camp Chase in November 1861. Friends and neighbors, including Jesse F. Phares, soon had petitioned for his release with the justification that although Hutton had voted for secession, he had not joined the Confederate Army. The petitioners also had pleaded that "his family are much afflicted with sickness," and that he had left "a widowed mother, & a wife & child needing his services."[43] Union authorities released Hutton in March 1862 after he had posted bond.[44] In spite of this, Confederate soldiers from the region knew Hutton's home as a rendezvous point for insurgent activity until the end of the war.[45]

Forty-four-year-old Samuel L. Wamsley was a brother of Andrew M. Wamsley. A prosperous farmer, Wamsley and his wife, Levina, lived next to the Phares family. They had two daughters, ages five and sixteen, and fourteen-year-old and ten-year-old sons.[46] He had served as a constable before the war.[47]

The four hostages arrived in Wheeling with a proposal. Captain Myers reported, "These prisoners desire that one of their number be permitted to pass through the lines to solicit the release of Phares and Bradley, for whom they are held as hostages." Col. Nathan Wilkinson, through whose custody the prisoners had passed in Clarksburg, added, "The General Commanding Dept. of West Va. [General Kelley] directs me to say that under the circumstances of the arrest of the in this named persons, he is of the opinion that his Excellency the Governor of West Virginia alone, has the right to grant the desire asked for."[48]

Governor Boreman agreed. This was not an unusual move. It was common for hostages in the nineteenth century and earlier to be allowed to negotiate for the release of the prisoners for whom they were held. From the first days of the Civil War, both Union and Confederate authorities used hostages for two reasons. The first was to guarantee good treatment of their counterparts in enemy hands by threatening hostages with the same punishment or treatment as those for whom they were held. The second was to use the hostages as leverage to win the release of prisoners in enemy hands. Sending one or more hostages as negotiators, while retaining others as surety, was part of this process of leverage. So it was that Boreman allowed Hutton and Andrew M. Wamsley to travel to Richmond to seek the release of Bradley and Phares. The practice was the rule, not the exception, as the governor used hostages as pawns in the game of war.

In the meantime, Jesse F. Phares, recovered from his wound, undertook his own efforts on behalf of his brother and George Bradley. Sheriff Phares went to Washington in October 1863 and met with Morgan Gar-

The old tobacco warehouse in Richmond, which became known as Castle Thunder during the Civil War, housed most of the political prisoners taken from West Virginia. (Anderson, D. H, photographer. Castle Thunder—Confederate prison. Richmond United States Virginia, 1865. [Richmond, VA: Anderson, No. Main St.; 1865?] Photograph. https://www.loc.gov/item/2015651771/)

rett, a recently exchanged political prisoner, to get information about the two. Garrett told Phares that the Confederates held his brother in Castle Thunder, the Confederate military prison for civilians in Richmond, and that he was well when Garrett left. Bradley was not so fortunate. Garrett reported that he had been unwell for some time.[49]

Two days after Sheriff Phares shared his findings with state leaders and the press in Wheeling, Alfred Hutton gave Boreman mixed news about his and Wamsley's efforts in Richmond. "I am pleased to inform you that we have been able to procure the release of John G. Bradly," Hutton wrote. "Wm. S. Phares was ordered to be released, but unfortunately for him, during his imprisonment, his course both in actions and sentiments was such, that the proof and memorials in his behalf, could not over come them, and the result is that he is still held." Hutton told the governor that he would continue to seek Phares's release or at least to have him placed on an exchange list. Noting that he was becoming sick, Hutton asked Boreman for more time. Then, in a hint at the ironic relationships of wartime, Hutton added, "I will return just as soon as I find that I can be of no more service to my friend."[50]

Eight days later, Andrew M. Wamsley continued the story. From his home, he informed Boreman of his and Bradley's arrival in Randolph County the previous evening. Wamsley related an arduous journey during which he had walked approximately one hundred miles from Milborough on the Virginia Central Railroad in Bath County, Virginia, while Bradley rode his horse. Wamsley noted that as a result he, too, was ill.[51]

Wamsley updated the governor on Phares and Hutton. "A. Hutton I left in Pocahontas [County] to get the releas[e] for Phares," he reported. "The authorities at Richmond agree to leave it to Wm. L. Jackson." Jackson had commanded the troops who had captured Phares and was then camped in Pocahontas County. Wamsley expressed confidence that Jackson would agree to Phares's release, but first Jackson had to deal with an invasion of the Greenbrier Valley from General Averell and a coordinating Union force from Charleston. By the time Wamsley wrote his letter, Jackson had suffered successive losses and the defeat of his regiment and others under the overall command of Brig. Gen. John Echols at Droop Mountain on November 6.[52]

As Andrew M. Wamsley waited for Phares's release, he pleaded with Governor Boreman to release his brother from the Atheneum. "I ask you as a friend to parole Samuel L. Wamsley in Wheeling untill Hutton can return," he petitioned. Wamsley explained that he and Adam See were free because they had served as hostages for Bradley, but that Samuel remained in prison as a hostage for Phares. "We have had a great deal of trouble with the authorities in Richmond besides a great expense," Wamsley continued. He told Boreman that his brother, too, had been unwell.[53]

While Hutton and Wamsley were in Richmond trying to win the release of Bradley and Phares in October 1863, George D. Mollohan contacted the governor from Castle Thunder at the instigation of Col. Robert Ould, the Confederate agent for exchange in Richmond. Mollohan complained that his "health is becoming much enfeebled and I greatly fear that a few months longer confinement here will result in my death." He wrote that Ould wanted him exchanged for Conrad Kuhl, whom US authorities held in Camp Chase, and asked for Boreman's influence in negotiating the exchange.[54]

It was not that simple, however. Kuhl was not a prisoner of war or a political prisoner. A military court had convicted Kuhl and sentenced him to be fitted with a ball and chain and assigned to hard labor for his role in the murder of a civilian orderly in the Union Army. In July 1861 Kuhl's father, Henry, and another man, Hamilton W. Windon, had waylaid the civilian after he had stopped at the Kuhl home in Braxton County for food as he was returning to camp from an assignment. The older Kuhl and Windon had decapitated the man with a scythe and mutilated and hid his body, and Conrad Kuhl had been present. Military authorities had hanged Henry Kuhl and Hamilton W. Windon.[55]

Boreman shared Mollohan's request with Col. William Hoffman, the US Army commissary general of prisoners, but he recognized the incomparable situations of Mollohan and Kuhl and used the hostage law as an alternative to gain Mollohan's release. "Some time ago Mr. Geo. D. Mollahan, a Union citizen of Braxton county was seized by a gang of armed rebels and hurried off to Richmond," recounted the *Wheeling Daily Intelligencer*. "As soon as his capture was known Gov. Boreman caused to be seized as hostages John Lawrence and Addison McLaughlin, two prominent rebels of the same county."[56]

As he undertook the seizure of the hostages, the governor carefully followed the process that he had established with Andrew M. Wamsley, Adam See, Alfred Hutton, and Samuel Wamsley. First, an affidavit had to be filed attesting to Mollohan's capture and requesting hostages. Mollohan's son, Harrison, then a soldier in the Tenth West Virginia Infantry stationed at Beverly, satisfied that requirement by swearing to an affidavit before John B. Earle, the circuit court clerk in Randolph County, on November 19, 1863. Harrison Mollohan named "Adison McLoughlin" and "John Laurence" as "persons of known disloyal sentiments."[57] McLoughlin, age fifty-five, was an attorney and salt maker at Bulltown. Laurence, at age fifty-seven, was a tanner and merchant in the same community.[58] S. A. Rollyson, a lieutenant in Mollohan's company, forwarded the affidavit to the governor and added that Mollohan was "requesting that those two citizens designated in said affidavit be seized and held by federal authority as hostages."[59] In spite of Judge John J. Jackson Jr.'s ruling in federal court that summer, the lines between federal and state roles in hostage-taking still blurred in the minds of the people in West Virginia.

Boreman issued a warrant for McLoughlin and Laurence on November 24. This warrant showed that the governor had settled upon boilerplate language in that much of the wording was the same as in his first warrants for hostages. It used language from the hostage law in establishing that a "loyal citizen" had been "seized and carried out of said county by soldiers acting under authority of the so called Southern Confederacy." It reiterated that the hostages were "persons of known disloyal sentiments," and it asserted that the taking of the hostages was "necessary to effect the release and safe rendition" of Mollohan. The warrant also made specific reference to the formal title of the hostage law and the date that it was passed. Finally, it was signed and sealed by the governor.[60]

This warrant differed from those for the Wamsleys, See, and Hutton in two important ways, however. Boreman did not address the warrant for McLoughlin and Laurence to any particular person for execution. Neither did he phrase the warrant as a request. Instead, the governor simply directed that the hostages be seized.[61]

While Boreman did not address the warrant to a specific person, he sent it to Rollyson. It ended up in the hands of Col. Thomas M. Harris, who commanded the Tenth West Virginia at Beverly. Harris, like Averell had two months before, forwarded the warrant to senior authority—in this case, Col. Augustus Moor, the senior officer then at Beverly. Moor returned the warrant to Harris without explanation or justification but with instructions to turn it over to Rollyson since the governor had sent it to him.[62] Soldiers of the Tenth West Virginia executed the warrant, and Moor returned it to Boreman.[63]

On December 5, the *Wheeling Daily Register* noted, "A man named Lorentz was brought to the city yesterday from Braxton County, as a hostage for Mr. Molohan, who was captured by Jones during his raid in May last." The report did not mention McLoughlin or McLaughlin.[64] Although state documents continued to refer to him as a hostage, no evidence exists that he ever came to Wheeling. Federal military prison records listed other political prisoners but not state hostages in the Atheneum during the Boreman administration. People across the state knew Addison McLaughlin as a prominent Whig and legislator who had represented Braxton, Gilmer, Lewis, and Nicholas Counties in the Virginia General Assembly at various times during the antebellum era. State leaders designated land he owned as the county seat for Webster County when it was organized in 1860, and they named the county seat, Addison, after him. [65] So, it may be that his prominence kept him from being imprisoned.

"Lorentz was paroled on condition that he would go to Richmond and secure the release of Molohan," the *Wheeling Daily Register* added.[66] Indeed, Governor Boreman paroled Laurence (whose name appears as Lorentz on the parole) on "his pledge of honor" for that purpose and authorized him to go to Richmond, provided he received "permission of the Commandant of some U.S. Military post" to pass through the lines. Boreman gave Laurence sixty days to accomplish his task. If he was unsuccessful, Laurence was expected to return to Wheeling and surrender himself to the governor.[67]

The *Wheeling Daily Intelligencer* picked up the story from there. "Lawrence thereupon started to Richmond through the mountains," the newspaper recorded. No account of the journey exists, but with less than a week of his parole remaining, Laurence "returned bringing Mollahan with him" in late January 1864.[68]

The hostage cases from Randolph and Braxton County arose just as West Virginia became a state. They further tested the hostage law in the aftermath of the federal court ruling in the George W. Thompson case. Gov. Arthur I. Boreman established a pattern of enforcement of the law that satisfied the goals of the law and at the same time provided for coordination with the US Army.

Governor Boreman's use of the hostage law also showed his state's dependence upon laws and precedents set by Francis H. Pierpont's Virginia government in dealing with the war and its effects. West Virginia was a creature of Virginia, and its fragile existence depended upon continuity as well as federal support. It also needed legitimacy in the eyes of its people and other states. The governor's success in executing the hostage law went a long way in proving West Virginia's legitimacy. If West Virginia could successfully protect its people and control dissidence, it would hold its own in the company of states and perhaps win grudging regard from the Confederacy and the Virginia government in Richmond. Reality dictated the need for such regard in matters of prisoner exchanges and humanitarian issues.

Nevertheless, the war was far from over when Laurence and Mollohan came back across the mountains. The legitimacy and existence of West Virginia was still delicate, and much depended upon its governor's power. That power grew, and it grew largely because of Governor Boreman's efforts to secure the state. The exercise of the hostage law played a part in that, and as the war progressed, new events precipitated new hostage cases. After the Jones-Imboden Raid, the next incident that led to the seizure of hostages came in July 1863. It involved another Confederate raid into Randolph County, but it caught up a pro-Union resident of Barbour County, and the resulting hostage case played out in that county.

CHAPTER 5

# Hostage Politics in Barbour County in 1863

Philippi, the county seat of Barbour County, earned distinction in the early weeks of the Civil War as the site of the opening battle in George B. McClellan's campaign to clear western Virginia of Confederate forces. Historian John W. Shaffer, who wrote extensively about the Civil War in Barbour County, commented, "Except for this footnote in history, Barbour's role in the war was insignificant."[1] While it is true that no major military engagements took place in Barbour County following the Battle of Philippi in June 1861, the geographic position of the county gave it importance to both the North and South and to the competing state governments at Richmond and Wheeling.

The Tygarts Valley River cascaded northward out of Randolph County and meandered through Barbour County into Taylor County, where the all-important Baltimore and Ohio (B&O) Railroad and its branch, the Northwestern Railroad, linked the region with the Chesapeake Bay in one direction and the Ohio River in the other. The fertile river valley produced crops and cattle, which both armies coveted, but it mostly provided a corridor of travel with turnpikes and minor roads leading to nearby towns, including Clarksburg, Grafton, and Independence on the railroad.

For the Confederacy, Barbour County meant a pathway for disrupting the railroad. Col. George A. Porterfield came through Barbour County when he took position on the railroad near Grafton in 1861, and he pulled back into Barbour County when Union forces pushed along the railroad in response (see appendix for a timeline of events in context with one another). Brig. Gen. John D. Imboden paused in Barbour County in 1863 as he waited for Brig. Gen. William E. Jones and contemplated an all-out assault on the railroad. The Tygarts Valley also led to the navigable Monongahela River and Pittsburgh.

For Union forces, Barbour County offered a route toward Beverly and the Allegheny Mountains. Brig. Gen. Thomas A. Morris followed that route under McClellan's command when he drove Porterfield from Philippi and

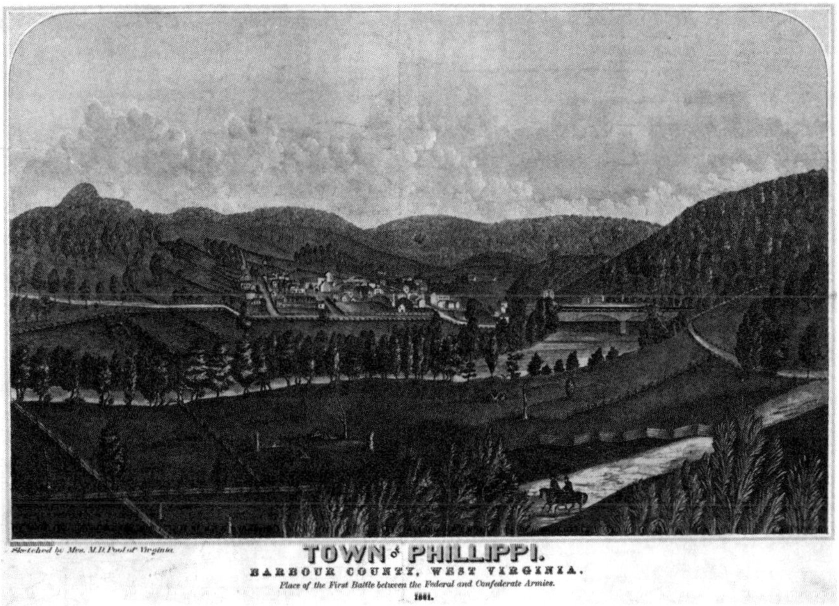


A late nineteenth-century view of Philippi, the county seat of Barbour County. Philippi gained notoriety as the site of the first conventional battle of the Civil War after Fort Sumter. (Town of Phillippi, Barbour County, West Virginia. [No Date Recorded on Shelflist Card] Photograph. https://www.loc.gov/item/2003674509/)

Barbour County held a strategic position for both armies throughout the Civil War (A. J. Johnson, *Johnson's Virginia, Delaware, Maryland & West Virginia.* [New York: Johnson and Ward, 1864] Map. https://www.loc.gov/item/lva0000096/)

pushed the Confederates from Laurel Hill on the eastern edge of Barbour County a month later.

After the opening actions in the war, Union troops mostly dominated the county, except when the Jones-Imboden Raid displaced them in the spring of 1863. The seemingly passive presence of the Union Army in Barbour County belied a significant role for the county, however. Barbour County gave the Union a strategic buffer between Confederate forces east of the mountains and in the Greenbrier and Kanawha Valleys and the B&O and Northwestern Railroads and Monongahela Valley to the north.

In this setting of Union occupation, an environment of retaliation, resistance, and insurgency grew as pro-Union and pro-Confederate citizens and expatriates postured and vied with one another for political, social, and economic position through political, legal, and extramilitary means. The *Wheeling Daily Intelligencer* reported in 1862 that "a most lamentable state of things exists in Barbour County." The newspaper claimed that 150 men had joined pro-Confederate guerrilla bands out of fear of being coerced into the Union Army. "Many of the men who left to join the guerrillas, were men who had been trusted and protected by the Union people," according to the *Intelligencer*. "They have now joined a set of merciless horse-thieves, and come back to destroy their old neighbors." The report continued, "The Union people have abandoned hope of living in peace, and are going into the army." That is to say that many men joined the army. On both sides, women and children were left at home while the men joined the fighting.[2]

West Virginia antiquarian Ruth Woods Dayton contributed, from a pro-Confederate perspective, to the accounts of women and children in Barbour County. Dayton's grandfather, Samuel Woods, served as a pro-secession member of the Richmond Convention and later as an officer in the Confederate Army in eastern Virginia, while his family remained in Philippi. Dayton wrote that her grandmother, Isabella Woods, "endured numerous insults and threats, as the feeling against all Confederate soldiers and their families was very bitter." Isabella Woods left her home in town and moved into the country. In her absence, her home "was broken into, damaged, and occupied by soldiers and northern sympathizers as well" and many "belongings were carried off, destroyed or burned." The family's temporary house was burned, and the Woods struggled for survival. Dayton recounted that her grandmother "collected some money that was owed Grandfather, but many people felt the War gave them an excuse to repudiate their debts and refused to pay anything." To add insult to injury, Samuel Woods was sued more than a dozen times in absentia in local court. "It was common practice to advertise and sell the household furniture of the Southern men who were away at the War," Dayton explained. Eventually, Isabella Woods and her children, like others, slipped through the military lines into the Shenandoah Valley to escape Barbour County.[3]

Commenting on this sort of environment, Daniel E. Sutherland wrote in *The Journal of Southern History* that "guerrilla war produced a pair of nasty mutations—community vigilantism and outright outlawry." Sutherland's study focused on areas in the Confederacy but his conclusions about guerrilla warfare apply perhaps even more among populations of mixed loyalties, such as in Barbour County. Civilians became victims in a war from which they had initially hoped to gain politically, socially, or economically. "Earlier advocates became disillusioned when the guerrilla struggle, feeding off its own excesses, began to hurt those it was supposed to defend more than it helped them," Sutherland observed.[4] Much of this unforeseen harm came from the tit-for-tat nature of guerrilla warfare, and hostage-taking played a significant part in this vengeance warfare.

The abduction of Sheriff James Trahern from his home in January 1863, which accelerated the passage of the state's hostage law, took place in this environment. Spencer Dayton, a Philippi attorney—and future grandfather-in-law of Ruth Woods Dayton—described that seminal event in hostage-taking in the county. "I have to state, that on Sabbath evening about 9 o'clock of the 4th instant, Mr. Trahorn's house, situated in a somewhat isolated section of Cove's settlement, was surrounded by about twenty-five or thirty mounted men, most of whom were leading horses other than the ones they rode, who demanded admittance immediately, threatening to break the door in, unless the request was complied with," Dayton began. Besides the sheriff and his family, James Harvey, a justice of the peace, and "Miss Bosworth," a teacher, were in the house. Harvey and one of Trahern's sons hid in the attic and managed to take with them about $1,000 in taxes, which Trahern had collected in the Elk Creek section of the county the previous day. Dayton reported that Harvey and the son "were not discovered by the rebels who announced themselves as belonging to 'Imboden's cavalry.'" Once in the house, the raiders grabbed an unhidden portion of the tax money, pilfered through the sheriff's papers and official papers that Harvey had in saddlebags, and took about $500 of merchandise from a store that Trahern kept in part of his house. "They compelled Mr. T to go along with them, first gathering together some five or six horses of his which they also took with them," Dayton continued.

Unionist leader Spencer Dayton became a key state senator following the Civil War and helped to end Radical Reconstruction in West Virginia. (Spencer Dayton of Philippi, Barbour County, Va. [WV], West Virginia and Regional History Center, West Virginia University Libraries, Morgantown, WV)

"They then proceeded to the house of John Shrayer [Shroyer], some half a mile distant, and took from him three horses, and thence went to the house of Henry Martin, a Union Magistrate, apparently for the purpose of taking him or his horses, but upon his breaking out of the house, and calling out lustily to some supposed friends to 'shoot the scoundrels' they beat a hasty retreat over the Laurel mountains."[5]

Dayton's perspectives on the war in Barbour County guided his account of the sheriff's capture. A glimpse at his view of the war is worthwhile since he continued to figure prominently in the saga of Barbour County's hostages. From the start of the secession crisis Dayton had been the county's most vocal opponent to Virginia's separation from the Union. Raucous secessionist meetings had taken place at the courthouse, and during one such meeting, Dayton had jumped from a window of the courthouse to escape angry reaction to his attempted support for the Union. When Virginia Unionists had planned the First Wheeling Convention in May 1861, five men had secretly met in Martin Myers's shoe shop in Philippi and chosen Dayton, H. L. Hoff, Joseph Teter Sr., and Rev. Alpheus Zinn as delegates to the convention. Shortly afterward, Confederate troops had occupied the town, and Dayton had been the only one of the chosen delegates to escape the watchful eyes of the Confederates and make his way to Wheeling.

Later, after the Confederate loss at the Battle of Philippi and the Union occupation of the town, Dayton attended the Second Wheeling Convention. With West Virginia's statehood, Unionist voters elected Dayton as the county's prosecuting attorney, and it was from that influential position as a court officer that he influenced the hostage situation in the county.[6]

The incident that Dayton described to the *Wheeling Daily Intelligencer* in January 1863 stirred anger and anxieties. False rumors reached Philippi that Trahern had been found hanging from a tree a few miles from his home, and the situation escalated. On the evening after Trahern's arrest, Union soldiers from Philippi confronted Henry Bowman and Henry Wilson and accused them of knowing beforehand of the raid against Trahern. Bowman, a Methodist minister, and Wilson, a Dunkard minister, were both in positions to hear news, often confidentially. Union accounts stated that Bowman and Wilson fled and were shot; Confederate reports contended that the men were murdered in vengeance.[7] At Gov. Francis H. Pierpont's urging, Union soldiers retaliated in the next few days. They took Barbour County residents David Anglin, Jacob Bolyard, William H. Dougherty, Samuel Elliott, Dr. Abraham Hershman, Peter Johnson, John Koonts, and Samuel Stalnaker—all county leaders before the war—and sent them to Wheeling as hostages for Trahern.[8]

John W. Shaffer, in *Clash of Loyalties: A Border County in the Civil War*, commented on the capture of Trahern and subsequent events. "In a war imbued with as much romanticism as the American Civil War, kidnapping and killings such as these are a stark reminder that the war in border regions like West Virginia was carried out with as much hatred and violence that people could inflict on their enemies," Shaffer wrote in echo of Daniel E. Sutherland's analysis of guerrilla warfare in the Civil War. "Almost every county in West Virginia includes in its history some account of atrocities committed by one side or the other, from burnings and bushwhacking to murder."[9]

With that opening act, Barbour County became a stage for hostage-taking in 1863, and the new hostage law scripted the action. The spring and summer Confederate raids in West Virginia set the scene. In early July, Brig. Gen. William L. Jackson drove northward with a cavalry force from Greenbrier Valley into Tygarts Valley. Jackson failed in his attempt to capture Beverly, but his men did take fifty-five prisoners, including William Price of Philippi. Price, a lieutenant colonel in Barbour County's militia, fell into the hands of the Thirty-Seventh Battalion, an undisciplined group that had originally been organized as a partisan ranger unit under the command of Lt. Col. Ambrose C. Dunn. Even as a regular battalion, the force was known among pro-Union citizens as "Confederate thieves" and in the Confederate Army as a rogue outfit. Indeed, General Jackson filed charges against Dunn following the raid because of his independent and uncoordinated operations.[10]

Price had been carrying mail between Beverly and Philippi when the raiders captured him. Local residents reported that the Confederates held the colonel in an attempt to exchange him for an officer of equal rank. Reports indicated that his captors treated Price "with more than the usual severity with which prisoners are treated at Richmond" because he "was from the start one of our zealous Union men, living in the midst of the rebels, of whose misdeeds, he kept the Government Authorities informed."[11]

Governor Boreman was very sensitive to the plight of part-time officers in Confederate hands, such as Price. According to reports, they were classed as political prisoners on one hand, but on the other, they were used to bargain for military captives. In an October 1863 letter to the US Army commissioner for exchange at Fortress Monroe, the governor expressed concern for these militia officers. "Some of these men have been captured, and it becomes a matter of interest to their friends as well as to those of the militia remaining at home, who also are bearing arms, to know whether provision has been made by the U.S. authorities for their protection while prisoners and for their exchange as soldiers captured in the Government service," Boreman urged. Boreman wanted assurance that men like Price would be treated as prisoners of war and not as spies or traitors.[12]

It took four months after Price's capture for the hostage law to be invoked in his behalf. In November 1863, Spencer Dayton filed an affidavit before a justice of the peace and named John Johnson, John Brown, William McClaskey, and William Hill as "persons of known disloyal sentiments, commonly reputed to be actively engaged, in promoting the rebellion, and the cause of the so called Confederacy, in opposition to the laws, and authorities of the United States."[13] As it turned out, Johnson, Brown, McClaskey, and Hill had already been taken as hostages for another Barbour Countian, John M. Corley, who was held by the Confederates for less than a week. So, a week later Union troops took Dr. Lorenzo D. Dolbeare, a Philippi physician; J. N. B. Crim, a storekeeper and a justice of the peace under the pro-Confederate Virginia government; Hiram Smith, also a pro-Confederate justice of the peace and a sergeant in the pro-Confederate militia; and John P. Thompson, a former justice of the peace, as hostages for Price. Authorities also retained McClaskey as a hostage for Price. The other hostages for Corley were released upon his release.[14]

Interestingly, it appears that the governor and the army sometimes took hostages in advance of the legal formality of an affidavit. Such was the case when soldiers seized Dolbeare four days before anyone filed an affidavit.

Dolbeare, a thirty-eight-year-old husband and father, was the son of Connecticut natives and had not actively participated in the secession movement or Confederate service. Earlier in his life, he had served as a constable in Harrison County, to the northwest of Barbour County, before following his father into medicine and studying at the Medical Department or National Medical College of Columbian College (now part of George Washington University) in Washington, DC. Upon his graduation in 1860, Dolbeare first opened a practice in Lumberport in Harrison County but soon moved to the sleepy county seat town of Philippi.[15]

The arrest of Dolbeare under the hostage law and the earlier arrest of Dr. Hershman by the army as a hostage for Sheriff Trahern pointed to a phenomenon of the war that struck at the very core of society. Combatants and their governments targeted physicians. This practice extended into twenty-first-century warfare and prompted study of this historic problem. Jason Cone and Francoise Duroch in *World Policy Journal* in 2013 explained that "medical facilities and staff are being targeted for what they appear to represent—assistance for the 'enemy'" and wrote that "states and non-state actors in their public discourse and their modes of military deployment" blurred the distinctions "between partisan deliverers of relief and impartial humanitarian actors."[16] In 1863, the targeting of physicians took place on the national as well as the state and local level. The case of the Confederate capture of Dr. William P. Rucker, discussed in chapter 2, prompted Lt. Col. William H. Ludlow, US Army agent for exchange of prisoners, to suggest to Maj. Gen. E. A. Hitchcock, commissioner for exchange of prisoners, that a Confederate physician be seized as a hostage for Rucker.[17]

While the adversaries in the American Civil War did not ordinarily kill physicians, their capture had the desired effect. The loss of doctors to a community resulted in difficulty for society and pressure upon political leaders to return doctors or to seek their return from the enemy. Ironically, Spencer Dayton, who had set in motion the legal process for taking hostages for William Price, became the leading voice in gaining the release of Dr. Dolbeare. On the very day of Dolbeare's arrest, Dayton sent an appeal to Governor Boreman for the doctor's release. "Dr. Dolbeare, I personally know, to be a physician having an extensive practice, over a large area of this county," wrote Dayton. He pointed out to the governor that the only other physician in the town, Dr. E. D. Talbot, suffered from infirmities of age and only occasionally visited a handful of nearby patients. Otherwise, the nearest doctor lived about ten miles away. Dayton told Boreman that Dolbeare "has, as I know from current report, frequently attended upon sick soldiers, of whom there are two posts, at this place and at Belington, some twelve miles distant, where there is now no resident physician." Dayton explained that a doctor who had practiced at Belington, farther up the Tygarts Valley from Philippi, had left the state and gone to New York until the war ended. Dayton viewed Dolbeare as "a very useful and even necessary member of our community."[18]

Dayton went on to cite a precedent from earlier in the war. The Barbour County sheriff, James Trahern, had been captured by Confederate soldiers, and another doctor, Abraham Hershman, had been taken as a hostage under the authority of the pro-Union government of Virginia. Dayton maintained that Gov. Francis H. Pierpont had set a policy that physicians were exempt from being taken as hostages and had released Hershman. Nevertheless, doctors still made tempting targets and bargaining chips, and Dayton had to convince Governor Boreman that West Virginia should follow Pierpont's precedent.[19]

While Dayton made a humanitarian appeal for Dolbeare's release, he stopped short of absolving him of disloyalty to the Union. "I know nothing of Dr. D's opinions upon the questions that have precipitated the war upon the country except from report; my intercourse with him upon public topics having been of a reserved character," Dayton wrote. "At the same time justice to him requires that I should state that I have heard him condemn the horse stealing and marauding going on in the country, and I have no reason to doubt his sincerity on the subject."[20]

Dayton ended his letter with assurances to the governor that he did not wish to interfere with civilian or military authorities. He made clear his support for the hostage law and for Boreman's administration.[21]

Six days later, six other Unionist residents of Barbour County added their pleas to the governor. D. M. Myers, N. E. Warder, Lewis Wilson, A. P. Wilson, Martin Myers, and Edwin E. Tutt complained that "Dr. Dolbeare is the only licensed physician in this neighborhood and has a very extensive practice and that, being taken away from us at this time, it has left many of his patients in a very critical condition." The petitioners told Boreman that Dolbeare's patients were "bound to suffer without his assistance, as in this county, unlike many others, we have but few physicians." They promised the governor that Dolbeare's release "would give general satisfaction to the loyal citizens of this community."[22] These men held important places in the pro-Union community and caught the governor's attention. D. M. Myers, an early resident of Philippi, served as circuit clerk. Warder held the office of constable. Lewis Wilson was the county clerk and a prominent miller. A. P. Wilson was a justice of the peace and another early resident. Martin Myers, the justice of the peace who had taken Dayton's affidavit attesting to Price's capture, had hosted the surreptitious Unionist convention in his shoe shop in 1861, and Tutt had been in attendance.[23]

In the meantime, the Union Army commander at Belington pushed back in defending his arrest of Dolbeare and the others. "I think I have made a good selection," Capt. Fenelon Howes told Boreman. "I have information that I deem reliable that William McClaskey, L. D. Dolbeare, and J. P. Thompson are in communication with the rebels every week." Howes claimed that the men informed the Confederates of Union troop movements in the vicinity and in the direction of the B&O Railroad. Howes reported to the governor that Confederate sympathizers in the area insisted that Price would not be released, and he added, "I think that there ought to have been more than five men taken as hostages for William Price."[24]

Howes seems to have taken the situation personally. A resident of Barbour County before the war, Howes commanded the company of the Fifteenth West Virginia Infantry in which Price's son, William G. W. Price, served as a lieutenant.[25] The captain not only knew the Price family personally but had belonged to the same Masonic lodge as Crim, McClaskey, and Thompson. The lodge had broken up at the outbreak of the war because of division among its members.[26]

In spite of the captain's adamant position, civilian calls for leniency increased, not just for Dolbeare, but for others, and the hostages for Price began to dwindle. Before the end of November, two doctors told of the poor health of John P. Thompson. James E. Reeves, a Fairmont doctor who had previously lived in Philippi, laid out his case—in vivid detail—to Governor Boreman that Thompson suffered from "pulmonary disease" and "cannot survive confinement." With an interest that seemed more scientific than humanitarian, Reeves added that Thompson's case had been published in medical journals.[27] Another doctor, T. Kennedy of Grafton, stopped short of calling for Thompson's release but simply said that "his health is not good," and that he had "been under treatment for disease of the lungs."[28] Henson L. Hoff, who had chaired the county's secret Unionist convention in 1861, personally delivered the doctors' letters to Governor Boreman along with his own letter on behalf of Thompson, stating that "it is the wish of the loyal men in his neighborhood that he should be released."[29]

Boreman also received requests for William McClaskey's release from two Unionists with statewide prominence. Samuel Crane, a resident of neighboring Randolph County, had been a contender for the Union Party nomination for governor in the state's first election and held the office of state auditor in West Virginia's first government. Gideon Martin was a member of the West Virginia House of Delegates and served as the chaplain of the Fifteenth West Virginia Infantry.[30] Boreman could not ignore their influence.

Then in late December 1863, D. M. Myers asked Boreman to release J. N. B. Crim and Hiram Smith. Myers verified that he had seen letters from William Price, and that Price was "in comfortable circumstances" and was "doing well." He also told the governor that the Confederates had housed Price with US Army officers, and that they treated him as a military prisoner.[31] This treatment of militia officers had been what Boreman had sought in his letter to the commissioner for exchange two months earlier. The governor bowed to the political influence and noted, "Crim & Smith released by me Dec. 22, 1863," the same day that Myers had sent his request.[32] Three months later, the Confederates exchanged Price, and he returned to his farm near Belington and was elected as a justice of the peace later in the year.[33]

No record exists of Dr. Dolbeare's release. It may be that Boreman had released Dolbeare in response to the petitions for his release—if not when the petitions were received, perhaps after Price's status as a prisoner of war became known. At any rate, tax records listed him as practicing medicine again in Philippi in 1864.[34] He remained only one of four physicians in the entire county and the only one at the county seat besides the aged Dr. Talbot. The others practiced in Burnersville, Meadowville, and Nestorville—ten to twelve miles away.[35]

Political, economic, and social influence figured importantly in the cycle of political captures, hostage-taking, and the exchange of prisoners and hostages. Initial captures took place to disrupt political, military, and paramilitary operations. The state selected prominent and influential hostages, such as physicians, because of the leverage their captivity had in negotiating their exchanges. This was the very idea behind the hostage law in Virginia and West Virginia. By its nature, this system stratified society—or rather reflected existing stratifications in society. Spencer Dayton illustrated this in an outline of the hostages for John M. Corley.[36]

Dayton used social class and lack of ties to the county in determining that John Brown "hardly deserves the honor of being taken [as a hostage] for a respectable man." He described Brown as a member of "a hard family of people" and claimed that Brown was "probably not much respected, even by the rebels." He portrayed Brown as an outsider in Barbour County.[37]

Dayton showed his racial prejudices in profiling William McClaskey. Although McClaskey held prominence as a merchant and a former deputy sheriff, the prosecuting attorney defined McClaskey as "active, smooth, pliant, obsequious, deceitful, unscrupulous, and untruthful; not a harsh or unkind man but a servile one." Dayton pointedly added that McClaskey was "supposed by some to have an infusion of negro blood in his veins & certainly having some of the foregoing characteristic qualities of that race, in his composition."[38]

Barbour County was the historic home of a community of mixed-race people known as the Chestnut Ridge People because of their original settlement in the Chestnut Ridge area northeast of Philippi. Hu Maxwell, prolific writer of county histories in West Virginia in the late nineteenth and early twentieth centuries, used the common and pejorative term *Guineas* in writing about the group. Maxwell traced the roots of the community to the Male (Mayle) family and fixed its origins in the county in the late eighteenth century.[39]

Avery F. Gaskins of West Virginia University studied the community quite extensively in the late twentieth century. He pointed out that in early British North America and the United States, interracial couples often sought the frontier as an escape from the prejudices of the coastal regions, and many of these people formed colonies in the southern Appalachians. Once settlement increased on the frontier, these families again became subjects of rejection and ridicule. This was the case for the Chestnut Ridge People. "The Guineas are a group of about 1,000 to 1,500 (an exact census is not available) persons of mixed Caucasian-Negro-Indian background," explained Gaskins. "Since the outside world discovered them, they have remained aloof and very intricately intermarried, so that the majority of them bear only a half-dozen or so family names." Gaskins wrote that an effort toward self-sufficiency had enabled the aloofness of the community, but that effort became hard to sustain. Gaskins continued, "By the end of the last century, civilization had hemmed them in, and they found themselves surrounded by unsympathetic and often hostile neighbors."[40]

Ruth Woods Dayton noted her family's interaction with the Chestnut Ridge People during the Civil War, and its experiences reflected both Gaskin's conclusions and the biases of Spencer Dayton. During the period in which her grandmother avoided Union-occupied Philippi, she depended upon the assistance of the Norris family, members of the Chestnut Ridge People "of good reputation." Pro-Union citizens of Philippi allegedly retaliated against the Norrises by burning their house.[41]

The so-called Chestnut Ridge People accounted for 1.4 percent of Barbour County's population of 8,958 people in 1860. While Chestnut Ridge was a historical center, people of mixed racial heritage lived throughout the county during the Civil War. The census listed the 126 individuals as "mulatto," as opposed to black or white. No free people were listed as "black" in Barbour County, but county residents enslaved 95 people of African descent. At 1.1 percent of the population, fewer African Americans (including people of mixed race) were enslaved than were free.

Spencer Dayton's prejudice toward people of African descent reflected the social and political realities of his county and West Virginia. His doubts about William McClaskey's worthiness as a hostage came from Dayton's assignment of mixed-race people and African Americans to lower social class, an assignment that he also made to those, like John Brown, who lacked economic standing and cultural graces. These social assessments influenced political rights and power as well. Only a little more than a decade earlier, Virginia had a property qualification for voting and holding political office, and the new state of West Virginia maintained the not-uncommon exclusion of African Americans from citizenship. Thus, the mixed-race people of Barbour County walked a fine line. If they looked white and followed European American customs, they enjoyed civil rights; if the community considered them black, their rights could be denied. This reality invited constant scrutiny from people like Spencer Dayton.

The text of the hostage law made no mention of race, but it implied that hostages would be white, and none of West Virginia's hostages were African American. As a pawn, a hostage needed enough political and social clout to make it desirable for the Confederacy and Confederate Virginia to want to trade one of their prisoners for the hostage. The clout also made it possible for hostages to act as negotiators for their own exchange. Citizenship instilled basic political power and a certain amount of clout, and African Americans could not be citizens. The hostage law also required that hostages be "persons of known disloyal sentiments." Citizens had the inherent responsibility of loyalty in sentiment while noncitizens, who were expected to be nondisruptive, held no such responsibility.

Women lived under a similar status. They were not full citizens. Their legal status was secondary. While the state expected loyalty from them, and authorities arrested many women for political crimes during the Civil War, none were taken as hostages. The state may not have believed them to hold sufficient clout, or some attempt at chivalry may have precluded women from being taken as hostages since a hostage's label as disloyal was not a criminal charge. The historical record does not make the reason for the exclusion of women clear.

The situation for African Americans in West Virginia went beyond racial ostracism. A different, but related, consideration was the relatively low presence of African Americans in the state. In a state with a population of about 377,000 people, those of African descent accounted for about 21,000 of that number or about 5.5 percent. These included about 18,000 enslaved individuals and about 3,000 free blacks.

Beyond the citizenship question, other considerations precluded African Americans as hostages. In raw racist terms, the exchange of whites for African Americans was not considered to be equitable in the atmosphere of the times. The assigned property value of enslaved people might have made them likely targets as hostages, but the state would not dare seize the slaves held by pro-Union people, and those of pro-Confederate West Virginians already were subject to confiscation under state law if they fell into Union hands.

So it was that, while being taken as a hostage was not desirable, it was considered honorable. Not everyone in Civil War West Virginia was considered honorable enough for the distinction. Nevertheless, Spencer Dayton was apparently mistaken in his assessment of McClaskey. The efforts by prominent Unionists for his release belied his insignificance in the county. Still, Dayton's analysis shows a tendency to assess the potential for men to be effective hostages.

Starkly divided Barbour County serves as a study in the process of selecting hostages. In both the cases of Sheriff Trahern and Col. William Price of the state militia, the state chose prominent and influential people as hostages to gain more leverage. That leverage entailed the use of local physicians to exert pressure on communities. Such hostage-taking was not without repercussions, for these important people were missed by people on both sides of the war. Some pro-Confederate residents were not valued outside of their own families and were not deemed to be viable hostages. They simply would not have caused the political and social pressure that state leaders sought to exert.

The situation in Barbour County also drew attention to the place of state militia officers among captives. They found themselves in the gray area between commissioned officers and civilians while off duty.

Facing such issues was important as West Virginia moved forward in the war as a new state. It depended upon the precedence of antebellum Virginia and the Restored Government of Virginia. At the same time, it was a separate state and needed to find its own way and assert itself as independent of Virginia. It still had far to go, and continuing hostage situations presented West Virginia and its governor with its own unique, precedent-setting crises.

The next situation that presented hostage cases for West Virginia's governor came two months after William L. Jackson's raid, which caught up William Price in July 1863. These cases unfolded in Gilmer County and adjacent Doddridge County—in the headwater regions of Little Kanawha River and Middle Island Creek—beginning in September 1863. While they emerged at the same time that Arthur I. Boreman dealt with hostage situations in Randolph, Braxton, and Barbour Counties, they took on a different character. Confederate guerrilla activity behind Union lines prompted them, and the state handled them directly with state troops rather than the US Army. As a result, new issues and questions arose that added still more layers to West Virginia's hostage saga.

CHAPTER 6

# Guerrillas and Retribution in Gilmer and Doddridge Counties, 1863–64

When the Jones-Imboden Raid crossed western Virginia in the spring of 1863, its farthest reach extended into the sparsely settled region between the West Fork of the Monongahela River and the Ohio River. The tributaries of these rivers almost touched here and would have except for the ridges and knobs that gave rise to them and kept them apart. Oil—petroleum as it was more often called in these years—occupied speculators at the outbreak of the war and held the attention of stalwart investors and the armies during the war. William E. Jones had gone after the oil fields near Parkersburg, if for no other reason than to keep them from benefiting the enemy.

"How rich men could content themselves to dwell in a place of this kind is a mystery of money getting that I cannot explain," commented a correspondent for the *Philadelphia Press* during the war. "If a man is nervous and not a believer in predestination he had better not venture far beyond the regions of Burning Springs (30 miles southeast of Parkersburg on the Little Kanawha River)." The reason for this was the presence of guerrillas in the backcountry. "In 1862 the guerrillas had complete possession of the country, and a man's horse was about as safe as the life of a lamb in a wolf-infested forest," the reporter wrote. "Even beyond that point [Burning Springs], and far on in the rich counties that are now regarded as neutral but dangerous ground, the military authorities are busily making arrangements for securing rebels and robbers."[1]

When Maj. Gen. George B. McClellan had moved his forces into western Virginia in 1861, the area came under Union control. Confederate activity had lapsed into resistance and insurgency. Much of this had been possible because of civilian support, but support of the Confederacy had never been universal, and the divided civilian population had fed the partisan activity. The state government in Richmond had taken advantage of the situation and encouraged and funded regiments in 1862 that skirted the boundary between regular and irregular—regular because they served strategic and tactical functions of the military leaders of the state and the Confederacy and irregular because the men of these regiments were undisciplined and independent in demeanor. These regiments were known as Virginia State Line units, and they made it possible for Confederate guerrillas to possess much of the country east of Parkersburg in 1862. However, that possession was much more tenuous than was supposed. The fact that the Confederacy had resorted to guerrilla activity meant that conventional units had not retained control. The state line regiments proved too hard to control, however, and by the spring of 1863, they had been brought under more direct oversight of regular Confederate commanders. Still, they kept much of their maverick nature.

In the case of the upper waters of West Fork River, Little Kanawha River, and Middle Island Creek, the Third Regiment of the Virginia State Line transformed into the Nineteenth Virginia Cavalry, a regiment that figured importantly in other regions in West Virginia's hostage story as well. The Third Cavalry acted as part of a larger brigade and served as an important reconnaissance force during raids into its members' home counties. After the Union Army repositioned itself and became more mobile in response to the Jones-Imboden Raid in early 1863, the Nineteenth stayed farther away from northwestern Virginia as a unit, but splinter groups played an important guerrilla role as men from the regiment visited their homes and engaged in their familiar irregular—and sometimes unauthorized—activities.

Noted West Virginia Civil War amateur historian Boyd B. Stutler summarized the role of one company of the Nineteenth Virginia Cavalry in the region. "Marauding groups such as the Moccasin Rangers, with an interchangeable membership, had a nuisance value to the Confederacy in that they terrorized the Union element . . . , but generally were not a credit to the Confederate cause," he noted. "It was a great time to pay off old scores, quarrels about line fences and neighborhood disagreements, and many of the acts of the rangers were more personal than political."[2] Local historians rebutted Stutler, however, and insisted that vengeance in the name of war was common on both sides. They contended that the Nineteenth Virginia Cavalry proved "invaluable to the Confederacy" and pointed out that the guerrillas "knew of all movement of troops and reported them" and "kept

The scene of the Confederate cavalry raid on Troy, West Virginia, in September 1863. (Heckert Family Mill and Home at Troy, Gilmer County, WV, West Virginia and Regional History Center, West Virginia University Libraries, Morgantown, WV)

the Union Home Guards from harassing the Confederate people."[3] Indeed, in the summer of 1863, Gen. Robert E. Lee commented that the Nineteenth Virginia Cavalry was "in a good position to watch the force of the enemy" for possible movements against Confederate forces in southwestern Virginia."[4]

So, the Confederacy enjoyed the advantages of a well-supported insurgent force in northwestern West Virginia in the early months of the new state. As in other regions, this insurgency led to the capture of pro-Union citizens and retaliation by the state government through the taking of hostages.

One such instance unfolded at dawn on September 11, 1863, along Leading Creek in Gilmer County (see appendix for a timeline of events in chronological context). A typical late summer fog hugged the creek bottoms as a company of the Nineteenth Virginia Cavalry under Capt. S. H. Campbell swept down upon the community of Troy, a pro-Union enclave in an otherwise heavily Confederate-leaning county. The Confederates robbed two stores, stole horses, and pillaged homes. When Campbell's men left the village, they took four local residents and three Union soldiers with them.[5]

The captives were a mix of men from prominent Union families. They included sixty-one-year-old Adam Heckert, owner of the mill along Leading

Creek in Troy; Peter Heckert, his sixty-seven-year-old brother; thirty-three-year-old Henry Messenger; and twenty-year-old Adam Gluck. Gluck had escaped the captivity of pro-Confederate guerrillas five months earlier, only to be caught up in the Troy raid. Three soldiers from the Sixth West Virginia Infantry—James White, Alex Goff, and James Robinson—happened to be in Troy and fell into Confederate hands as well.[6]

Members of a Union home guard pause during their pursuit of Confederate guerrillas in the Little Kanawha region (Squad of Citizen Homeguards, Joseph H. Diss Debar Collection, West Virginia State Archives, Charleston, WV)

Local Union home guard commander David Heckert made oath before L. T. Bougham, a justice of the peace in bordering Ritchie County, five days later and asked that hostages be taken for the four civilians. He identified R. A. Benson, Joseph M. Wood, William W. Yerkey, N. Smith, Sylvester Stump, J. A. Campbell, John Woofter, George F. Bush, George H. McQuain, Edgar M. Wolf, John Wolf, William S. Wright, G. W. Goff, Abraham Bush, and H. A. Goff as disloyal persons and petitioned the governor to seize them under the hostage law. Boreman complied and sent an order to Lieutenant Heckert the following day for the arrest of the hostages. His force from Gilmer County and a Ritchie County home guard unit, known as the Bone Creek Guards, accomplished the task, and the hostages arrived at the Atheneum in Wheeling on the evening of September 21.[7]

The nature of hostage-taking in West Virginia placed influential men in the state's grasp because of the leverage they provided in winning the release of those in Confederate custody. This meant that many hostages also possessed the influence to bargain for their own release. Within two days of the arrival of the Gilmer County hostages in Wheeling, moves began to win their freedom. On September 23, Abraham Bush, who had been sheriff of Gilmer County before the outbreak of the war, offered to go beyond Confederate lines to negotiate for the freedom of Henry Messenger and Adam Gluck. Abraham and his brother, George F. Bush, both wealthy farmers, posted a $5,000 bond to show their good faith, and the former sheriff promised to return to prison if his efforts failed.[8]

Friends of the hostages also began campaigning for their release. On October 2, 1863, Clarksburg attorney Charles S. Lewis lobbied his old friend, Nathan Goff, a member of the West Virginia House of Delegates, on behalf of John Wolf. Lewis, a former state legislator and former congressman, had served in the Second Wheeling Convention, and he was well connected in Unionist circles. Lewis knew Wolf, a former resident of the Clarksburg area, and pointed out that the hostage was aged and infirm.[9]

A second letter to Goff followed Lewis's that day. Luther Haymond added his support for Wolf's release. Haymond held great influence with Goff. He worked with Goff as cashier of Merchants' National Bank in Clarksburg, a bank that Goff had founded and served as president.[10]

Another Clarksburg resident, John Irwin, wrote to Daniel Haymond, a state senator from Ritchie County, on the same day. Irwin, believing that Wolf was a hostage for Troy residents Adam Heckert and Daniel L. Steinbeck, cited confusing, secondhand reports that the Confederates had freed Steinbeck and Heckert. Irwin asked Haymond to assist Goff and state senator Edwin Maxwell from Harrison County with efforts to release Wolf. Irwin reinforced his request with a supporting statement from William W. Warder, a Gilmer County justice of the peace who had served in West Virginia's constitutional convention. Warder observed that "Mr. W[olf] was at home and very quiet—behaving himself very well" since the start of the war.[11]

A different appeal followed three weeks later on October 26, 1863. John Bennett of Steer Creek in Calhoun County wrote to West Virginia's adjutant general, Francis P. Pierpont, nephew of Governor Pierpont, and inquired whether a petition on behalf of the hostages had been received from members of the home guard at Troy. Bennett showed particular interest in Sylvester Stump, a nineteen-year-old neighbor who had taken grain to the mill at Troy for his father and neighbors on the day that hostages had been taken and had been caught up in the dragnet as a stranger in town. While pro-Union residents held varying opinions about the hostage law, Bennett expressed the fear of "all union men on the border" that the taking of hostages resulted in Confederate retaliation against them. Bennett's plea reached Governor Boreman, and he ordered Stump's release.[12]

Meanwhile, the stresses of the Troy raid and the seizure of hostages from the community tore open rifts within the Unionist population in Gilmer County. The divisions centered on rivalry between the Holt and Cox families, led by J. F. W. Holt and Philip Cox. Both families enjoyed political power that extended to Wheeling, but they leveled charges of disloyalty to the state and the Union against one another. The accusations spilled onto the pages of the *Wheeling Daily Intelligencer* from October through December of 1863. While members of the respective families alleged subversion and sedition on the part of the other family, the crux of their rivalry lay in competition in the mercantile trade and control of the sheriff's office and, through it, the collection of taxes in the county. The resulting grudges stretched back as far as 1830. The bizarre exchange in the pages of the newspaper ended as suddenly as it began with a retraction by George K. Cox of his family's charges against the Holts.[13]

The mudslinging between the Cox and Holt families caught up many of the people who were involved in the hostage situation in Gilmer County, as they allied themselves with one family or the other. Among those who initially endorsed the Holts' contentions were Adam and Peter Heckert. Beyond the implications for the feud, this is significant in that it suggests that the Heckerts were free from Confederate captivity by October 1863.[14]

As the new year began, it became clearer that the Heckerts had returned home, but Gluck and Messenger remained as prisoners of the Confederacy, and the hostages still waited in Wheeling. George H. McQuain, William W. Yerkey, John Woofter, John Wolf, Joseph M. Wood, George F. Bush, Edgar M. Wolf, and William Wright wrote to Governor Boreman on January 13, 1864. They had pieced together information about Gluck and Messenger and forwarded it to the governor. The hostages hoped that the release of the Heckerts, together with their cooperation, would lead to their release. They told Boreman that Gluck and Messenger were held in Richmond and had been classed as prisoners of war. The detainees in Wheeling told Boreman that the Confederacy would exchange Gluck and Messenger only for Confederate soldiers, not for civilian hostages like themselves. The reason for the designation is unclear.

The hostages also shared news about their comrade, Abraham Bush, who had gone south to seek the release of the two Union men. Bush was a prisoner of the Confederates in Staunton. The group explained that "the South regard us as thare enemys" because "we have all taken the oath of aligence and voted for the amended constitution and for your honer and have ben taxpayers to this Government and have ben law a biding men and our interest is in West Virginia and not in the South."[15]

Irony tinged Bush's capture by the Confederates. A year and a half earlier, Union military authorities had ordered his arrest with claims that Bush had feigned his loyalty to the Union and had consorted with Confederates guerrillas.[16] "As there has been a good deal of this duplicity on the part of prominent Citizens of Gilmer County," wrote Col. Thomas M. Harris, commander of the Tenth West Virginia Infantry. "I think it would have a Salutary Effect to make a few Examples and I do not know of a more suitable person to begin with than Mr. Abraham Bush Ex Sheriff & c." [17] Bush had been ill at the time of the arrest order in 1862 and had avoided confinement at that time.[18]

Boreman apparently acceded to the entreaties of the hostages and released five of them—the Wolfs, Yerkey, Wright, and George F. Bush. In February 1864, forty-seven soldiers from Company G of Tenth West Virginia Infantry at Beverly, led by Capt. J. M. Ewing, took issue with the freeing of the hostages. The men—all from Gilmer County—protested to Boreman that while the five former hostages enjoyed their freedom, Adam Gluck and Henry Messenger were still suffering in Libby Prison. The soldiers asked for the taking of Salathiel G. Stalnaker, Lemuel Stump,

E. T. Stout, and Milton Norris, who "had supported secession from the start," as new hostages.[19]

Adam Gluck's brother, Sgt. J. C. Gluck, elaborated in a cover letter to the petition. In a discourse that hinted at his future life as a state legislator, the sergeant explained that when he had left home for the army, seventeen-year-old Adam had remained to support their large family; their father was too old to do so alone. Gluck wrote that after "a lawless prowling band of demonized marauders in human form" had captured his brother in September 1863, his family had no news of his condition. "Is it lawful[,] right or reasonable that while we are protecting the persons and property of rebbels & rebel sympathisers in our midst that those demons in human form be allowed to carry or drag away the few civil citizens we have left to take care of the soldiers families?" he demanded. "Is there no remedy for such a barbarous course of conduct[;] is there no one to make atonement for those sins[?]" Gluck sermonized, "Yes varily we have them in our midst[;] we have those in our midst who was actively and industriously engaged in passing the disgraceful ordinance of secession[.]" He contended that these men had falsely sworn allegiance to the United States and West Virginia in order to avoid confiscation of their property under a state law aimed at Confederate sympathizers. "Compel those to make atonement for the sins of their brethren & the floods of treason will soon cease to overspread our country & our honest loyal citizens will prosecute their business without fear of molestation," Gluck concluded.[20]

While J. C. Gluck fretted about his brother, Adam Gluck and Henry Messenger joined most of the inmates of Libby Prison as the Confederate Army shipped them to Georgia in the spring of 1864. They crowded into Camp Sumter—Andersonville—and shared the hardships of that infamous place. Messenger died from dysentery in July 1864. Prison records listed him as a civilian despite reports of his status as a prisoner of war. Gluck died from scurvy in October 1864. He was designated as a private in Company G of the Tenth Virginia (West Virginia) Infantry. Regimental muster rolls never showed him as a member of that unit. Perhaps the Confederates mistook him for his outspoken older brother.[21]

Fear and uncertainty certainly grasped the citizens of Gilmer County, regardless of their political persuasions, but the feelings were not restrained by county boundaries. The anxieties of war spread across the upper Little Kanawha River and neighboring regions in 1863 and 1864. Confederate partisans passed in and out of the county, aided by their sup-

An 1864 map shows Gilmer and Doddridge Counties butted against one another between the West Fork of the Monongahela and Ohio Rivers. (A. J. Johnson, *Johnson's Virginia, Delaware, Maryland & West Virginia.* [New York: Johnson and Ward, 1864] Map. https://www.loc.gov/item/lva0000096/)

porters, and Union troops—many recruited locally—policed the area with the assistance of willing residents. In this atmosphere, Union soldiers found a suspected Confederate spy, a stranger dressed in gray, in Gilmer County in the fall of 1863 and took him to West Union, the seat of adjoining Doddridge County. The Northwestern Railroad, the branch of the Baltimore and Ohio that connected the main line with Parkersburg, passed through West Union, and Union forces maintained a substantial presence there. The US commander found no cause to hold the suspected spy and released him. That did not satisfy some, and the man was found murdered outside of town. Suspicion fell on two soldiers of the Sixth West Virginia Infantry, a loosely disciplined regiment of local origin. The commander deferred to civilian jurisdiction in the matter, and the county coroner ordered the arrest of the soldiers. Although Doddridge County was largely pro-Union, significant numbers of its people questioned the authority of the state government, and local officials did not act concertedly. Unconditional Unionists equated this with weak loyalty and were outraged by the coroner's course. Ephraim Bee, a member of the West Virginia House of Delegates, represented their view. "If the government will not protect them, the people of Doddridge county will rise *en masse* and clear the county of rebels and sympathizers," he wrote. "We would have no raids and incursions if it were not for these sympathizers amongst us."[22]

People like Bee were not just reacting to moderate Unionism on the part of county and township officers; real Confederate sympathy and collusion did exist in Doddridge County. Company D of the Nineteenth Virginia Cavalry, under Capt. John Righter of nearby Marion County, regularly worked there. The activities of Righter and his men especially concerned state and federal leaders because they took place deep within Union territory and affected both the Northwestern Railroad between Clarksburg and Parkersburg and the main line of the Baltimore and Ohio (B&O) Railroad between Fairmont and Wheeling. In his home county, the *Fairmont National* accused Righter of conducting a "hellish system of warfare," and his reach extended into Doddridge, where he had recruited a number of men.[23]

The *Fairmont National* story mentioned the Ashcraft family in connection with Righter. The family was numerous in Doddridge, Harrison, and Marion Counties, and Jeremiah and Preston Ashcraft belonged to the Nineteenth Virginia Cavalry. Residents in Doddridge County watched the family with trepidation. The head of the Ashcraft family in Doddridge County, Uriah Ashcraft—along with Absalom Ash, George W. Kile, and Samuel Loy from his neighborhood—had come under suspicion of stealing horses for the benefit of the Confederacy in August 1862 and spent four months in Camp Chase before being released on an oath of loyalty to the Union.[24]

When a horse-stealing raid took place in the McElroy Creek area in the northern part of the county in October 1863, the Ashcrafts received the blame. A group of women rallied and went before the justice of the peace, Jacob Yeater, at Yeaters Mills (Center Point) on November 2 and testified against the Ashcrafts and several of their associates.

Matilda Williams spoke of personal animosities with the Ashcrafts and her fear of them. Her husband served in the Union Army, and she told of the Ashcrafts' disdain for him. According to Williams, Uriah Ashcraft had fumed that "if any man had of sworn that Isaac my husband had turned out to be such a man he would not believed it." She added that Stephen Ashcraft, a nephew of Uriah, had said that he could not believe that Isaac Williams "was any such a man as he turned out to be to fight against his country."[25]

Tensions over enlistments in one army or the other pervaded the border region and created resentments between families, which the women and children left at home had to bear. Isaac Williams had joined the Union Army and served in Company A of the Fourteenth West Virginia Infantry. The company drew many recruits from Doddridge and Harrison Counties. While men in many West Virginia regiments served in the state and could visit families during regular leaves (sometimes unofficially), Company A was posted far from home in eastern Virginia. This left the soldiers' families without the vigilance of husbands and fathers.[26]

The absence of husbands and fathers thrust women and children into the roles of defenders of families in the culture of the time. With the perception that women and children lacked physical prowess and skill with firearms, men who became predators on the home front often intimidated and victimized families where females dominated. Gordon B. McKinney wrote about another Appalachian border region, western North Carolina, which bore amazing similarities to West Virginia. According to McKinney, "women in the region were physically threatened and attacked; social, political, and economic divisions abounded; deprivation and scarcity became the normal pattern of life; and the mountain counties were a center for deserters and Unionist sympathizers."[27] While Doddridge County was a center for Confederate sympathizers, the plight of women resembled that of the women in McKinney's article. Families headed by women resorted to the means at their disposal. These often were legal and economic means, which frequently proved more effective than the use of direct force.

Williams continued her testimony with the claim that Uriah Ashcraft had bragged in October 1863 that "the Rebels would be in here as thick as bees then the big wigs would have to fight or worse." She stated further that Ashcraft actively worked against Union Army recruitment and supported deserters from the army.[28]

The animosities between the Williams family and their pro-Confederate neighbors existed between other families as well. Tensions also ran high between the Kile (Kyle) family and the Ashcrafts. Azariah Kile, the husband and father of the family, belonged to the West Virginia Exempts, an independent battalion that provided security for the state properties in Wheeling and served as the guard for the Union provost marshal there. As such, men in the unit often made arrests for the provost marshal and guarded the Atheneum, the military prison in Wheeling. Uriah Ashcraft and his cohorts passed through the Atheneum on their way to Camp Chase and likely encountered Kile.[29]

Martha E. Kile, just eleven years old, led in her family's complaints before the justice of the peace. She testified that John Trader had passed by her house on McElroy Creek the previous summer, hid behind a bush, and "snapped" his gun (pulled the trigger with a primer cap affixed but without the gun being loaded) toward the house. She testified that her sister, Mariah M. Kile, could corroborate her report.[30] Their mother, Nancy Ann Kile, swore that children came into the house and told her that Trader had snapped his gun. She went to the door and saw Trader hurry away. She claimed that George W. Ashcraft had recently cheered for Jefferson Davis and the Confederacy in the presence of her and Elisa Jane Coffman. She also said that three armed men had passed her house the previous Saturday and asked where the Ashcrafts lived.[31]

Ruth Bates, a neighbor of the Kiles, followed with an affidavit that Uriah Ashcraft and his sons frequently passed her house in the direction of M. C. Syms's residence just before the raid. Syms had lost a horse to the raiders.[32] Belinda Booher told the justice of the peace that Uriah Ashcraft had wished "that hell might open and swallow all such which was Union men." Booher also stated that Ashcraft had traveled past her house "too much for any good" and at "unusual hours of the night."[33] At the same time, Elisa Jane Coffman swore that on the day after John Brown's store had been robbed in October, George W. Ashcraft had been heard huzzahing Jefferson Davis and the Confederacy.[34]

Others followed with their accounts. Susannah Coffman provided further context and added to the players in the raid. She told the justice of the peace that at the time of the raid, John W. Swiger came to her house when her husband was not at home and asked for a drink of water.[35] Sixteen-year-old Sary (Sarah) Jane Shields reported that on the night of the raid, "John G. Dye was a long with them at my fathers house and was blacked."[36] Her father, Thomas Shields, contended that a man whose hand size matched that of John G. Dye left a handprint on his fence the night of the raid.[37]

With these affidavits, the women of the McElroy Creek area availed themselves of legal means to fight their enemies in the absence of physical power. Yet, according to Altina Waller, in her groundbreaking work in *Feud: Hatfields, McCoys, and Social Change in Appalachia, 1860–1900,* the use of the legal system to remedy difficulties was the rule and violence was the exception in Appalachian society as a whole, not just among women. "Far from ignoring the legal system, . . . residents appear to have been quick to resort to litigation, sometimes over slights and insults which seem, from a twentieth-century perspective, trivial."[38] The violence and lawlessness in counties such as Doddridge was a product of war, whether because of blurry patriotism or because of opportunism on the part of unscrupulous people.

The women of McElroy Creek targeted their antagonists with trivial detail. They complained primarily about the Ashcrafts, and it became clear from their stories that the Ashcrafts exemplified a common phenomenon in border regions during the Civil War. In this phenomenon, families and individuals who did not fit into mainstream society sided against the dominant side in their county or region, whether Confederate or Union. This occurred because these families and individuals perceived offenses—political, social, or economic—against them at the hands of more affluent or influential people. The war provided the underdogs opportunities for revenge against the powers that be, often through irregular warfare under the guise of support for a particular side in the war.

Eight days after the group of women and children gathered before the justice of the peace in November 1863, Jacob Yeater sent the depositions to Lt. Jesse F. Snodgrass of the Second West Virginia Exempts and asked that they be used "to our benifitt."[39] Local officials lacked the strength to enforce the law without the support of the military, and those, like Yeater, who derived their authority from the state of West Virginia, felt particularly vulnerable to pro-Confederate attacks. Snodgrass, who had farmed in the McElroy Creek area before the war, became a contact for local residents who sought a connection with the military establishment in Wheeling.

Indeed, Snodgrass enjoyed growing influence in Wheeling. He worked closely with state leaders in protecting them and government property. This took Snodgrass into the political arena, and he gained a reputation as a public speaker, a reputation that benefited him in his career as a Methodist Episcopal minister after the war. In the winter of 1863–64, Snodgrass rallied a crowd at the Rough and Ready Hose House, a fire station in the northern section of Wheeling, just before a city election, and called for "exterminating all rebels and suffering none but good Union men to rule over us."[40]

Yeater contacted Snodgrass again after Christmas in 1863 when he forwarded another mass appeal from Doddridge County in the form of a petition. Yeater asked the lieutenant to hand it to Gov. Arthur I. Boreman.[41] The petition, signed by twenty-nine men, called upon Governor Boreman to arrest and hold C. R. Gain, Thomas Swagger (Swiger), William M. Bonnell, Samuel Beverline, and Thomas Ash as hostages. It alleged that Gain, Swagger, Bonnell, Beverline, and Ash were "violent Sesestionist and unprincipold Scoundrells and leaders in the Rebell cause and threatens the peace and property of the poor soldier and his helpless family that is left among us." The petitioners complained that they felt "that we are in a helpless condition" because "our sons, brothers and neighbors has volunteered in the service of our country and has left their familys with the few union men that is left at home." The signers explained that the "Rebells has come and stolen our property and carried it away to Dixey and they are fed and harberd by the Rebells and Simpathizers amongst us." They told the governor that they were "in a helpless condition and at the mercy of those prowling Hell hounds and Sesesh amongst us."[42]

Yeater added his personal request that Snodgrass verbally ask the governor to remove Gain, Swagger, Bonnell, Beverline, and Ash from the area. The justice of the peace expanded upon the local political and security situation. He noted the arrests of two other Confederate sympathizers, J. C. Morgan and Galen Prunty, apparently without Snodgrass's assistance. He also spoke of his involvement in efforts to thwart local elections under the authority of the state government in Richmond.[43]

A second petition from Doddridge County reached the governor a week later. It, too, called for the arrest of Gain, Swagger, Beverline, and Ash but left Bonnell off the list. The petition asked Governor Boreman to exile the men from the state and called them "Rebells of the deepest dye and suspicious persons." It told the governor that the exile of the four men would "confer a favor on a healpless Loyal and out raged community." Seventy-five signatures appeared on this entreaty, and they included Jesse F. Snodgrass; his captain, Perry G. West; and four other officers and noncommissioned officers of the Second West Virginia Exempts.[44]

The affidavits from the women of McElroy Creek and the subsequent petitions named networks of family and neighbors who had longtime relationships, both positive and negative. The written pleas held much between the lines. As Altina Waller pointed out, in small, close-knit Appalachian communities, "everyone could be—and usually was—aware of the circumstances and individuals involved in any case being considered."[45] Though not polished in their words, the petitioners in Doddridge County shaped their images as victims and astutely used the hostage law through their local judiciary, which served as a conduit to state government. "Yet mountaineers respected the letter and spirit of the law as well as a kind of commonsense justice based on familiarity," Waller explained. "Respect for an abstract, written, legal tradition came from a strong eighteenth-century English heritage, which endured remarkably well in spite of an illiterate oral culture."[46]

This mix of formal and informal justice complicated matters for Governor Boreman. He, after all, had served as a circuit court judge in more cosmopolitan Parkersburg and as a legislator in the staid halls of Richmond. It was not so much that Boreman was unfamiliar with traditional, rural justice in western Virginia and West Virginia, but a subtle attempt to manipulate the hostage law lay within the Doddridge County entreaties. No one was identified as being arrested by the Confederates. Instead, the affidavits and petitions documented a broad reign of terror. Another month passed before the governor acted on the pleas. To satisfy the form of the law and the governor's hostage policy, Snodgrass went before the secretary of state, J. Edgar Boyer, on February 16, 1864, and swore that Gain, Swagger, Bonnell, Beverline, and Ash were "persons of known disloyalty."[47] That opened the door for taking hostages, but Boreman carefully adhered to the law and made sure that the hostages were linked to specific captives in Confederate hands. The governor did not want the hostage law used as a purely vindictive measure against general pro-Confederate activity. He used Thomas Hill and Ducket Gatrell, whom Confederates had seized from Doddridge County but had not been identified in the appeals from the county, for that purpose and issued an order for Snodgrass to arrest five men as hostages for the two Unionists.

Hill's case had received some notoriety the previous fall when Rev. John Hussey, a Presbyterian minister and a member of the US Christian Commission from Ohio, stopped at Wheeling after his release from confinement at Richmond. Hussey had been captured while tending wounded soldiers at Chickamauga and had spent time at Libby Prison and Castle Thunder. "In prison Mr. Hussey met with Thomas Hill, a citizen of West Virginia, who like himself was simply a citizen and who had never been connected with the army, but who had been violently taken from his peaceful home down in the back country, simply because that by reason of his uncompromising Unionism he was obnoxious to the secessionists," newspaper accounts related. "Mr. Hill is a man of high character and has been guilty of no crime whatever, never having been even charged with any."[48]

Hill, in fact, had been in the wrong place at the wrong time. He was a bridge builder, and Brig. Gen. Benjamin F. Roberts, commander of Union forces in the region in the spring of 1863, had employed him to work for the army. Soldiers under Brig. Gen. William E. Jones had captured him at work during Jones's raid toward Parkersburg in April 1863.[49]

Hussey provided a detailed description of an "absolutely incredible" prison life. He told of unbearable stench among prisoners confined in a single room and unbearable heat in the summer and unbearable cold in the winter. Boarded windows allowed very little light, and the men suffered from endless disease, especially lung ailments. Everyone was covered with lice. Hussey noted that political prisoners were "treated worse than any other class of prisoners" and were subjected to "inhuman tortures of hunger and exposure." The normal food ration consisted of a small, half-loaf of bread and two ounces of meat once every twenty-four hours.[50]

Such stories increased the public rhetoric against the South and resulted in new calls for retribution. "The question naturally comes up to an Union man's mind in this shape, viz—why are our West Virginia fellow citizens, who are non-combatants, permitted by us to be taken to Richmond, thrown into those hellish prisons and tortured as they are?" asked Archibald Campbell, the editor of the *Wheeling Daily Intelligencer.* "Why is it that hostages from among the most influential rebels in West Virginia cannot be seized and put in prison, and made to use their influence to get these men released?" The editor added, "This thing has been done once or twice with signal success, and why cannot it be done again?"[51]

Campbell, of course, knew of past hostage-taking, but he knew little or nothing of the incidents that arose in the fall of 1863 and the hostage dealings that were under way at that time. Pressure from the media, nevertheless, had a strong political effect on Boreman's reactions to the Confederacy taking civilians and motivated his action on behalf of Hill and Gatrell in February 1864.[52]

The hostages whom Boreman chose represented a segment of Doddridge County society who lived on the periphery in the 1860s. Life in the county centered on West Union, the county seat, and adjacent areas on the Northwestern Turnpike and the Northwestern Railroad, and in general residents of the remote McElroy Creek area felt marginalized. Within the community, still further segregation took place, and those who sided with the Confederacy were the most separated from the mainstream. Like the Ashcrafts, they considered themselves underdogs in Civil War West Virginia. Samuel Beverline, for instance, had enjoyed status before the war as a justice of the peace. That meant that he also served on the county court, a petit court and governing body for the county. The takeover of local politics by the pro-Union government of Virginia and later the government of West Virginia displaced him from that status.[53] For some, however, Confederate sympathies were a symptom, not a cause of their marginalization in their community. The Swagger family owned substantial amounts of land in the county before the war but lost much of it due to debt. Some of that loss was because of debts owed to the Bates family. In one case, Thomas Swagger had lost 144 acres of land because of a debt of just $16.31.[54] Such experiences left families with memories of prominence and influence while they struggled with a lack of practical power. Participation in pro-Confederate activity restored some of their power and allowed them the chance for material gain. Their former prominence and influence stamped them with enough notoriety to be placed in the pool of hostages.

Lieutenant Snodgrass executed Governor Boreman's order to seize the hostages on February 25, 1864. Snodgrass reported that he had arrested Bonnell and Swagger. He could not find Gain, Beverline, and Ash. The lieutenant billed the governor $3.50 for expenses.[55]

While three of the designated hostages became lost in the fog of war, the murkiness of the situation did not end there. Within a month, doubts arose over Bonnell's disloyalty to the Union and, thus, his suitability as a hostage. Lieutenant Snodgrass looked into the matter and in March 1864 wrote to Jacob Yeater, whose word Snodgrass had trusted in the selection of hostages in Doddridge County. In his answer, the justice of the peace defended the choice of Bonnell as a hostage. Yeater insisted that "there is not [a] Loyal Man that knows him in McClellan Township that Can Regard him as such nor hant for the Last two years." Bonnell generally spoke in favor of the Confederacy, kept company with Confederates, either voted against statehood propositions and pro-Union candidates or did not vote, and on one occasion refused to take a loyalty oath, according to Yeater. The magistrate further described an incident during a township election in which Bonnell took the loyalty oath required of voters and then hawked and spat in front of Yeater before going to vote.[56] At the same time, two other Unionists, Andrew J. Bates and Vincent A. Glover, claimed that in September 1862 Bonnell had bragged about interactions with Confederate insurgents and had shared the band's countersign with the pair. They said that Bonnell had threatened to shoot them if they divulged the secret.[57]

As questions swirled over Bonnell's case in the spring of 1864, ten men wrote to Governor Boreman and told him that Thomas Swagger had never taken arms against the federal government, the state of West Virginia, or the pro-Union Virginia government. The writers, five of whom were related to Swagger, explained that he had been caught up in a horse-theft raid and been arrested. They told the governor that horse thieves had stopped at Swagger's blacksmith shop and done some work, and that rumors circulated that Swagger had aided them and concealed stolen horses. They noted that Swagger had been released on bond and implied that his release was a sign of doubt of his guilt.[58]

Friends of Bonnell and Swagger not only attacked the allegations of disloyalty against the two men, they called into question the legitimacy of the petitions that had called for the arrest of the hostages. They charged that a dead man's name had appeared on one petition and that two names had been placed on a petition without the men knowing its purpose.[59] Jacob Yeater took the charges head on and obtained affidavits from the two men, James Morgan and Aaron Swiger, that confirmed they had asked Yeater to place their names on the petition.[60]

In commenting on the pushback from the hostages' supporters, Yeater told Lieutenant Snodgrass that "Strange things will Some times hapen so we will have to do the Best we Can under Such Circumstances." Coincidentally, as the justice of the peace wrote to Snodgrass, a leading supporter of the hostages, a man named Shields, arrived at Yeater's home, and Yeater read him the correspondence with Snodgrass. Afterward, Yeater informed the lieutenant, "Old Blackhawks friends is at work again for him and they have run McClellan Township from one end to the other for siners to a Petition and have got 6 siners and 4 of them is as mean a Rebels as there is in the Township or in Prison at Wheeling." He told Snodgrass that Shields's allies had been harassing those who did not support their cause.[61]

The work of "Old Blackhawk" bore new fruit as four women—Mary Beverline, Dorcas Prunty, Sarah Loughry, and Elizabeth Allen—wives of Union soldiers, contended that none of the men who had been designated as hostages, whether in actual custody or not, had threatened Union soldiers' wives or property.[62] These statements countered claims and fears that women and children were at risk from Confederate sympathizers while their husbands were away in the Union Army.

On a more substantial level, three prominent Unionists and supporters of West Virginia in the county appealed to the governor on behalf of the hostages. Of the three men, Boreman especially trusted Chapman J. Stuart. He was the judge for the Fourth Circuit—which included Doddridge, Gilmer, Pleasants, Ritchie, Tyler, and Wetzel Counties—at the time and had served in the constitutional convention for West Virginia. Stuart had represented Doddridge, Harrison, Ritchie, and Wood Counties in pro-Union Virginia's state senate from 1861 to 1863 and had been a member of the Second Wheeling Convention (over which Boreman had presided), where he had been a guardian of civil liberties. Before that, he had served at Virginia's secession convention as a Unionist. During the 1850s, Stuart had been the prosecuting attorney for Doddridge County. Floyd Neely was less well known but no less a supporter of the Union. Neely was colonel of the Eighteenth West Virginia Infantry and had served as sheriff from 1860 until West Virginia became a state; he had earlier been sheriff from 1852 until 1856. The third man, Benjamin H. Maulsby, was a justice of the peace, a merchant in West Union, and an agent for the B&O Railroad. The trio assured the governor that they believed that he had ordered the taking of the hostages based on the best information available to him and with the best interests of the state in mind. Nevertheless, they told Boreman that "the parties who petitioned for the arrest of the parties named did not act advisedly." Stuart, Floyd, and Maulsby reinforced the notion that citizens' names had been added to petitions without their knowledge, contrary to Yeater's contentions. They also pointed out that William M. Bonnell had voted against the secession ordinance and had "nearly in every instance" supported the Union Party in state politics. Regarding Thomas Ash, Samuel Beverline, and C. R. Gain, the three Union leaders told the governor that although Ash, Beverline, and Gain had been imprisoned as suspicious persons early in the war, they had been released after taking loyalty oaths. The occasion for opposition against them was their election to township office in 1863. While Stuart, Neely, and Maulsby believed that the previous imprisonment of the men had disqualified them from office, they did not believe that the men's candidacies and election merited their seizure as hostages. "We are satisfied that the parties named entered into the matter intending to live up in good faith to the obligations they took, and had faithfully been living up to their obligations since their release," they told the governor. They added that Ash, Beverline, and Gain had taken office with good intentions and were willing to resign if the governor wished. On the other hand, they reiterated charges that people's names had been added to petitions without their knowledge and said that "a very bad state of affairs" existed in McClellan Township. Stuart, Neely, and Maulsby concluded that the whole situation was irrelevant at any rate because, according to them, Gatrell and Hill no longer were in Confederate hands, and no hostages should be held for them.[63]

The circumstances of Gatrell's release are unclear, but Thomas Hill had in fact been released, not because of the taking of hostages by West Virginia, but through the efforts of the US Army. Maj. Gen. Benjamin F. Butler, Union commissioner of exchange, had exerted pressure on Col. Robert Ould, Confederate agent for exchange in Richmond. Hill had been offered paroles by the Confederate military but had refused. In exasperation, authorities in Richmond had made Hill subject to conscription into their army (as, in their view, a resident of Virginia). Butler intervened at that point and threatened to hold hostages for Hill if the Confederates did not exchange him. That threat had the desired effect.[64]

The release of Gatrell and Hill eased pressures upon Governor Boreman, but he and Lieutenant Snodgrass felt embarrassed. The apparent deception on the part of Doddridge County Unionists for political and personal purposes brought greater scrutiny on the county, and the cases against supposed Confederate sympathizers unraveled further. This included the focus upon the Ashcrafts. Family patriarch Uriah Ashcraft had been captured by the Union Army in May 1864 once again for "complicity with horse thieves" and was confined at Clarksburg. Governor Boreman prevailed upon Maj. Gen. Benjamin F. Kelley, commander of the Department of West Virginia, to order Ashcraft's release. The governor explained that Lieutenant Snodgrass knew Ashcraft and had vouched for him after investigating the situation. Boreman accepted Snodgrass's conclusion that "some evil person" had implicated Ashcraft in a letter that Union authorities had been allowed to intercept. The author of the letter had since fled beyond Confederate lines and could not be confronted.[65]

The active cycle of charges and countercharges among the people in the upper reaches of the Little Kanawha River and Middle Island Creek in the aftermath of West Virginia statehood in 1863 and 1864 was deceptive. It suggested a balance between Union and Confederate strength and between support for Virginia versus West Virginia. In fact, it reflected a weakened Confederate role in the northwestern part of the state. By no means did the area enjoy peace. Instead, Gilmer and Doddridge and other remote counties experienced a common phenomenon in the aftermath of active war. Guerrilla warfare set in. The Confederates resorted to it to preserve some role in otherwise Union-controlled areas. Guerrilla fighting at least disrupted the Northern war effort and occupied forces that could have been used elsewhere. Former Virginia State Line units, particularly the Nineteenth Virginia Cavalry, with its knowledge of the people and geography, served the Confederacy well in this regard.

As generally happens, some took advantage of the chaos in the rear areas of war. Outlawry took place, sometimes under the guise of military authority. Beyond outright violence and robbery, intimidation occurred. Threats of violence and political repercussions were common. Arrests and hostage-taking played well in this atmosphere. The state hostage law allowed for pro-Confederate and anti–West Virginia residents to be detained and pawned, but it also opened the way for revenge. In an area where Confederate threats were acute but fleeting, the use of the law to level false or at least questionable accusations was common. Old political social and economic grudges were settled. Yet, a price was paid. State leaders felt used. Such use brought embarrassment, and this led to distrust of supposedly supportive local Unionists. New political alliances formed. Ephraim Bee was one such political casualty as he lost his legislative seat to Joseph H. Diss Debar, whom many in the Union Party coalition viewed as more progressive as opposed to hardline. This became particularly important as West Virginia looked toward the end of the war and postwar governance.

The end of the war was still a year away, however. Brutal, personal warfare still took place in Gilmer and Doddridge Counties and in other parts of the state. Indeed, during the entire time that Governor Boreman considered the pleas and contentions in his files from these counties from 1863 to 1865, still others arrived on his desk. Perhaps some of the most brutal and personal accounts came from the region of the South Branch of the Potomac River in the area tucked between Maryland and Virginia known as the eastern panhandle. From there, new and ever unique hostage cases developed.

CHAPTER 7

# Rebel Rangers, Union Scouts, and Hostages on the South Branch

If a traveler left West Union in Doddridge County in 1863 and rode east along the Northwestern Turnpike, they would pass through Clarksburg and Grafton, cross over Cheat River near Rowlesburg, go in and out of western Maryland, and reach Romney in Hampshire County three days later. Romney lay in the center of the Appalachian Mountains, east of the Eastern Continental Divide, where the South Branch of the Potomac River formed a broad valley parallel to the Shenandoah Valley just to the east. The waters of the South Branch joined with those of the North Branch and eventually flowed past the nation's capital, but the country of the South Branch was very different. For that matter, it was quite different from Doddridge County. The region existed in relative seclusion. The Baltimore and Ohio skirted it to the north along the North Branch of the Potomac, and the Parkersburg and Staunton Turnpike threaded through the mountains to the south, but otherwise, besides the Northwestern Turnpike, only the Seneca Road, pushing into the valley from the west, provided a way in and out.

Five years before the start of the Civil War, a contributor to the *Washington Evening Star*, under the pen name "A Mountaineer," described the area and extolled the virtues of a "romantic and picturesque" region. "The face of the country is broken with high mountains," the correspondent wrote. "No pen can describe the grandeur of the scene which is presented from the top of one of these peaks on an autumn evening, when the dying leaves of the forest present every imaginable hue, while the setting sun, shooting his silvery rays upon the landscape, throws additional splendor over the view, and the mountain peaks seem to look down with a frown

Romney, the principal town in the South Branch Valley, during the Civil War. (Waud, Alfred R., Artist. View of Romney, VA. Hampshire County. United States Romney West Virginia, None. [Between 1861 and 1862 January 10]. Photograph. https://www.loc.gov/item/2004660441/)

upon those beneath." Readers in Washington learned of fine springs, including mineral springs; mountain trout; abundant game; fine grazing lands with fat cattle; fields of clover, timothy, and bluegrass; bumper crops of corn and wheat; and iron ore and coal beneath the ground. Hastily mentioned were mountain hazards such as long winters lasting until the end of April, bears, wolves, and rattlesnakes, and not mentioned was the subsistent existence of many of the inhabitants.[1]

On the eve of secession, the county seat towns and a few along the railroad enjoyed prosperity. In Romney, for instance, the Virginia Hotel boasted the best food available, choice liquors, an experienced bartender, and an enlarged stable. Jacob Vanmeter shipped sixty head of cattle to New York. The antislavery, procolonization writer Rev. William Henry Foote headed Potomac Seminary. Romney Classical Institute and Springfield Academy offered secondary education. David W. Entler opened a new blacksmith shop, and a foundry, tinsmith, druggist, carriage works, dry goods store, and an insurance agent advertised in the town's newspaper. People in the outlying country either struggled or succeeded depending upon the richness of their land and their proximity to markets.[2]

Conditional Unionism prevailed in varying degrees early in 1861. Henry G. Davis—budding railroad baron, future US senator from West Virginia, and Democratic candidate for vice president in 1904—led the most stalwart Unionist movement. Others favored preservation of the Union along with states' rights and slavery. In the end, the area's delegates to Virginia's convention on secession voted against leaving the Union but signed the secession ordinance when it was a fait accompli.[3]

Many people were reluctant secessionists, but key leaders in the restoration of Virginia's government to the Union and in the creation of West Virginia also lived in Hampshire and neighboring Hardy Counties. The region was a crossroads of political sentiment, but the proximity of the South Branch, as locals refer to the region, to the B&O Railroad and the northward course of its river gave it a connection to the North and made it vital to the security of the railroad as well. Northern forces cordoned the railroad and patrolled southward into the valley to fend off Confederate attacks. Southern troops frequently sprinted northward in efforts to disrupt the railroad. Both sides used the South Branch as a hiding place to deceive opposing forces in the nearby Shenandoah Valley or in the counties west of the mountains.

Participants in these military actions reached above Romney and gave further descriptions of the South Branch and its people. The South Fork

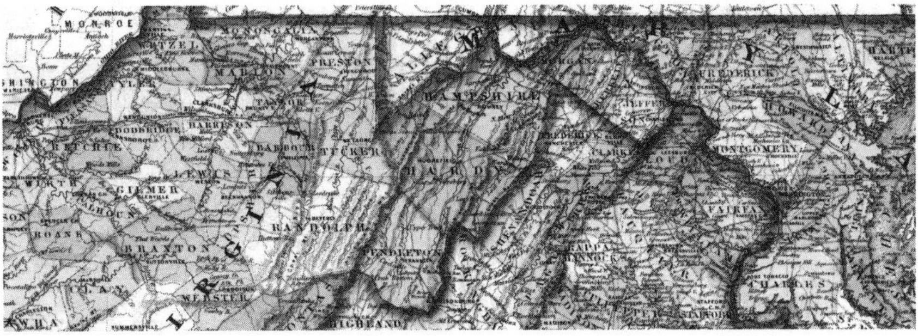

An 1864 map shows the South Branch region centered between West Virginia, Virginia, and Maryland (A.J. Johnson, *Johnson's Virginia, Delaware, Maryland & West Virginia.* [New York: Johnson and Ward, 1864] Map. https://www.loc.gov/item/lva0000096/)

joined the main river at Moorefield, and upon one Union soldier's posting to that town, he gave an account of the upper valley:

> This is the county seat of Hardy county, a very pretty town in one of the most fertile and beautiful portions of the valley of the South Branch of the Potomac. The people are generally wealthy, and before the war, owned large numbers of slaves. . . . We soon after started up the South Branch Valley. As far as Petersburg, the country is pretty good, but above that, it is one of the poorest in the world. It is surprising that the people can scratch a living out of the hills in times of peace, to say nothing of war and its devastations.[4]

A correspondent for the *Cincinnati Gazette* elaborated upon Petersburg. "This place is not the city of Petersburg in the southern part of Virginia, but a dilapidated town of some three hundred inhabitants, in Hardy county, at the junction of Tunay [Luney] Creek with the south branch of the Potomac," the writer noted. "The Potomac is a strong stream here, difficult to ford when the streams are swollen."[5] Beyond Petersburg, the North Fork of the South Branch merged with the river. The main stream of the South Branch came northward past Franklin, the county seat of Pendleton County, a place more like Virginia mountain towns than West Virginia towns along the B&O Railroad or on the banks of the Ohio or Monongahela Rivers. Time moved slowly there, and the war challenged the tranquility of the village and its surroundings.

The invasion of conventional armies forced the people of the South Branch to take sides as danger threatened their lives. Besides uncontrollable pressures, deliberate choices placed people on opposite sides. Certainly, their political sympathies came into play as partisans sought to harass their enemy armies, but, as in other parts of West Virginia, old social and economic rivalries motivated residents. Some chose sides to gain advantages in marketplaces and county seats, but others joined the side opposite their antagonists. In the active front of war, this choosing of sides resulted in violence as often if not more than political competition. Early in the war, militia units joined the fighting. Then, the Virginia State Line units and the regiments that evolved from them invited locals who sided with the Confederacy. When West Virginia was formed, home guard or independent scout companies supplemented the reactivated state militia on the Union side.

John D. Imboden, who later became famous for his coordinated raid across the mountains on the eve of West Virginia statehood, proved especially successful in organizing irregular units in the South Branch and Shenandoah regions. "I do not propose to rely much on military science, but mainly on great celerity of movement, sleepless vigilance, good marksmanship, and plenty of old-fashioned rough-fighting and bushwhacking to make our country too hot for our enemies the Yankees," Imboden insisted in the spring of 1862. "I therefore want men who will march all night or sit behind a bush all day, and a good marksman with a double-barrelled shot-gun."[6]

One company of irregulars that organized under Imboden's call quickly stood out. Known as McNeill's Rangers, the company became part of the Eighteenth Virginia Cavalry in 1863 when the regular army incorporated the state line units. McNeill's Rangers received its name from its commander, Capt. John Hanson McNeill. The company certainly met the demands put forth by Imboden, but it did not fit the stereotype of backwoods guerrilla units. John McNeill came from an affluent, educated family, and he led his men as an experienced captain. McNeill, a native of Frederick County, Virginia, had lived in Hardy County as a young man, but had moved west in the 1850s. He and his wife first settled in Kentucky and then moved to Boone County, Missouri, in 1854. There he became a leading cattle breeder with statewide reputation. He was elected as a vice-president of the Missouri State Agricultural Society. The family moved to Daviess County, Missouri, and McNeill was president of the first county fair in 1856 and led the creation of the Daviess County Agricultural and Mechanical Society the following year. With growing affluence, his son, William, attended college. At the outbreak of the war, John McNeill received an appointment as captain of a cavalry company in the pro-Confederate Missouri State Guard, and his sons served with him in the company. His son, George, was killed; William was wounded, and John and his son, Jesse, were captured. They made their escape from detention in St. Louis and headed back to Virginia in early 1862. Shortly after their arrival in Hardy County, they organized their partisan company. The band proved different than the typical bushwhackers, though. They did not merely fight pro-Union home guard units and harass Unionist citizens as most other partisan units did. McNeill's Rangers took on conventional Union forces and participated in coordinated operations against them. They disrupted enemy supply lines and posed a constant threat to the B&O Railroad.[7]

By 1863, McNeill's successes brought much attention. Robert E. Lee expressed his gratification for the captain's "gallant conduct" and hoped that he would "continue to harass the enemy as much as possible."[8] Confederate Secretary of War J. A. Seddon called McNeill a "very brave and enterprising partisan officer."[9] The Union also took note. "This McNeill should be taken as an example by our men," commented an observer in New Creek, on the North Branch of the Potomac. "He is doing his party vastly more service with less than fifty men than the whole Keys Battalion is doing the Government."[10]

The success of McNeill and his men gave them key roles in important Confederate actions in 1863 (see appendix for a timeline of events in chronological context). They served as scouts on Gen. William E. Jones's leg of the Jones-Imboden Raid in the spring, and the company rode with J. E. B. Stuart's cavalry screen during the Gettysburg Campaign that summer. In September, McNeill received the lion's share of the credit for infiltrating the camp of Union troops who had been sent to Hardy County to surprise Confederates under General Imboden, including McNeill's company. The infiltrators, numbering about 180, left 30 Yankees dead or seriously wounded and carried away 160 prisoners (out of seven companies), 46 horses, and assorted equipment. The Confederates lost three men.[11]

General Imboden reported to Robert E. Lee that the Union expedition against his men had been guided by a "Union man."[12] Both sides greatly resented the assistance that local residents gave to their enemies. They stayed on guard against such people and looked for ways to put an end to their endeavors. Shortly after the raid into the Union camp, McNeill's troop captured Michael Yoakum in Rockingham County, Virginia. Yoakum lived in Hardy County, which neighbored Rockingham. The Confederates called the eighteen-year-old a "swamper and murderer."[13]

Confederate guerrillas such as McNeill's Rangers kept the eastern panhandle of West Virginia and the Shenandoah Valley unbalanced until the end of the war. (Photograph, "War in Western Virginia—Rebel Guerillas Watching a Wagon Train Going through a Pass in the Blue Ridge Mountains," *Frank Leslie's Illustrated Newspaper*, August 23, 1862. West Virginia State Archives.)

The Yoakums, in fact, suffered from a reputation in their community, even among Unionists, for intimidating and stealing from their neighbors. They countered that their detractors were pro-Confederates and false Unionists who sold stolen cattle to the Confederate Army. The Yoakums claimed that they had been victims of robbery and theft. Such claims and counterclaims stemmed from political, social, and economic rivalries between families before the war.[14]

When Michael Yoakum fell into McNeill's hands, Alfred Yoakum went before Abijah Dolly, a justice of the peace at Greenland Gap, on September 28, 1863, filed an affidavit, and asked that the governor take hostages for his son. He identified Thomas Seymore (Seymour), Felix B. Welton, and Job Welton as "persons of known disloyalty," and Governor Boreman honored the father's request three days later.[15]

The proposed hostages for Michael Yoakum were influential farmers in Hardy County, and they all lived in the Luneys Creek area. Sixty-year-old Thomas Seymore was Job Welton's father-in-law. Job Welton, thirty-seven, had recently inherited his father's substantial holdings, which included land and herds in multiple counties. His uncle, Felix B. Welton, forty-seven, was a Presbyterian elder and a frequent visitor to Richmond before the war. He also was known to harbor wounded members of McNeill's Rangers.[16]

The taking of hostages for Michael Yoakum soon became controversial. The governor called upon Col. James A. Mulligan to seize the hostages. Boreman believed Mulligan to be in command of US forces at Petersburg.[17] Mulligan, of the Twenty-Third Illinois Infantry or Irish Brigade, actually commanded the Second Division of the Department of West Virginia, based at New Creek. Quite coincidentally, he had commanded the Twenty-Third Illinois at the First Battle of Lexington, where John H. McNeill had been wounded and captured in Missouri. The governor's warrant ended up in the hands of Maria Yoakum, Michael's mother, and she delivered it to Col. Joseph Thoburn of the First West Virginia Infantry, who commanded the Second Brigade of the division at Petersburg.

Thoburn followed a similar course as Union officers in Randolph County. He questioned the governor's use of the US Army in enforcing the hostage law and forwarded the warrant through military channels. "Gov. Boreman of course has no authority to order Col. Mulligan to arrest parties for him, and the parties he wants arrested are far from being the worst of this locality,"[18] Thoburn told an officer at departmental command. Thoburn obviously resented Boreman's involvement in federal military affairs and wanted to make a point. The truth of the matter was that Boreman had not ordered the taking of the hostages but had requested the army to seize them. Mulligan shared his subordinate's viewpoint. He referred the warrant to his superiors and advised if hostages were taken that the local commanding officer should choose them. The colonel stated that Seymore and the Weltons had taken the prescribed loyalty oath and that the judge advocate assigned to the division had vouched for them. Mulligan added that he had personal knowledge of the men's "good character."[19]

So it was that Colonel Mulligan discouraged the holding of Seymore and the Weltons. "However there are persons in the neighborhood of Petersburg to whom the law of retaliation would well apply, in proper punishment for their own insidious sins against the Government," he told officers at department headquarters in Cumberland, Maryland.[20] In concurrence, Thayer Melvin, assistant adjutant general for the department, returned the warrant to Mulligan by order of Brig. Gen. Benjamin F. Kelley, the department commander, with instructions to request Thoburn to "name two or more persons in or about Petersburg, who by reason of their known sympathy with the Confederacy, evidenced by giving aid or comfort to the rebel soldiers, or guerrillas" as hostages.[21]

Colonel Thoburn suggested Jesse Fisher and William Van Meter of the Moorefield area as hostages.[22] He noted that five "rebels" had recently been at Van Meter's home and explained, "Those who entertain our enemies in our midst are the ones who should suffer." Interestingly, the colonel crossed out the words "if any" after the word "suffer."[23]

Colonel Thoburn's recommendations, along with Boreman's warrant, bounced their way back through the chain of command to Mulligan and then to department headquarters. Melvin issued orders for the arrest of the hostages and instructed Thoburn to send the correspondence and orders in the case, along with the governor's original request, to Boreman.[24]

The contradiction in the selection of hostages pointed to an ongoing dilemma in hostage-taking. The governor depended upon local residents in counties distant from Wheeling to determine likely candidates as hostages. The criteria called for persons of known disloyal sentiments, and supposedly loyal people could satisfy their own prejudices and grudges by labeling personal enemies as disloyal. On the other hand, Union Army officers defined loyalty by whether loyalty oaths had been taken and by people's cooperation with the army. The state and federal definitions did not always match.

In some ways, the Union Army handled West Virginia's hostage requests in the South Branch region the same as those in Randolph County, but stark differences surfaced with the commanders in the South Branch. Union officers quickly asserted their authority over the use of their troops as in Randolph County, but they were less diplomatic about it. This suggested a resentment of Governor Boreman and his government. Different field commanders were involved, and that may explain part of it, but Thayer Melvin and General Kelley played parts at the top of the Union command in both instances. It may be that the commanders in the South Branch knew more about the hostages than the commanders had in the Tygarts Valley, and their objections may have been based on an understanding of the local situation. This may have included knowledge of the animosities between the Yoakums and their neighbors and the possibility that Alfred Yoakum's nomination of hostages was intended to settle old scores. The fact that the South Branch was more distant and that Governor Boreman was not as familiar with the area and its people may have complicated matters. It also is true that at least one Randolph County hostage, Alfred Hutton, had a record of suspected disloyalty with Union commanders independent of his state record, and Union commanders may have been more willing to accommodate the governor in that case. All of these are considerations in the differences in approaches by the Union chain of command in the two regions. It also may be a simple matter that some unknown difficulty between the state and the army on another matter made officers feel less cooperative at the time of the Yoakum situation. Union commanders in the South Branch faced more immediate partisan activity, and they simply may have been so occupied with the almost constant fighting there that they did not take time for the niceties of politics.

The army's selection of hostages was not beyond question either. William Van Meter was not a civilian when Thoburn chose him as a hostage. William Van Meter, twenty-four years old, had grown up in Hardy County. His parents, Garrett and Elizabeth, were rich farmers and owned sixteen slaves. The son, however, had left home before the war and moved to Texas. In June 1861, he returned to Virginia and joined the Twenty-Fifth Virginia Infantry (CSA). He was captured at the Battle of Rich Mountain in July 1861 and was paroled but was rearrested in Beverly in May 1862 and sent to Camp Chase for violating his parole. Van Meter was exchanged in August 1862 but was captured again while on hospital duty at Antietam. After a sojourn in a US Army hospital in Frederick, Maryland, he was paroled again. By then, his enlistment had expired, and he joined McNeill's Rangers but soon transferred to the First Texas Cavalry for a brief stint. By late fall in 1863, he was back with the Twenty-Fifth Virginia and was listed on duty in eastern Virginia in November and December 1863. Perhaps he, like many Confederate soldiers, visited home—with or without leave—for short periods between the fighting and fell into Thoburn's net. At any rate, the Union Army should have classed Van Meter as a prisoner of war when he was arrested as a hostage in December 1863.[25]

Twenty-nine-year-old Jesse Fisher had a less sensational record. A cousin of the Weltons, his father, George, was a wealthy farmer, and his family had servants, both African American and white, including fourteen slaves. Fisher was a private in Capt. Isaac Stickley's pro-Confederate company of the Fourteenth Regiment of the Virginia Militia, which saw active duty early in the war but was overshadowed by state line units and their successors later in the war.[26]

Two months and six days had passed since Yoakum's father had appealed to the governor for help in freeing his son. Boreman had not stayed idle during that time. His impatience got the better of him, and he issued a second warrant. This time he sent it to Capt. E. C. Harper, commander of a particularly effective state independent scout company in the area. The governor again included Seymore and Felix B. Welton in the warrant but added Streit Cunningham, a wealthy, fifty-three-year-old Moorefield area farmer, to the list.[27] The new order did not reach Harper before Thoburn's hostages arrived in Wheeling, but it brought one last jab from Thoburn. Harper reported back to Boreman that, upon learning of the new warrant, Thoburn "didn't deem it necessary to take any more" hostages.[28] While Thoburn resisted the governor's authority over federal troops, he had no problem interfering with an order from a state commander-in-chief to state forces not in federal service.

Once Thoburn's hostages were in prison in Wheeling, William Van Meter offered to go beyond the Confederate lines to negotiate for Yoakum's release so that he and Jesse Fisher might be released. Van Meter promised to return if he was unsuccessful. He apparently convinced Governor Boreman to allow the trip, but unlike others who made similar efforts, Van Meter did not return. He was back with his regiment by the start of 1864.[29]

Meanwhile, Michael Yoakum suffered a vengeful captivity. Soon after his capture, his mother discovered from friends and neighbors the path of McNeill's force after it had seized her son. She followed it to General Imboden's camp fifteen miles south of Harrisonburg, Virginia. Maria Yoakum described the scene to Colonel Thoburn, who reported it to his superiors as useful intelligence. She saw McNeill and his men, well dressed and with fine horses, preparing for another raid into Hardy County. At the same time, the balance of Imboden's brigade, which she estimated as half the size of Union forces in Hardy County, "looked very badly and dead horses were lying all round his camp."[30]

In this desperate setting, Imboden treated his prisoners harshly. "She says her son is in chains in the woods, stripped of part of his clothing & in a wretched condition generally," recounted Thoburn. "She thinks he cannot live long unless something is done for him." Yoakum's mother saw two other civilian prisoners in the same condition.[31]

Maria Yoakum learned that Imboden intended to try her son in a court-martial for murder and treason with the possible penalty of death by firing squad. With the same apparent knowledge and influence that gained Mrs. Yoakum access to Imboden's camp, the family availed themselves of the civilian court system in Confederate Virginia on behalf of their son. They also gained the attention of Robert E. Lee. In January 1864, General

Lee confronted Imboden about the case and bluntly tutored the Staunton attorney and former state legislator in the law:

> General: I have been informed that you have in arrest a citizen of Hardy County named Michael Yoakum, who is charged with outrages committed upon the persons and property of some of our citizens of that county, and that you propose trying him before a court-martial. I am also informed that a writ of habeas corpus has been sued out by Yoakum, to which you have made return claiming jurisdiction over the case. You have the power to afford immediate protection to our citizens against threatened or attempted violence, but where an offense has been committed by one not in the military service of the United States or our own you have no jurisdiction to try the offender by a court-martial. You can arrest and deliver him to the civil authorities, who alone are competent to try him. If the facts of this case be such as I have represented them above I desire that you will surrender the accused to the civil authorities, in obedience to the writ, to be disposed of by the court having jurisdiction.[32]

A circuit court released Michael Yoakum, and he returned home to a region that remained chaotic. Control of local government alternated between pro-Confederate Virginia and West Virginia, and for a time Hampshire County had two county seats, one in Confederate hands, and one in Union hands. Legislators represented the South Branch counties in both Richmond and Wheeling. Confederate military forces sustained supportive government officials, and West Virginia tried to assert its authority in the area with the help of the US Army.

The justice of the peace Abijah Dolly stood out among those who asserted West Virginia's authority in the South Branch. His judicial role made him a defender and arbiter for Unionist rights and concerns, but he also waded through tension and conflict as a township supervisor and thus a member of the county board of supervisors. Dolly's influence reached beyond the local level, however. He had sat in the West Virginia Constitutional Convention and knew the state's leaders.[33]

The Confederate Army targeted Dolly as a state and local leader under the West Virginia government. The *Wheeling Daily Intelligencer* noted an instance of this in 1863. "We learn that our old friend Abijah Dolly, member of the late Constitutional Convention, from Hardy county, made a very narrow escape not long since from the clutches of the rebels," its editor recorded. "Mr. Dolly resides in the very midst of a venomous nest of rebels, but so far has luckily managed to elude them."[34] The escape made the Confederates even more determined, and they posted a $2,000 reward for Dolly, dead or alive. The justice of the peace did not stay in his own house for some time afterward.[35]

Violence in the region intensified during election season, and candidates and poll officials lived in danger. In Pendleton County, two independent scout companies, assisted by two others in neighboring counties, made sure that pro-Union elections took place in the largely pro-Confederate county. Known as swampers, the members of these same home guard units prevented elections under the Richmond government from occurring.[36] Shortages of food and supplies resulted from the state of war, topography, distance from the railroad, and the fact that federal permits were needed to ship south of the B&O Railroad. This made the atmosphere more tense. Many people took to the roads in attempts to find needed goods, and their transience raised suspicions of spying or scouting.[37] The paranoia led to increased arrests on both sides, and the hostage law came into play. Confederates raided the North Fork section of Pendleton County and took away twenty-eight-year-old Samuel M. Day and thirty-six-year-old John Greenawalt, laborers on their fathers' meager farms in November 1863.

The state's response reveals a canned, impersonal approach to very personal, tragic circumstances. "Enclosed I send you warrant for the arrest of some rebels as hostages," AG Francis P. Pierpont directed Capt. E. C. Harper, commander of one of the independent scout companies in Pendleton County. "You will have the enclosed affidavit filled up and sworn to by some good man."[38] It does not appear that the state government used fill-in-the-blank hostage affidavits in every case, but this occasion suggests that in the chaos of war, state officials sometimes streamlined the hostage-taking process. As a result, Joel Siples (Siple), Andrew W. Dyer, and Robert Phares joined the ranks of state hostages.[39] Dyer was Pendleton County clerk and a school commissioner. Phares was the county's sheriff before the outbreak of the war.[40]

The region did not relax as 1863 came to an end. Union Brig. Gen. William W. Averell launched a noteworthy cavalry raid from New Creek and moved up the South Branch against the Virginia and Tennessee Railroad at Salem, Virginia. As 1864 began, Maj. Gen. Fitzhugh Lee retaliated against Union forces in the area for Averell's expedition, and Brig. Gen. Thomas L. Rosser, in command of the Laurel Brigade under Lee, haunted the South Branch and the North Branch until the end of the war. Larger Confederate forces under Jubal Early darted in and out of the upper Potomac region as he parried with the Union Army in the Shenandoah Valley, and as he pushed toward and then away from Washington. McNeill's Rangers often aided Early, and in an attack on Union defenders at Mt. Jackson in early October 1864, Capt. John McNeill was mortally wounded.

In the meantime, Abijah Dolly found respite in politics—the very thing that had brought him danger. Voters elected him to the West Virginia House of Delegates in November 1863, and while he was in Wheeling, at least, Confederate raiders could not molest him. The presence of Rosser's brigade complicated his life when he returned home from the state capital, however. On November 28, 1864, Rosser surprised New Creek in Hampshire County and defeated the Union garrison. He took many prisoners, several cannons, and hundreds of horses while destroying much property of the B&O Railroad. The prisoners included several civilians. "That old hero, Abijah Dolly, formerly a member of the West Virginia Legislature, was one of the prisoners taken from New Creek," reported the *Wheeling Daily Intelligencer*. Abraham Hinkle, who was visiting New Creek from Pendleton County, described his experience as one of the captives. Drunken soldiers drove the civilians through mud, with the flat of a saber enforcing their commands. A major was in charge and led the ordeal. "This fellow searched and robbed with his own hands eighteen or twenty citizen prisoners taking everything of value found upon their persons," Hinkle wrote. "Although thrice ordered by General Rosser to send his prisoners to the front, he refused to obey until he had finished his pocket picking." The undisciplined scene allowed most of the prisoners, including Dolly, to escape. "He made his escape, ran on ahead of the rebels, reached his farm, and drove off and concealed all his stock before the rebel advance came up," the *Daily Intelligencer* crowed.[41]

Despite Dolly's escape, he became the object of a new hostage situation. Prominent Unionist James Carskadon, noting his own "narrow escape" in the New Creek attack, sent a letter to Governor Boreman two days afterward asking for hostages to be held for civilians taken by Rosser's men. Carskadon requested that Boreman seize Hardy County residents Benjamin Cunningham, Jonathan Seymore, and Parsons M. Taylor—as well as William G. Van Meter and Streit Cunningham, who had slipped out of the earlier hostage net—as hostages for Dolly. He also wanted George W. Washington, John M. Pancake, William S. Taylor, Elijah Rinehart, Okey Johnson, James Sheetz, Hugh Perrill, Benjamin Grayson, and Jesse Davis—all residents of Hampshire County—as hostages for Frederick Hufman, John Little, Upton Buxton, Andrew J. Roby, Gillmore F. Sims, and John Garret.

Carskadon conceded, "Quite a number of the prisoners both citizens and soldiers have escaped and have arrived here [New Creek] and we have a report that Dolly has escaped." Still, he pressed for hostages before he knew who was actually in Confederate custody. Carskadon feared that those in captivity would be pressed into the Confederate Army.[42]

James Carskadon, a Hampshire County farmer, was born in the county in 1819. He had become politically active in antebellum times and was elected to the Virginia Senate in 1860. As a member of the Virginia General Assembly who remained loyal to the United States, he attended the Second Wheeling Convention in June 1861 and participated in the creation of the pro-Union Virginia government. Carskadon chaired the Union Party convention in Hampshire County in 1863 and attended the state convention of the National Union Party in Parkersburg in 1864. He represented Hampshire, Hardy, Morgan, and Pendleton Counties in the West Virginia Senate at the time of the attack on New Creek and was in a position to gain the governor's attention.[43]

The senator learned more about the captives in the week after the attack on New Creek and followed up with an affidavit before a notary public in Hampshire County, Thomas P. Adams. John Little remained on the list of captives, and Carskadon added Isaac D. Caldwell and James T. Crawford. At the bottom of his affidavit, he explained to Boreman, "Many of our citizens have been released, the above only being retained." Carskadon also amended his list of requested hostages. He no longer called for the hostages for Dolly and took John M. Pancake, William S. Taylor, Benjamin Grayson, and Jesse Davis off the list. He added James Parsons and Isaac Pancake of Hampshire County.[44]

Senator Carskadon told the governor, "There were quite a number more citizens taken off but they were not citizens of this State."[45] Thomas P. Adams disputed this statement. In his own letter to Governor Boreman, Adams claimed that Carskadon had purposely left some captives out of his affidavit, and Adams arranged for a second affidavit "naming all, whether friends to us or not." The notary public told the governor that Carskadon "was only working for one or two of his own political supporters." Adams hoped that Boreman would view the new affidavit as an effort by him and his supporters to do their "duty to all parties without having an ax to grind at the expence of any neighbor."[46]

Adams's resentment of Carskadon apparently stemmed from rivalry over federal patronage. Patronage through the Republican Party and its state affiliate, the Union Party, provided a means for winning votes not only for the parties but for staving off Confederate influence. Those who controlled patronage wielded much power. Adams had just been elected to the West Virginia House of Delegates from Hampshire County, but his greater influence came from his federal board of trade post. Through the position, he controlled treasury department permits on the B&O Railroad in the New Creek area and decided who was allowed to ship goods south of the railroad. The Carskadon family also enjoyed federal power with a number of revenue appointments being distributed through the family.[47]

George W. Tuxworth and John Hughes of Hampshire County put their names on the affidavit that Adams arranged. It still named Little, Caldwell, and Crawford but added A. J. Tuxworth, J. H. Dallman, E. B. Davis, J. T. Corbitt, and C. B. Reynolds to Carskadon's list of captives. Adams included a clipping about Rosser's raid from a Richmond newspaper, but ironically, it supported Carskadon's position. The news report gave Ohio as the residence of Tuxworth and Corbitt. It said that Dallman and Davis were from New York and that Reynolds lived in Pennsylvania. They likely were travelers on the railroad. Both Adams and Carskadon came up short in their lists. The newspaper story also included A. Shellenburger of Hampshire County, William Tetterburn and Amos Peters of Hardy County, and Pascall B. Gentry and Lewis Simon of New Creek among the prisoners as well as nine others from Marshall, Monongalia, Ohio, and Preston Counties in West Virginia and fourteen more from Indiana, Maryland, Ohio, and Virginia. The report stated these men were sent to Castle Thunder via Staunton to be held as hostages for pro-Confederate residents in Union hands. It also noted that an unspecified number of unnamed African Americans, "slaves stolen from their masters," had been captured in the New Creek raid and taken to Castle Thunder.[48]

In the Adams affidavit, the idea of using medical doctors as leverage resurfaced. Suggested hostages included Dr. Groves, Dr. McNemar, and Dr. Ewing. The affidavit also kept Okey Johnson, George W. Washington, and James Parsons from Carskadon's list and added Jonathan and Thomas Seymour; Job, Cyrus, and Abraham Welton; Aaron Clark; George Cunningham; and John and Abe Johnson.[49]

As the captives from New Creek languished in Castle Thunder and their hostages sat out the war in the Atheneum, the cycle of action and reaction continued in Hampshire, Hardy, and Pendleton Counties. In January 1865, members of McNeill's Rangers, now led by Jesse McNeill, targeted men of the West Virginia independent scout companies under Capt. John Yoakum and Capt. James Rohrbaugh in their Hardy County homes.

Rohrbaugh recalled the raid in vivid detail. "On the 10th of this month, a party of rebel cavalry numbering about fifty men, made an incursion in our neighborhood," Rohrbaugh began. "After taking Henry Goldizen & Bethuel Watts, members of Capt. Yoakum's company, prisoners, and killing Michael Yoakum, brother of the Captain, they came to my father's place, robbing me, my brother Samuel, and my sister Belinda Idleman, a widow, of all they could get a hold of." Rohrbaugh listed a vast amount of food, cloth, leather goods, and ammunition, which the Confederates destroyed or carried away. He continued in a tragic vein, "They went to the house of Isaac Hartman, one of my men, and after pursuing him some distance into the woods, killed him, apparently after he had surrendered, for he was shot in the face on the left side of his nose, taking from him his revolver; all his money & his & Geo. Day's clothing."[50]

Captain Rohrbaugh's account provided an example of the attacks and counterattacks that happened daily in guerrilla warfare and which gave rise to many of West Virginia's hostage cases. It was a pro-Union perspective. Contrasting accounts gave the pro-Confederate side. A story of the January 10 attack appeared in the *Richmond Enquirer:* "A portion of Captain McNeil's company—some 25 or 30 men—under command of Lieut. [Isaac] Welton, made a desent [*sic*], on Tuesday the 10th instant upon a squad of Swamp Dragons on North Fork, Pendleton county, killing three and capturing two," it reported. "A man named Yoakum and another named Branneman, both notorious among the 'Dragons' for their thieving operations, were among the killed."[51]

Thus, while McNeill's men had turned Michael Yoakum over to General Imboden in 1863, only to see him released, they took no chances this time. They meted out the death penalty without waiting for a trial.

McNeill's Rangers lost their commission in the Confederate Army in February 1865, but that did not end their eye-for-an-eye actions. When the opportunity arose, Jesse McNeill served cold revenge upon General Kelley for the 1862 arrest of his mother (Jemima Cunningham McNeill), sister, and brother as they had been traveling along the B&O Railroad from Ohio to reach the camp of the rangers. Mrs. McNeill and her children had escaped and reached her husband and son, but plans for vengeance developed. On February 22, 1865, they were fulfilled when the rangers made a daring incursion into Cumberland, Maryland, headquarters of the Union Department of West Virginia. The Confederates came away with General Kelley and Maj. Gen. George Crook. The two generals spent a month in Confederate captivity until being exchanged.[52]

Some in the hostage drama in the South Branch never came home. Samuel M. Day, the Unionist captive from Pendleton County, went to the Confederate prison in Salisbury, North Carolina. Confederate authorities did not list him as a civilian. They categorized him as a prisoner of war based on his membership in the militia. Yet, Day did not belong to any of the active state home guard companies known as independent scouts. The Confederates listed him as a member of the Forty-Ninth Virginia Militia, the formal militia organization to which all adult men belonged, and which had gone dormant and was ignored by the State of West Virginia. Day was exchanged in March 1865 and was sent to a US military hospital in Baltimore. He died later in the month. His father, Leonard Day, who had desperately sought his son's release through the taking of hostages, now stepped forward to claim his son's personal effects. His son was buried in Baltimore.[53]

In its first issue after the war, the *South Branch Intelligencer* in Romney published a poem by R. J. Coffey entitled "Hope" at the top of its first column:

> When all around seems dark and drear,
> And sadness settles on the heart,
> And want and wretchedness appear
> To crush and wound the tender smart;
> Hope comes to us on golden wings,
> And whispers of celestial things.[54]

The war ended, and the people of the South Branch grasped at hope, but before that happened, personal warfare and hostage-taking continued in other parts of the state. Dark and drear prevailed. Vicious personal warfare, similar to that on the South Branch of the Potomac River, took place on the opposite corner of the state, where West Virginia, Kentucky, and Ohio came together. Starting with violence against still another West Virginia sheriff late in 1863, this fighting gave rise to several hostage incidents in the early half of 1864—incidents that added another file to Governor Boreman's thickening collection of hostage cases.

CHAPTER 8

# The Plight of Southwestern West Virginia in 1864

While people in the South Branch Valley lived in fear and anger over the constant fighting and the prospect of being imprisoned either as political prisoners or hostages, a similar guerrilla warfare prevailed in southwestern West Virginia along the borders of southern Ohio and Kentucky. Gov. Arthur I. Boreman, in his address to the state legislature in January 1864, outlined the situation:

> Notwithstanding all that has been done by Government troops and State companies, some portions of the State are still infested with bands of marauders, who rob and plunder the people and carry off large quantities of their property beyond the lines. They do not commit as many murders as formerly, but they still continue the nefarious practice of capturing our citizens, and especially the civil officers of the State, whom they carry off and throw into loathsome prisons, there to linger, and in many instances to die for want of the absolute necessities of life.[1]

Boreman focused on a recent incident in Putnam County. Located on the lower Kanawha River between Charleston and the Ohio border, Putnam County lay in Teays Valley, the bed of a prehistoric river that sloped westward toward the Ohio River in defiance of the northwestwardly flowing Kanawha. The valley made Putnam County an attractive farming region and provided a path for the antebellum James River and Kanawha Turnpike and for railroad speculation before and after the Civil War. On the day after Christmas in 1863, a Confederate force of about 150 men raided Winfield, the county seat, robbed a store, and took away horses. They then crossed the river into Red House and vandalized the telegraph office and cut telegraph lines. When they left, they took with them the sheriff, William H. Shaw (see appendix for a timeline of political and military events in context with West Virginia's hostage saga).[2]

The Confederate raiders acted under the command of Col. Milton Ferguson as part of the Sixteenth Virginia Cavalry, another amalgamation of former Virginia State Line units. Maj. Gen. Sam Jones, in command of the Confederacy's Department of Western Virginia, had sent Ferguson to the lower Kanawha Valley in late December to divert Union attention from southwestern Virginia.[3] William H. Copley, West Virginia state senator from neighboring Cabell County, had keen knowledge of Shaw's capture and the work of Ferguson's men. Copley told the Wheeling press that Ferguson and his regiment had been actively "stealing everything he could carry away and foraging upon the people" in the region for the past month and had eluded the Thirteenth West Virginia Infantry in its attempts to stop the Confederates. The *Wheeling Daily Intelligencer* related the legislator's news and noted the role of Ferguson's raiders in Shaw's disappearance. "As the rebel Government at Richmond has offered a thousand dollars reward for Sheriffs, Mr. S is doubtless closely confined in some Richmond prison."[4]

Ferguson owed his success to his knowledge of the region. He was a resident of Wayne County, and many of his men came from the same area. They had many friends and supporters, and the governor addressed this as he continued his speech to the legislature. He blamed the seizure of people and property on the communication and supply network that Ferguson had with local people. Boreman struck at the heart of the relationship between Confederate sympathizers and the capture of pro-Union residents:

> It is absolutely necessary to our peace, and to the continuance of civil organization in many of the counties that these captures cease, and I intend, if it be possible, that they shall cease. If the disloyal among us will not give information of the presence of these bands in the neighborhood, a sufficient number of them not less than two for one, shall be arrested and imprisoned until the captured loyal person is returned.[5]

Boreman cited the hostage law and his use of it. He introduced a new concept of the law, however. The governor stated his preference that the law be preemptive rather than punitive:

> The disloyal in our midst can prevent these captures in another way, and that is, by making proper representations to their rebel leaders. It is known that they keep correspondence with them. This is not denied by many. If they wish to remain in our midst in peace, they must secure that peace by preventing the forcible abduction of our loyal people. This they can do, for in nearly every case when hostages have been arrested it has secured the safe return of the captured party; and it seems to me that the same influence that can effect the release can prevent the capture.[6]

Although Boreman espoused the hostage law as a deterrent of Confederate arrests of Unionist citizens, he did not hesitate to use it as a reactionary measure. He ordered the arrest of Alexander W. Handley of Teays Valley, Mordecai A. Summers of Winfield, John B. Crawford of Winfield, John M. Handley of Mason County, Jesse Timms of Buffalo in Putnam County, J. L. Bronaugh of Buffalo, George W. Summers of Mud River in Putnam County, J. M. Reece of Mud River, and B. F. Sterrett of Buffalo as hostages for Sheriff Shaw. Alexander Handley's son was a lieutenant in Ferguson's command.[7] Boreman later added William M. Bonnell of Doddridge County to their ranks.[8] The *Wheeling Daily Intelligencer* noted the arrival of the hostages at the Atheneum on January 29, 1864. "They are all prominent rebels and no doubt will be the cause of a safe and speedy return of Mr. Shaw," the newspaper reported confidently. It continued to advocate the use of the hostage law from its relatively safe position nestled between Ohio and Pennsylvania. "This plan of arresting hostages for Union men will do incalculable good," the Republican journal editorialized. "It will convince Union men everywhere, and particularly those performing the dangerous and vexatious duties of sheriff, that the State intends to protect them at all hazards and it will show the rebels that they are not to be permitted to drag loyal citizens from their homes with impunity."[9]

Residents of Putnam County and vicinity had a different point of view. Led by Joseph C. Gary, a justice of the peace, petitioners recounted the seizure of their sheriff to Governor Boreman but asked him to reconsider use of the hostage law. They believed that the arrest of the hostages could "in no wise affect the fate of their valued friend, Mr Shaw." They added their view that the hostages had no influence with Confederate authorities and had no "friends who can in any wise forward the release of their most esteemed friend William H. Shaw." The men expressed fear that the taking of hostages would result in more pro-Union people being taken by the Confederates. "It is well known to your Excellency that these guerillas and marauders

An 1864 map shows the counties of southwestern West Virginia with Kentucky and Ohio just to the west. (A. J. Johnson, *Johnson's Virginia, Delaware, Maryland & West Virginia* [New York: Johnson and Ward, 1864] Map. https://www.loc.gov/item/lva0000096/)

have on several occasions made inroads into this part of the country and carried away citizens and property & that they can do so again."[10]

Several weeks later another petition made the same case but undoubtedly carried more weight with the governor. It included the signatures of seventeen men in Kanawha, Mason, and Putnam Counties. Some of the most prominent men of the state were among them. Benjamin H. Smith of Charleston, US attorney for the District of West Virginia, former Virginia legislator, and Boreman's future opponent for the governor's office in 1866 was one. John Hall, president of the West Virginia Constitutional Convention, from Mason County was another. Perhaps the most venerable, however, was George W. Summers of Charleston (not the hostage). Summers had been a powerhouse in the antebellum Whig Party in Virginia. He had served in the Virginia House of Delegates and in the US House of Representatives. Summers had been the Whig candidate for governor in 1851. He had served as a Unionist member of the Richmond Convention and attended the Peace Conference in Washington in 1861. These petitioners repeated a refrain that Boreman read again and again from both bona fide Unionists as well as from Confederate sympathizers who claimed loyalty to the state and the Union to gain the release of hostages. They insisted that the hostages are "personally known to us, that they are peaceable law abiding & useful citizens of their respective counties; and that whatever their feelings or sympathies may be we are satisfied they were in no *manner* privy to or aided in the seizure of said Shaw." The Unionists did not argue that the hostages were completely loyal to the

Union but took the position that beliefs alone were not sufficient cause for men to be imprisoned. They, too, questioned the efficacy of the hostage law. "We are satisfied that the policy of arresting & imprisoning our own citizens as hostages can only result in checking if not destroying in them any germ of loyalty to the government which we all feel should be encouraged & promoted," the petitioners reasoned.[11]

Meanwhile, politics also came into play for the Confederates as William H. Shaw waited in Libby Prison. After his arrival in Richmond on January 25, 1864, the sheriff wrote to his wife and his friends to apply pressure for the release of the hostages who were held for him. His wife in turn contacted Boreman. This was a common approach for civilians in Confederate hands and had the blessing of prison officials.[12] The indirect manipulation from Richmond did not work. Not only did West Virginia keep its hostages, the US Army took two of its own.

Brig. Gen. E. P. Scammon, Union division commander at Charleston, ordered the arrest of R. T. Harvey, a wealthy forty-eight-year-old Putnam County farmer, and Chapman W. Maupin, a fifty-two-year-old farmer and merchant in Cabell and Mason Counties. Both men had sons in the Confederate Army. On January 25, Scammon wrote a blind letter to the "Confederate Commander in Southwestern Virginia." That happened to be Sam Jones, based at Dublin, on the Virginia and Tennessee Railroad. The Union general alerted Jones that Maupin would come across the lines under a flag of truce with the eventual goal of traveling to Richmond to bargain for Shaw's release. Scammon used the opportunity for comment on the sheriff's captivity. "The capture of Mr. Shaw cannot, I think, have been authorized by you," he wrote. "His detention can serve no end, save that of provoking retaliation upon such civilians as may sympathize with his captors, and who, but for such useless acts, would be permitted to remain in tranquility."[13]

Col. George S. Patton (grandfather of the World War II general) of the Twenty-Second Virginia Infantry received Maupin within Confederate lines and passed him along to department headquarters with the comment that Maupin was "reported as a strong Confederate sympathizer, which I am satisfied is the case." Patton also noted Maupin's earnestness in his efforts to gain Shaw's release. Maupin had twenty days to accomplish his mission and went on to the Confederate capital.[14] Within six weeks, Maupin returned to Charleston and turned himself over to Scammon, as agreed beforehand. He was unsuccessful in winning Shaw's freedom. Nonetheless, Brig. Gen. George Crook, in command of the Kanawha

Division at the time, ordered the release of Maupin and Harvey. Confederate authorities "expressed to him [Maupin] their utter indifference as to the fate of the citizens of West Virginia claiming the protection of the federal government & inside their military lines, asserting that the more of her citizens the state chooses to arrest and imprison the better it would be for their cause."[15]

Maupin was not the only person to encounter seeming indifference from the Confederate government in the Shaw case. Congressman Samuel A. Miller and state senator William W. Newman, both of whom represented the Kanawha Valley in Richmond (the region was represented in Washington and Wheeling at the same time), ran into a stone wall. The provost marshal general, Brig. Gen. John H. Winder, rebuffed the politicians on instructions from Secretary of War James A. Seddon just days after Maupin's return to West Virginia. Seddon wrote:

> The policy of the Government in matters of this description has been adopted after mature consideration. It cannot recognize the right or the power of the enemy to coerce us into terms by the arrest of non-combatant private citizens. This mode of warfare seems peculiarly acceptable to them and if tolerated must be prosecuted on our part on very unequal terms. In the interests of our citizens, unfortunately beyond the pale of protection by our armed forces, we cannot permit ourselves to be seduced into even a quasi recognition of such arrests as legitimate acts of war.[16]

The position of the Confederate War Department rang hollow, however. The Confederates readily took political prisoners and hostages. In the same month, for instance, Maj. Gen. Benjamin Butler ordered the arrest of three prominent residents of Portsmouth, Virginia, and the Virginia General Assembly in Richmond called for the Confederate Army to take hostages for them. The Virginia legislators did not assume the authority for the state to take hostages itself, unlike West Virginia.[17] In one example of Confederate hostage-taking, two Union soldiers went to Castle Thunder as hostages for two Portsmouth women who were held in irons by the United States. They in turn had been arrested in retaliation for the lynching of an African American member of the Fifth Ohio Infantry. The Ohioan had been murdered in revenge for the execution of a Georgia infantry soldier for reported atrocities.[18]

Perhaps the objection of the Confederate government to hostage-taking lay in its practice by a state government. Certainly, it objected to the use of hostages when African American Union soldiers were taken. The Confederate Congress formally expressed outrage that "refined and delicate ladies have been seized, bond with cords, imprisoned, guarded by negroes, and held as hostages for the return of re-captured slaves" by the Union Army.[19] The pro-Confederate Virginia General Assembly joined in and lamented that "refined and virtuous women have been brutally insulted, and, manacled by rude, unfeeling soldiery, have been led captive from their homes as hostages for negroes."[20]

Confederate congressman William Porcher Miles of South Carolina, perhaps in ignorance of actual military practice, but more likely in a grandstanding speech to stave off political and diplomatic criticism, justified civilian arrests and hostage-taking. "This government has observed all laws, but the enemy's disregard of them renders it necessary that we should advance our retaliation *pari passu* with his measures," he told his colleagues. "When one belligerent ignores all laws, the other is relieved from all obligation to observe them."[21] Col. Robert Ould, agent of exchange in Richmond, more truly captured the Confederacy's history on the matter. "My own conviction in this class of cases is clear that we should not be deterred from the arrest and detention of domestic traitors because the enemy seizes and holds one or more of our citizens as hostages for such parties," he advised Seddon. "It is true that it is hard upon the hostages, but yet it is only one of the many forms of suffering which the cruelty and malignity of our foe inflict upon the people."[22]

Ould's remarks came early in 1864 in response to the capture of another West Virginia sheriff, A. J. Stephenson of Nicholas County. Soldiers under Brig. Gen. John Echols had seized Stephenson, and Boreman had ordered the arrest of sixty-three-year-old Edward Campbell, former county court justice, and fifty-one-year-old farmer Dickson McClung. Unlike Sheriff Shaw, however, Stephenson was quickly released, and the hostages were sent home.[23]

With the failure of the US Army to gain Shaw's release through Maupin's mission, the state government stepped up its efforts. On March 16, 1864, Governor Boreman allowed three of West Virginia's hostages for Shaw—Alexander and John Handley and Jesse Timms—to travel to Richmond to try again for Shaw's release.[24] No word was received for several weeks, and then, in late April, the *Point Pleasant Weekly Register*, published in Mason County, next to Putnam County, announced, "We understand from a gentleman who came down the Kanawha on Saturday last [April 16], that W. H. Shaw, Esq., Sheriff of Putnam county, who was cap-

Union soldiers routing Confederates on the waters of the Guyandotte in southwestern West Virginia. (Photograph, "Surprise of Rebels Between Hurricane and Logan, Western Virginia, by a Detachment of Colonel Piatt's Zouaves [Thirty-Fourth Ohio Volunteers], Under Lieutenant Rowe," *Harpers Illustrated,* January 18, 1862. West Virginia State Archives, Charleston, WV.)

tured some time in December, by the rebels and taken to Richmond, has been released and is now at his home in Winfield." The newspaper soberly noted, "We understand that he gives a sad account of his sufferings and the treatment of our prisoners in Richmond."[25] After a brief rest, Shaw traveled to Wheeling on April 21 and reported his return. The Handleys and Timms had gone back to Wheeling as promised and waited for their own release. When Governor Boreman officially learned of Shaw's return, he ordered the freedom of all of the hostages for the sheriff.[26]

On the day after the Handleys and Timms left Wheeling on their mission to free Sheriff Shaw, another incident took place in southwestern West Virginia that placed new hostages in the Atheneum. In March 1864, Confederates in Wayne County were lying low. Colonel Ferguson and thirty-nine of his men had been captured the previous month in the Laurel Creek area of the county by elements of the Fourteenth Kentucky Infantry. A Union probe through Wayne and Cabell Counties on March 16 through March 18 encountered no opposition. "There was no force at the town, nor had there been any there or in Wayne County since the Sixteenth Virginia was routed by Colonel Gallup from Louisa, Ky," reported Col. John J. Hoffman of the Second West Virginia Cavalry upon unexpectedly finding no enemy at Trouts Hill (Wayne Court House). "The force reported under Colonel French as marching down Guyandotte [River] was not heard of either by Colonel Brown or myself, and we were both satisfied that there is no organized force in that region." Hoffman continued, "There is in Wayne and Cabell Counties a considerable number of the Eighth and Sixteenth Virginia Cavalry at home on furlough, but so scattered through the hills that it is almost impossible to capture them with a mounted force, but can be effected much easier with small squads of infantry who are acquainted with the country and the residences of the men."[27]

The scattered and dormant nature of the Confederate troops in the area was deceptive, and Hoffman understood the Confederates' guerrilla tendencies there. In fact, Confederates in the area had regrouped under William S. "Rebel Bill" Smith. William Smith had been associated with the Eighth Virginia Cavalry, and after the loss of Milton Ferguson, he had filled the void of leadership. Although he held no official commission, Smith fancied himself as Colonel Smith and operated his band as the Big Sandy Rangers.[28]

According to family and local tradition, William S. Smith had long been something of a rebel. He had left home at seventeen and worked his way along the Ohio, Mississippi, and Missouri Rivers as a riverboat hand. Smith had worked for a sutler at Fort Leavenworth for a time and then had gone to California in 1850 to search for gold. In 1851, Smith supposedly killed a man in a shootout in San Francisco and then escaped back east to Wayne County. When war came, he had joined the Fairview Rifles, which was inducted into the Thirty-Sixth Virginia Infantry. It later had become part of the Eighth Virginia Cavalry.[29]

Several Unionists stood as counterparts to Smith and Confederate activity in the region. Quebec native John Adams was perhaps the most vocal. Adams had come to Wayne County from Vermont in 1857 as one of the first settlers of Ceredo, an experimental, abolitionist farming community that Massachusetts congressman Eli Thayer had founded.[30] Mostly New Englanders had come to the community, and it had drawn opposition at the start as older residents of Wayne County resented the "Yankee invaders."[31] Open opposition had waned as the people in the area had seen the potential economic benefits of the community, but resentment had stayed just beneath the surface and erupted again with secession and war. As a member of the board of the Ceredo Land Company, John Adams was a leader and a symbol of the community. He had been active in the war, especially as adjutant for the 167th Regiment of the West Virginia Militia. In that role, he had worked tirelessly in 1863 and 1864 to enlist pro-Union militia members and to install officers in Wayne County. He regularly corresponded with state leaders about Confederate raids and pro-Confederate thievery in the county—and the work of William S. Smith. One letter summed up the situation and Adams's views of it:

> They deride our new State & Government[,] never vote, but secretly assist all rebel raids; they can stay & live at home securely while our Union people hide about where they can. As the case is now in our Co. the Secessionists are *secure* on their farms, secure their crops, ride good horses, make money & in fact appear to be *Lords* of this Country. How long? Do you think the Union men here will endure this State of Affairs? They are beginning to think that the Rebels ought to have *different rights* to what they now enjoy in this Co. We want all Rebels & their assistants hung or sent out of our Co. never to return.[32]

Thus, Adams became a special enemy of the pro-Confederate population. He relocated his family across the river in Ohio and carefully went about his business in Wayne County.[33] On March 17, 1864, Adams's care was not sufficient. Smith and his men found Adams and took him prisoner.[34] Governor Boreman responded by ordering the taking of hostages, and John N. Smith, William Stewart, and Erbin Walker were arrested by Capt. Benjamin R. Haley and independent scouts in Wayne County.[35] John N. Smith was the father of Rebel Bill. The father, a native of Pennsylvania, was sixty-nine years old and a substantial farmer near Trouts Hill. He had owned slaves in 1850 but seems to have turned away from slaveholding by 1860. Besides the "colonel," at least one other son served in the Confederate Army. Milton Ferguson was a next-door neighbor.[36] Sixty-seven-year-old William Stewart, a native Virginian, was another well-to-do farmer in the vicinity of Trouts Hill.[37] Erbin Walker, former postmaster of Savage Grant, was sixty-one years old.[38]

Four months passed without word of Adams. Rumors circulated that Rebel Bill and his men had murdered the Unionist. Meanwhile, attention shifted to the hostages. Benjamin R. Haley—who commanded the independent scouts who had arrested Smith, Stewart, and Walker—led thirteen others in appealing to the governor for the release of "those old men." The petitioners cited the rumors of Adams's murder and claimed that the hostages were "innocent of any knowledge of the whereabouts of

Mr. Adams or who his murders [*sic*] were." They excused the three men of collaboration with the Confederates and insisted that "they may have been surrounded by a strong rebel influence and may have drifted a little with the current that surrounded them, but we do not believe they have aided or assisted in the rebellion except by sympathy."[39] The trouble was

Confederate citizens and soldiers under guard (Joseph H. Diss Debar Collection, West Virginia State Archives, Charleston, WV)

that the hostage law did not require hostages to contribute to the Confederacy. It simply required that they be of known disloyal sentiments.

Two days later, on July 12, 1864, B. D. McGinnis, a lawyer in Guyandotte in Cabell County, provided a cover letter for a second petition. It specifically asked for John N. Smith's release. McGinnis admitted that he knew nothing personally about Smith. Nevertheless, he told the governor that the older Smith was "represented as deprecating the course of his rebel son who is acting as Colonel of the rebel forces in that county." McGinnis introduced the petition with a refrain of the fears of pro-Union citizens in the area. He wrote, "The citizens desire me to assure your Excellency that they are not in the main opposed to taking hostages, but that they regard this as a most inopportune time—as it subjects them to being arrested in retaliation—there being no Federal troops in that county to protect the citizens."[40]

The petition itself showed a group of men who were motivated more by fear than sympathy for John N. Smith. The signers said they had "been acquainted with said Smith a number of years before the war & ever since the rebellion and have always found him to be an honourable peaceable and quiet citizen and in our opinion it would prevent the destruction of the union citizens of this section of country if you should see proper to release said Smith and let him return home to his family." They shared their anxiety that "Colonel" Smith "is now at this time in our neighborhood and affirms that if we the undersigned do not get his father released immediately that he will take us off to some Southern prison there to be kept til his father is released." The men closed their plea with the prediction that they would be forced to flee to Ohio and leave their property exposed to Smith and his followers if the governor did not free the father.[41]

Before the month ended, the situation came to a close, and it did not turn out well for John Adams's family. His body, found twelve miles from where he had been captured, was riddled with bullets. The governor ordered Smith, Stewart, and Walker released. The man for whom they were held was no longer a captive.[42]

The discovery of Adams's body did not make Rebel Bill more cautious, nor did the release of his father instill mercy in him toward the pro-Union people of Wayne County. He made the abolitionist community of Ceredo his special target. "A few days ago the notorious rebel Bill Smith, with about sixty men, made a raid on Ceredo, situated on the Ohio river, in Wayne county in this State," began a story in the *Wheeling Daily Intelligencer* on September 24, 1864. The home guard captain, Benjamin R. Haley, and eight of his men fell into Smith's hands. They had been stationed at Ceredo to protect the town. The raiders took away all the male residents, except for two old men, robbed the post office and stole horses and money from the people of the community. "The loyal citizens have been greatly annoyed for the want of necessary protection, ever since March or April last, the country being overrun by guerrillas, committing depredations of the most shameful character, such as murdering citizens, robbing houses of bed clothing and their valuables, and taking money from citizens," the *Daily Intelligencer* reminded its readers. "It would be a great relief to the loyal citizens of Wayne county if the military authorities could possibly spare soldiers sufficient to protect said county from the bands of guerrillas that are continually infesting the county, and driving the loyal citizens away from their homes."[43]

When the November election came in 1864, Smith and his guerrillas "were prowling about all the voting precincts in the county." This dampened the turnout in Wayne County. Ceredo's residents rose in defiance, however. Many who had fled the town returned to vote. They cast their votes entirely for Abraham Lincoln.[44]

Two months later, Governor Boreman once again presented a message to the state legislature. He reviewed 1864 and reported on the state of affairs as it stood at the beginning of 1865. "Notwithstanding the people in some sections have been subjected to rebel raids, robberies and murders, it is gratifying to know that a great portion of the State is enjoying comparative peace and security, and is receiving considerable accessions to the population and is rapidly advancing in wealth and prosperity," Boreman told the legislators. The governor devoted most of his address to the economy and public works. It seemed that the war was winding down.[45] On the same day, the *Wheeling Daily Intelligencer* noted, "We learn from members of the Legislature, and others, from the border counties, that large numbers of rebel soldiers are coming in and giving themselves up at the various outposts in this Department." It continued with an account of a Confederate lieutenant who "recently came into Wayne county, accompanied by a dozen or fifteen other rebel soldiers" who took the loyalty oath. "They say they are tired of fighting for nothing and freezing to death," the newspaper gloated.[46]

The reports proved premature, though. James H. Ferguson, representing Cabell County, told the West Virginia House of Delegates in February 1865 that "every part of the county of Wayne, on the Ohio river was held by guerrillas." He also said that Union troops held only one town in Cabell County, Guyandotte. "The rebels have their headquarters up in

Logan county, and they make forays down toward the Ohio River, stealing, murdering, and devastating the country," Ferguson elaborated. "They enter the houses of loyal citizens and steal household furniture and bed clothing, and frequently strip women and children of wearing apparel."[47]

William S. Smith, least of all, accepted "peace and security." While Delegate Ferguson described the situation in his district, reports reached the newspapers of another raid on Ceredo by Smith. The "colonel" and his men invaded the town and went to the home of Jack Meadows and killed him. Meadows's wife killed one of the attackers with a revolver and wounded another. One of the Confederates struck her leg with a gun and broke it. Smith and his men forced her and her children from the house and burned it.[48]

"Since the murder of poor Jack Middaughs [Meadows] and the burning of his house by guerrillas, the people of this village are awed into a painful condition of fear and dread," a correspondent from Ceredo wrote to the *West Virginia Journal* in Charleston. "Nearly all the truly loyal and best men have left, under the belief that any of them may be the next victims of Bill Smith's barbarity, as it is understood he has threatened that others must share a similar fate."[49]

West Virginia did not apply the hostage law in retaliation. Smith and the Confederates had taken no one into captivity. Neither did the state respond with added force. The governor and his administration were looking ahead to the end of the war.

Before Governor Boreman closed his file on Wayne County, indeed while he actively worked with it, papers from still other files lay strewn across his desk. At the same time that the governor waited for news about Sheriff Shaw and John Adams in March 1864, yet another case reached his office from the other end of the state. This one came from Berkeley Springs in Morgan County. Confederate raiders struck a blow by carrying away two West Virginia legislators and a prosecuting attorney, and another hostage case was born.

CHAPTER 9

# The Union League Raid in Berkeley Springs in 1864

The nineteenth-century artist-correspondent David Hunter Strother, known by the pen name Porte Crayon, toured the Piedmont and Blue Ridge region of Virginia from Charlottesville to the Potomac five years before the Civil War. *Harper's New Monthly Magazine* published his account, as he was a regular contributor. One leg of the trip held special importance for Strother. It took him to his hometown, just two and a half miles from the Potomac River and the Maryland border. Known as Berkeley Springs by the post office department but incorporated as Bath, the town had developed around one of the many springs in the mountains of Virginia that were believed to have healing properties. Thomas, Lord Fairfax, had owned the springs in colonial times, and George Washington had visited it as early as 1748 as part of the party that had surveyed the area for Fairfax. Washington's brother, Samuel, had been one of the town's trustees when the Virginia General Assembly chartered it in 1776. George Washington himself had owned a house and two lots in the town and other property nearby. The *Maryland Gazette,* in 1784, described Berkeley Springs as a place of "general good and national grandeur" that mimicked European resorts "on a plan of propriety and decorum."[1] It was intended for the upper classes, not the middle classes.

"But the old times have passed away," Strother wrote. "The brave, the gifted, the gay, the beautiful of the old days gone to one common resting-place." He added, "There are new times now, new hotels, new bath-houses, new fashions, new manners, new people at Berkeley."[2] By 1856, the town and the springs had become more commercial, less famous, and more middle class. The Baltimore and Ohio Railroad passed nearby and brought visitors from across the country. Strother's father, John, owned the main spa and a four-hundred-room hotel, but others dotted the town. These included Strother's nearest rival, O'Ferrall's Coffee House—kept by John O'Ferrall, state legislator and clerk of the circuit and county courts for many years.

In the frenzy of John Brown's raid, the election of 1860, and secession, Berkeley Springs stood in the balance. It served as the county seat of Morgan County, and its geographic position—not just walking distance to Maryland but only eight miles from Pennsylvania—placed it in a hot seat between North and South. A correspondent to the *Richmond Daily Whig* put the county on middle ground in the fall of 1860. "No, sir, I tell you the sturdy yeomanry of little Morgan, like the illustrious sire for whom she is named, have the good and glory of their country at heart," the writer told the rest of Virginia. "The people are becoming fully awakened, aroused, and made conscious of the desperate effort that is being made to rend asunder the ties that bind us, and 'let slip the dogs of war.'" The correspondent singled out Charles O'Ferrall, son of the hotel proprietor, as a spokesman for moderation. The nineteen-year-old county clerk delivered the keynote speech at a John Bell rally in Morgan County two weeks before the presidential election.[3]

Morgan County, like Virginia as a whole, gave a majority vote to Bell in the election. Although the county's delegate to the Richmond Convention in 1861 supported secession, the voters overwhelmingly supported the Union in the statewide referendum in May 1861 (see appendix for a timeline of key events). The people of the county were less enthusiastic about separating the county from Virginia and placing it with West Virginia, however. The county sent no delegates to the Wheeling conventions in May and June 1861. It was represented in the West Virginia Constitutional Convention, but its inclusion in the new state was conditional upon a majority vote in the eastern panhandle in favor of the state constitution. A pro-Union meeting in the county in December 1863 reflected the sentiment in the county and suggested a class divide that pitted the business and laboring people of the county against the old Virginia gentry. Resolutions from the meeting noted that the county had "given over one half of their fighting population to the cause of the Union, and not over a dozen to that of the rebellion, whilst their superiors have nevertheless upheld the rebels in business denied to union men."[4]

Leaders among the Unionists represented the business working class. There was John Strother, venerable colonel from the War of 1812 and owner of the Berkeley Springs Hotel, whom Confederate raiders whisked away to be tried for treason in September 1861. He was released on bond only to have his hotel robbed by Confederate soldiers. His son, David Hunter Strother, became a Union officer and served on the staffs of generals George B. McClellan, Nathaniel Banks, and David Hunter. Aaron Bechtol, a native of Morgan County, represented it and Hampshire, Hardy, and Pendleton Counties in West Virginia's state senate. Bechtol, an old Whig and supporter of John Bell, operated a coach service that linked Berkeley Springs with the railroad at Martinsburg and Hancock, Maryland.[5] Joseph S. Wheat, a farmer and son of an early innkeeper, served Morgan County in pro-Union Virginia's House of Delegates and in West Virginia's House of Delegates.[6]

Bechtol and Wheat stood out as the leading voices for Unionism in Morgan County. When they were not in Wheeling, their presence at pro-Union meetings was presumed.[7] Early in the secession crisis and the war, these gatherings were termed Union meetings. In 1863, they also were commonly called Union Party or statehood meetings. By 1864, the name *Union League* was increasingly applied to them. Whether Union Leagues were formally organized or not is unclear. The labels *Union, Union Party,* and *Union League* were used interchangeably in West Virginia.

"Whether they called themselves a Union League or a Loyal League, organized societies dedicated themselves to promoting fealty to the Lincoln administration's policies and combating subversive acts mushroomed throughout Northern counties and small towns in the first half of 1863," explained Paul Taylor in *The Most Complete Political Machine Ever Known.* Spurred by a grassroots movement that originated in Illinois, the organization of these clubs, based on secret societies of prewar years, coincided with the early operation of the Emancipation Proclamation and military conscription. Though separate, they were contemporary with the more elite Union League Clubs of Boston, New York, and Philadelphia. The creation of a Grand National Council during a convention in Cleveland in May 1863 gave greater impetus to the movement.[8]

As the Union League was preparing to fully organize on the national level in the spring of 1863, a Union general gave the movement an important endorsement in the area that soon became West Virginia. From his headquarters in Buckhannon, Brig. Gen. Benjamin S. Roberts, commander of the Fourth Brigade, called for the organization of Union Leagues in Barbour, Braxton, Gilmer, Lewis, Randolph, and Upshur Counties, which were within the reach of his command. Roberts relied upon Union League volunteers to escort fifteen prisoners to Wheeling during the Jones-Imboden Raid just a few weeks later. He could not spare soldiers for the task.[9] Union League clubs sprang up as grassroots organizations elsewhere in West Virginia by the end of the year, and the editor of the *Wheeling Daily Intelligencer,* Archibald W. Campbell, served on the Union National Committee.[10]

The Berkeley Springs area was ripe for Union League activity. Although frequent combat in the vicinity discouraged visits to the resorts, Morgan County had been exposed to new thought and beliefs through the years because of ongoing interaction with people from throughout the country and even the world. Even during the war, news and recent innovation reached the county before more remote parts of West Virginia because of its location near the B&O Railroad and the Chesapeake and Ohio Canal and its proximity to the National Road. So, the planting of the Union League in the area is unsurprising. Union League meetings increased as the presidential election of 1864 approached. Aaron Bechtol and Joseph S. Wheat, the local legislators, actively participated. Their presence at a meeting on the night of Saturday, March 19, 1864, proved historic.

Confederate leaders were fully aware of the Union League and considered it a subversive organization in West Virginia. After all, they believed that West Virginia belonged in Virginia. So, the Union League became a target for the Confederates. Twenty-eight Confederate troopers raided the meeting of the Union League in Berkeley Springs on March 19. One detachment held the members at gunpoint while another rounded up their horses, which were hitched nearby. When they left, they took Bechtol, Wheat, Robert Finn (the county prosecuting attorney), and Thomas Shives, the league president (sometimes recorded as Shriver or Shrieves), with them.[11]

Maj. Gen. Franz Sigel, then in command of the Department of West Virginia, quickly learned of the raid and telegraphed Brig. Gen. William W. Averell at Romney within hours. "About 40 rebels made a dash into Bath and captured the Union League representatives, among them Wheat and Bechtal," Sigel wired. "Do all that you can to intercept them." Sigel told Averell that the Confederate force had headed toward Winchester. The major general thought the matter was sufficiently important to notify the US Army chief of staff, Brig. Gen. George W. Cullum, in Washington.[12]

Four days later, Morgan County sheriff Lewis Allen provided a civilian account of the foray in a letter to Gov. Arthur I. Boreman:

> About half past 8 o'clock a party of armed Rebels thirty in number under command of traitors from this town and county made a raid upon the Union

> League which was in session, being the regular meeting night in this town, capturing the whole number present but getting off with only our Prosecuting Attorney Robert Finn, Senator Aaron Bechtol, Joseph S. Wheat, our delegate, one very inoffensive young man, Thomas Shives, and two soldiers of 15th West Va infantry captured in town, together with a number of horses. The men after their capture were robbed of their valuables, even a portion of their clothing. The hats were taken from the heads of our men and their coats and shawls from their backs and mounted upon stolen bare-backed horses to ride notwithstanding the severe coldness of the night. They stold about 16 head of horses mostly from civil officers of our county.[13]

The raid into Berkeley Springs threw the Union side into a minor panic, but Confederates celebrated. "Our gallant friend, Major O'Ferrall, visited the scenes of his boyhood the other day, 'on business' connected with his profession; and on Saturday evening last, concluded to 'break up' 'a Union League' which met in his native town, Bath, in Morgan County," gloated the *Rockingham Register* in Harrisonburg, Virginia. "So, taking 29 or 30 of his command he slipped in and captured the following parties [Bechtol, Wheat, Finn, and Shives], who were brought to Harrisonburg on Wednesday afternoon."[14]

The Harrisonburg editor's "gallant friend" was none other than Charles O'Ferrall, the former clerk and innkeeper's son from Berkeley Springs. Twenty-three-year-old O'Ferrall commanded an independent battalion of the Virginia Cavalry, which bivouacked at New Market, nineteen miles north of Harrisonburg. O'Ferrall left his own published account of the incursion forty years later, far removed from the heated atmosphere of war and after he had served as a US congressman and a Bourbon governor of Virginia. His version followed the apologist vein of the New South and carefully downplayed political motives and personal violence in the raid.

O'Ferrall attributed the raid to a need for horses. He explained that in the late winter of 1864, many of his men had no horses. Horses had died or been disabled, and replacements were expensive and hard to find. The Confederate cavalry troopers were hard-pressed to furnish their own horses. "It had been reported to us that on a certain Saturday night in every month an organization of citizens, called a 'Union League,' met in the Odd Fellows Hall in the town of Berkeley Springs, my home; that its members were generally countrymen and rode into town to the meetings on their horses," O'Ferrall explained. "I did not like to raid my old friends, but I argued that they were Virginians, and as they had contributed nothing toward the support of the Confederacy in her struggle it would not be wrong for me to impress a few of their horses for my dismounted men."[15]

O'Ferrall handpicked twenty-eight men and further exhausted the battalion's horses by making an eighty-five-mile sprint to find additional mounts. The troop paused eighteen miles from Berkeley Springs at dawn two days later and secluded itself until late afternoon. It then moved quickly toward town. One party headed to the hitching posts near the meeting place, and another targeted the meeting. The troopers overpowered a sentinel and stormed up a stairway to the second floor with guns drawn and burst into the meeting room.[16]

A daughter of one of the Union League members slipped away and rushed to alert a Union cavalry unit at Sir Johns Run, just two miles away. So, the raiders left town in a hurry with Bechtol, Wheat, Finn, and Shives and the captured horses in tow. "I was really sorry we had captured Senator Bechtol and Delegate Wheat with the Leaguers," O'Ferrall wrote with a revisionist perspective. "They had been friends of my father during his lifetime, and my friends after his death until I became a 'rebel.'" He continued in hindsight, "In my heart I wanted them to make their escape, which they could easily have done during the night as we were passing rapidly along the mountain roads, with thick undergrowth on the sides—in fact they had every opportunity; but they could not summon sufficient courage to make the attempt, and daylight found them still prisoners in our hands, and I was compelled to send them and Finn to Richmond."[17]

By sunrise on March 20, 1864, O'Ferrall's force was thirty miles from Berkeley Springs. He confirmed in his account that Averell had dispatched cavalry from Romney, and they were only an hour behind the fleeing Confederates. O'Ferrall's party eluded the Yankees, however, by slipping into a defensible gorge and resting until late evening. The raiders then moved along until they reached Confederate lines.[18]

According to newspaper reports, Union authorities quickly took several Confederate sympathizers, including two young women, as hostages for the captured men. Revised stories later explained that the people were not hostages but had been arrested and taken to Cumberland for giving aid and information to the raiders.[19] O'Ferrall pointed out that the two young women were his sisters. He had briefly visited them and his younger brother during the raid. O'Ferrall insisted, however, that none of the women whom Union soldiers arrested had aided him or his men. He credited Col. David Hunter

Strother, "a gallant Federal officer" and acquaintance of the O'Ferralls, with interceding and gaining the release of the prisoners within a few days.[20]

Others in the Confederacy were not as gracious as O'Ferrall in his later accounts. Ten days after the attack on the Union League meeting, Lt. J. R. Nunn, provost marshal at Harrisonburg, contacted Brig. Gen. John D. Imboden. Imboden was then the commander of the Valley District of the Confederate Army. Apparently unaware of the nuanced differences between West Virginia and the pro-Union government of Virginia, Nunn reported that Bechtol and Wheat—members of the "bogus Virginia legislature"—Finn, and Shives were in his guardhouse. Nunn referred the general to two "very respectable and reliable citizens of Morgan County," familiar to Imboden, who had left their homes "partly because of these men." The lieutenant claimed that Bechtol had led a pillaging party that had destroyed a large part of the property belonging to one of the expatriates.[21]

Without hesitation, Imboden ordered Nunn to send Bechtol, Wheat, and Finn to Virginia Governor William Smith in Richmond. Imboden reasoned that the three men were traitors to the state. He, too, used the favorite Confederate appellation of *bogus* when referring to West Virginia or pro-Union Virginia, but he recognized the distinction between the two and noted Bechtol and Wheat as members of the "bogus legislature at Wheeling" as opposed to Alexandria. He instructed Nunn to send Shives to Castle Thunder for "aiding and abetting the public enemy and being a member of a treasonable organization known as the Union League." The general added, "I earnestly request the authorities at Richmond not to release these men without giving me the opportunity of proving their offenses."[22]

Nunn sent all four men to the governor the next day instead of just the three public officials. He did not escort the prisoners himself or forward them through the provost marshal's office in Richmond. A sergeant delivered them to the state's commander in chief. The sergeant carried an audacious note from Nunn in which he asked the governor for a receipt for the prisoners. Smith offhandedly sent all four to Castle Thunder. In contrast to Nunn's course, the provost marshal of Richmond, Maj. Isaac H. Carrington, followed protocol and reported to the governor through his superior, Brig. Gen. John H. Winder, the Confederate provost marshal general, that the four men from Morgan County were securely housed in "Eastern District Prison," the official name for Castle Thunder.[23]

Meanwhile, efforts began almost immediately to win the return of the captured men. Governor Boreman wrote to Simeon S. Buzzerd, postmaster of Berkeley Springs and Wheat's son-in-law, on March 25, 1864, and asked

Union soldiers interrogating a citizen prisoner from the Potomac region. (Waud, Alfred R., Artist. Provost Marshal—and police of Alexandria searching and examining a prisoner of war, United States, Alexandria Virginia, 1861. [ca. July]. Photograph. https://www.loc.gov/item/2004660107/)

him to talk with Col. David Hunter Strother about the situation. Buzzerd did so, and Strother conferred with General Sigel. Buzzerd, Strother, and Sigel concurred that hostages should be taken for the seized men.[24]

Sheriff Allen shared in that concurrence. In his letter to Boreman, he cited the governor's annual message that January and his promise to hold hostages at a ratio of at least two-to-one for Unionists who fell into Confederate hands. "This promise made us feel determined to do our duty to our country and state and now that our brethren have been ruthlessly snatched from the bosoms of helpless families, their valuable services deprived us, the loyal people of our county look to you for that redress promised and which all feel you will accord," Allen wrote. He promised that if the taking of hostages "fails to accomplish the much desired end[,] rest assured that although Morgan County has given nearly one half of her fighting population to the cause of the Union she will find still a number sufficient to protect herself from Rebel thieves."[25]

On March 25, Buzzerd made specific recommendations of hostages to the governor. In a unique move, he included people outside West Virginia.[26] Fifty-year-old A. Stephen Dandridge headed the list. Dandridge lived at the Jefferson County estate, which his great-grandfather, Revolutionary War general Adam Stephen, had built. He enslaved sixty-six people there. Dandridge had been active in Whig politics early in life and in the Democratic Party later but had not held any office besides district school superintendent. He seemed more interested in his plantation and was active in the Valley Agricultural Society. Dandridge was a brother-in-law to Zachary Taylor's daughter, Mary Elizabeth, and of R. M. T. Hunter, Confederate senator and former Confederate secretary of state and former speaker of the US House of Representatives. Dandridge had invited J. E. B. Stuart to establish his headquarters at his estate in 1862 and had given a horse from his stables to Robert E. Lee.[27]

Nathan White, a forty-six-year-old Charles Town attorney, came next on the list. He was a native of Montgomery County, Maryland. Before the war, White had served as a director of the Charles Town branch of the Valley Bank in Virginia with Dandridge and John W. Kennedy, who became a circuit court judge under the West Virginia government. Five people labored as slaves for White.[28]

Rev. A. H. H. Boyd, a Presbyterian minister in Winchester, Virginia, was third on the list. He was born near Martinsburg, Virginia (now West Virginia) in 1814 and attended the University of Edinburgh in Scotland. Boyd returned to the United States and became a pastor in Leesburg and Middleburg, Virginia. He then went to Harrisonburg and had been pastor in Winchester since 1842. Boyd enjoyed notoriety throughout Virginia. He was a patron of Richmond Musical Academy. At the General Assembly of the Presbyterian Church in 1856, Boyd successfully argued against a resolution that declared slavery to be a sin, but the assembly voted not to enter Boyd's pro-slavery report into the minutes. Early in 1863, a rumor circulated around the state that he had been killed by Union pickets for not heeding their order to stop. In fact, one of Boyd's slaves had been killed. Boyd was targeted in part because of his famous brother-in-law, Charles J. Faulkner, Confederate officer, former Confederate diplomat, and former US minister to France.[29]

Buzzerd also listed Philip Williams, a Winchester attorney. Williams enjoyed statewide prominence in Virginia as well. He had been commonwealth attorney in Shenandoah County and represented that county in the state legislature before moving to Winchester. He served as a trustee of Winchester Academy and as a state delegate to the World's Temperance Conference in 1853. Williams was a close associate of Waitman T. Willey, one of West Virginia's US senators, in the temperance movement during the 1850s. He was an active Whig in the 1840s, and during the 1860 presidential campaign, he was known as a pro-Union speaker and supporter of John Bell. [30] "Mr. Williams was well known for his devotion to the Southern cause," according to a local historian. "Though never in the service as a soldier, his aid went out fully to the cause."[31] Buzzerd noted that Williams had sons in the Confederate Army.[32]

Buzzerd next listed Robert Y. Conrad, fifty-nine-year-old Winchester

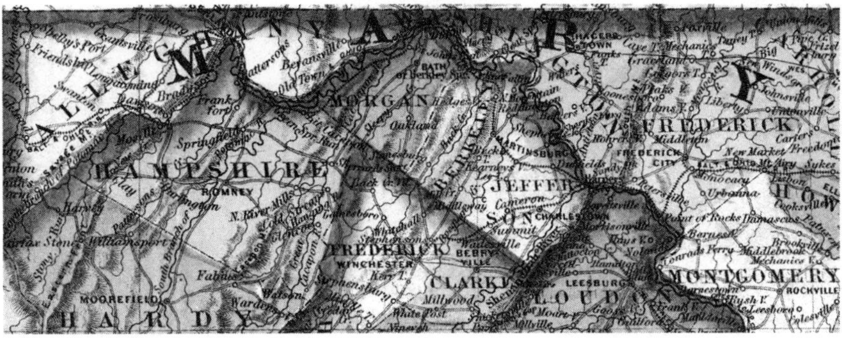


Morgan County and vicinity in 1864. (A. J. Johnson, *Johnson's Virginia, Delaware, Maryland & West Virginia.* [New York: Johnson and Ward, 1864] Map. https://www.loc.gov/item/lva0000096/)

attorney and a member of the Richmond Convention in 1861, where he had served on the Committee of Federal Relations. Conrad had voted against secession but had signed the secession ordinance. He had five sons in the Confederate Army.[33]

Finally, Buzzerd recommended Robert C. Gustin. He was a Winchester attorney and former resident of Berkeley Springs.[34]

Two of the proposed hostages were what might be termed the "usual suspects" in popular culture. Boyd and Conrad had been held by the US Army as hostages from January until earlier in March 1864 for an army recruiting agent, William N. Dooley, whom the Confederates had captured near Winchester as he tried to enlist African Americans. In that case, General Sigel marked Boyd and Conrad as "rank secessionists."[35]

Buzzerd also wrote to Judge John W. Kennedy, West Virginia's circuit judge in the area, about the situation, and Kennedy hastened to Wheeling to meet with the governor. Kennedy claimed jurisdiction over Morgan County at the same time that Judge Richard Parker, sitting in Winchester, held court for Morgan County on behalf of Confederate Virginia.[36]

Four days later, Buzzerd went before Justice of the Peace Aaron Faris and filed an affidavit that formally called for the taking of his six choices as hostages.[37] Boreman issued a warrant the same day. The governor carefully crafted the document, and it differed from other warrants, orders, and requests for hostages in the past. The paper included the official seal of his office and was addressed to the "Military Authorities U.S. in the Department of West Virginia." It did not bother with niceties in federal and state relations. The warrant "hereby ordered" the US Army to take the hostages, and the army obliged.[38] Lt. Col. W. C. Starr, department provost marshal, forwarded Boyd, Williams, Conrad, Dandridge, and White to Boreman under guard on April 16—"They having been arrested at your request."[39] A week later, General Sigel directed Starr to certify to the governor that the five men had been taken as hostages "as directed in the within warrant." Gustin's name had been crossed out.[40]

The process stands out in the hostage saga. Unlike other cases, the federal government did not question or dance around the authority of West Virginia's governor to ask the army to take hostages and hold them. In this case, the US Army not only acknowledged the governor's request, it acceded to his direction. The army's acquiescence made it possible to reach beyond West Virginia's borders for hostages and overlook the governor's lack of authority over residents of other states by shading the taking of Boyd, Williams, and Conrad under the guise of federal authority. The handling of the matter suggests the importance the army placed upon the case. It perhaps thought it important to win Bechtol and Wheat's return, but more likely was embarrassed by the taking of the Union citizens under its nose so soon after the capture of generals Crook and Kelley in Cumberland, Maryland. The army also may have seen an opportunity to put pressure on the Confederacy in a contest of civilian captures and exchanges at a time when it suffered from labor shortages.

Before Colonel Starr sent the hostages from Cumberland to Wheeling, humanitarian pleas began on their behalf. One came from none other than Col. David Hunter Strother, the famous artist-correspondent Porte Crayon. Strother knew A. Stephen Dandridge personally and provided him a letter of reference, dated April 16, 1864, and addressed to Governor Boreman. He asked that the governor provide Dandridge "the most liberal and lenient treatment that your views of public duty will permit." The colonel assured Boreman that Dandridge was "a man of honor" and that "his word may be implicitly relied on." Strother contrasted Dandridge's opinions during the Civil War with his actions and found his behavior "mild, considerate & inoffensive." He went further and generally endorsed Conrad, Williams, Boyd, and White. Although Strother did not know the men as well, he knew the region and their standing there. He concluded that, regardless of their relations with the Union, "their private reputation is unblemished and that they may be safely trusted to any extent that your Excellency may see fit."[41]

The common practice of sending hostages to Richmond to negotiate

Life in military prison was much the same for civilians whether they were prisoners in Richmond, as depicted here, or inmates in the Atheneum in Wheeling. (The Union prisoners at Richmond, Virginia, 1862. Photograph. https://www.loc.gov/item/2002736811/)

the release of Union prisoners took place in this case as well. Less than a week after the hostages arrived at Wheeling, Governor Boreman paroled Conrad and Dandridge and sent them to the Confederate capital—with the noted condition that General Sigel consented. Again, this episode showed an unusual amount of cooperation between the governor and Union commanders considering past army criticisms and reticence toward West Virginia's hostage-taking. The governor, as was usual, gave the parolees sixty days to accomplish their mission or to return to prison. The remaining hostages were the governor's guarantees for the paroles.[42]

Philip Williams, A. H. H. Boyd, and Nathan White remained in the Atheneum while their comrades made their way to Richmond, and David Hunter Strother's vouch for them apparently had no effect on the governor. The three men asked the governor for their own paroles in a polite letter to Boreman on April 23. If paroles were not possible, they at least wanted housing elsewhere. "We are all advanced in years, and as we are not arrested for any offence, but only to procure the release of W[heat]. & B[echtol], we take it for granted that you do not desire to punish us, but only to take the most effectual means of procuring their discharge," they ventured. The hostages expressed confidence that their request would not affect the mission of White and Dandridge, and that Confederate authorities were treating Bechtol and Wheat humanely. Thus, they believed their request was justified. The men also pointed to their certainty that the Union prisoners were not confined with criminals. They contrasted this with the fact that they were "confined in a common room with offenders of all classes, with murderers, thieves, burglars, soldiers who have been convicted of various offences (and of both armies) and citizens." The confinement tried the sensitivities of the gentlemen, especially Reverend Boyd. "We are obliged to hear most awful curses and imporcations, and as a matter of course, the prison is infested with vermin, and it is much crowded, so much so, that we fear our health will suffer," the hostages told the governor. They added, however, "We are treated as well as we could expect in our condition, confined in such a place and in such company." The men concluded with assurances that they posed no threat to Wheeling or West Virginia. None of them had held office under the Confederacy or in fact had held state office in over thirty years, they explained.[43]

Arthur I. Boreman did not respond, and Williams, Boyd, and White sent a more urgent letter the following week. The minister and two attorneys asked that the men be moved to a more comfortable room in the jail if parole was not possible. They wanted out of the Atheneum. "The place is very uncomfortable, and in order to keep it ventilated, the windows are required to be hoisted and the damp cool air blows immediately upon us, in consequence of which our health is suffering, all of us laboring under colds," the men pleaded. "The change is desirable not only on account of our health, but that we may escape the blasphemy and obscenity which we are so constantly obliged to hear in this place."[44]

While the hostages waited in vain for an answer from the governor, wheels were turning in Richmond. An influential Winchester resident pressured the Confederate government to make concessions that would lead to the release of his fellow townsfolk. "These gentlemen, as you may know, are amongst our most worthy and influential citizens, and I had promised their friends to lay their case in person before you," Judge Richard Parker wrote to Confederate Secretary of War James A. Seddon on April 19.[45] Parker had been a circuit court judge since 1851 and still held court in the name of Confederate Virginia for Clarke and Frederick Counties as well as Berkeley, Hampshire, Jefferson, and Morgan Counties in the area claimed by West Virginia. Parker and Seddon were fellow alumni of the University of Virginia law school and were contemporaries in the Virginia Democratic Party. Both had served districts in Virginia in the US House of Representatives at the same time. So, Parker was both frank and friendly in his letter to Seddon.[46]

Parker played down the importance of holding Bechtol and Wheat. "The persons taken by O'Ferrall were taken at a point where if they had influence, they could not exert it injuriously, but the two whom I have named have not the smallest influence even over their immediate neighbors," he wrote in contrast to the importance that West Virginia and the federal government placed upon the two legislators.[47]

The judge's diminution of the value of Bechtol and Wheat as prisoners prepared the way for his next argument: The practice of taking political prisoners harmed the Confederacy. "In this kind of warfare the South, as a general thing, is placed at the greatest disadvantage in the character of the persons arrested, and again because the inevitable consequence of these mutual arrests will be to remove or drive from our border nearly our entire male population," Parker contended. "Our difficulties along the border are sufficiently great as they are, and we feel that our freedom from arrest and imprisonment should not be dependent upon the action of every military officer, however young and indiscreet they may be."[48]

The last statement was an ironic jab at Major—now Lieutenant Colonel—Charles O'Ferrall. Judge Parker had appointed the teenage O'Ferrall as circuit court clerk to fill his father's unexpired term before the war. Still, the judge assigned responsibility for an awkward and dangerous situation to the young officer and at the same time, in another twist of irony, pointed to restraint on the part of the Union Army. Parker told Seddon that after the arrest of the hostages, General Sigel had "professed an unwillingness to initiate such a condition of things, and declared that their action was merely retaliatory and adopted in self-defense." The judge added, "But as matters now are there is not one of us who is secure for a day."[49]

Parker concluded with two specific recommendations. First, to curb the rashness of young Confederate officers, he suggested that the authority to arrest civilians be limited to department commanders. Second, in still a third ironic point, the judge opposed calls for the Confederate government to turn Bechtol and Wheat over to the Virginia government in Richmond to be tried for treason against the state. Parker warned the secretary of war that such a move could be embarrassing to the Confederacy and insisted that the national government was the "sole party on one side" of the war. Virginia's interests in the conflict were protected by the Confederate States of America, he wrote.[50] This was an interesting point coming from the judge who had presided over the trial of John Brown and his cohorts for treason against the state of Virginia for their raid on Harpers Ferry in 1859.

The secretary of war noted on Parker's letter, "I do not differ materially in opinion," and Sydney S. Baxter, a special commissioner in the Confederate War Department, launched an investigation into the status of Bechtol and Wheat. Secretary of War Judah P. Benjamin had asked Baxter, a former Virginia attorney general, in 1861 to delve into delicate cases involving political prisoners, and Baxter had filled that role without pay since then.

When Robert Y. Conrad and A. Stephen Dandridge arrived in Richmond, they found a favorable climate. Dandridge reported, "Mr. Conrad and I went to Richmond, had an interview with the Secty. of War, found him disposed to release the citizens captured at Bath and to stop the arrest of all citizens."[51] At Seddon's direction, Assistant Secretary of War J. A. Campbell ordered General Winder on May 2 to release Bechtol, Wheat, Finn, and Shives. Citing Baxter's report, Campbell noted that there was "no cause exhibited by the Military Authorities for the arrest or detention of the persons named."[52]

Arthur I. Boreman, in the meantime, turned up the heat in the situation. Unaware of events in Richmond, until Conrad and Dandridge reported to him on May 17, the West Virginia governor issued a proclamation on May 14 that designated thirty-six Morgan County residents, including three women, as "enemies of the state." He gave them sixty days to appear before the circuit clerk in the county and take a loyalty oath to the United States and West Virginia. Otherwise, they faced imprisonment. The list included Robert C. Gustin and Charles O'Ferrall.[53]

Boreman's move came three days before Conrad and Dandridge sent him word of the release of the prisoners. The paroled hostages had learned of the order from the assistant secretary of war to release Bechtol, Wheat, Finn, and Shives and left Richmond on May 3. Conrad explained that they had traveled toward Staunton but "became entangled in the Military Lines." Instead of heading toward Wheeling, the two returned to their homes, reaching them after a nearly two-week journey.[54]

Both Conrad and Dandridge sent letters to the governor that apprised him of the release order. Dandridge explained that they had arranged a meeting with Secretary Seddon upon their arrival in Richmond and found him already disposed to free the Berkeley Springs men. Conrad elaborated and revealed the influence that Parker's thinking had upon the secretary of war. "This discharge is founded upon the principle that in this time of war all arrests of non combattants for merely political opinions should be avoided," he told Governor Boreman. "I trust you will exert your influence with the Military Authorities of the United States, to induce them to adopt the same rules so vitally important to our border people."[55]

Campbell's order to release Bechtol, Wheat, Finn, and Shives dictated that "they will be conveyed to the lines as soon as convenient and practicable & released."[56] However, a quick release was neither convenient nor practical. Col. Robert Ould, the Confederacy's chief agent of prisoner exchanges, arranged for the men to go to Fortress Monroe by truce boat, but fighting along James River forced the boat to return to the Confederate capital before it could reach the Union stronghold.[57]

In the meantime, the hostages grew anxious. Conrad discussed the situation with Boreman by correspondence from Winchester and told the governor that he awaited "confidently some communication from you—that you regard my parole as discharged."[58] For his part, Dandridge explained to Boreman that he had reached his home "expecting to hear of the return to their homes of the Bath citizens—and of the hostages held for them." He asked the governor to inform him as soon as Bechtol, Wheat, Finn, and Shives had returned and the hostages were free. Dandridge volunteered to return to Richmond to "ascertain the cause of delay" if the prisoners did not arrive home soon. He believed that his presence might remove any "obstacles thrown in the way." This offer included a request for the extension of his parole in case of delays on the road to and from Richmond.[59]

Dandridge did not return to Richmond, but his anxiety continued. A month passed since the order to release the Union prisoners, and he pressed Colonel Ould about the matter. In exasperation, Ould blamed the Union for cutting transportation between Richmond and the coast. "There has been no default on the part of the Confederate authorities," he assured Dandridge. "As soon as intercourse is resumed, these men will be sent."[60]

Two more weeks passed before Bechtol, Wheat, Finn, and Shives gained their freedom. US Sanitary Commission official Amy Morris Bradley described the ordeal of the four men before reaching Union lines. According to her account, the civilians, along with fifty-six prisoners of war, left Richmond on June 26 under an escort of Confederate cavalry. With the prisoners on foot, the entourage headed toward Alexandria rather than Fortress Monroe. "Some of the prisoners were illy able to perform such a journey,"

Bradley wrote. "Nearly all of them being destitute of shoes, and some of them being almost naked." Bradley's sensational report alleged that the riders goaded the prisoners and lamented the effect of this upon the more aged Bechtol and Wheat. "The prisoners reached our lines in safety at last, however, and these unflinching West Virginia patriots are now at their homes, almost wrecked physically but unbroken in spirit," she pontificated. "Their voices, and, if necessary, arms, will be wielded again in that young but promising commonwealth, in defence of the principles in vindication of which they have braved the perils of the traitor's sword, the loathsome and galling bitterness of the tyrant's dungeon, and the taunts, jeers, and inhuman barbarity of the pliant dupes of treason and secession."[61]

After the prisoners returned to Berkeley Springs, Joseph S. Wheat soon traveled to Wheeling. He gave an interview to the *Wheeling Daily Intelligencer* in July and substantiated portions of Bradley's story but downplayed others. "Being somewhat advanced in years, he was not able to stand the march," the Wheeling newspaper confirmed. "He looks decidedly the worse of the wear," the article reported. "Prison life does not seem to have agreed with him." Nevertheless, the newspaper continued, "Mr. Wheat says that he was not used roughly on his trip—not half so much as he expected, and certainly nothing like he would have been a year or two ago." The *Daily Intelligencer* saw the comparative lenience as a sign that the South was losing the war.[62] It also might have been more directly a reflection of the direction of Confederate policy away from holding civilian prisoners.

The newspaper could not resist its own sensationalism, however. It credited Governor Boreman and the hostage law with the release of the four men from Berkeley Springs and attributed to Wheat a bravado that likely did not exist in the circumstances. "He told his fellow prisoners when he entered the room [at Castle Thunder] that he had not come to stay long with them," the *Daily Intelligencer* maintained. Wheat supposedly said that he had "left a Governor at home who was not in the habit of permitting people to be stolen without at least making an effort to get them back again." The story reported that most of the political prisoners were from other states, and that they were surprised when the men from Berkeley Spring gained their liberty. "Other prisoners seemed to think that West Virginia was sure enough a live state, and that she exercised an influence in the capital of rebeldom which states of larger growth and larger pretensions had not so far exercised."[63]

Governor Boreman ordered the release of the hostages when he received word on July 9 that Bechtol, Wheat, Finn, and Shives were within

Union lines.[64] That did not end the ordeal for the hostages, however. The *Wheeling Daily Intelligencer* noted that Reverend Boyd was immediately rearrested. The case involving William N. Dooley had not been resolved, and Boyd was again held as a hostage for him.[65]

Boyd apparently received his freedom within four months because, ironically, he, along with Conrad and Williams, once again found themselves in Union custody on November 8 at the order of Gen. Philip Sheridan. "They were allowed each to take a carpet-bag of clothing and some bed-clothes, and were told they might expect a long sojourn in Yankee land," the *Richmond Daily Dispatch* reported. "No reason was assigned for their arrest."[66]

The war ended, and the former hostages tried to return to normal life. Philip Williams chaired a meeting in Winchester on May 20, 1865, at which moderates opened the door to reconciliation with the United States and cooperation with Francis H. Pierpont's Virginia government, now occupying the government offices in Richmond. Robert Y. Conrad figured prominently at the meeting and offered resolutions against any remaining spirit of rebellion.[67]

Both Williams and Conrad put their sentiments into practice that fall when they ran for office under the United States and the Pierpont regime. Williams ran unsuccessfully for the state senate, and Conrad won a seat in Congress.[68]

While the hostages from the Berkeley Springs case, like most other former hostages across West Virginia and Virginia, achieved a sense of normality in the aftermath of war, it was only a sense. The war had changed much for everyone in the two states, but the hostages also struggled to recover from their experiences. Some never fully recovered.

Two of the hostages from Winchester suffered poor health from their imprisonment. Rev. A. H. H. Boyd died on December 16, 1865, at age fifty-two. The *Staunton Spectator* commented on his unusual wartime experience: "He was selected, with two or three others, as a sort of hostage, or rather subject of vicarious punishment, for the people among whom he lived; and the hardships of imprisonment hastened his end."[69]

Although Philip Williams tried to adapt to postwar reality, he, too, suffered ill health. Williams dramatically died on April 2, 1868, in the Woodstock, Virginia, courtroom, where he had argued his first case in 1823. A local historian noted Williams's former status as a hostage and recalled, "He suffered unjust imprisonment in a loathsome place in Wheeling, W.Va.; his fellow prisoners from Winchester being Rev. Dr. Boyd, Robert Y. Conrad and others." The historian believed that "Mr. Williams never fully recovered from the effects of his prison life."[70]

Death and hardship stalked the former hostages and the former political prisoners for whom they were held. Boyd, Conrad, Dandridge, White, and Williams were not alone in their struggle to move beyond the war. Some never did. George Buchanon died as a hostage in Wheeling. His death was not the end of the matter, however, and because of him and his situation, the hostages' captors did not easily move beyond the war either.

CHAPTER 10

# Governor Boreman and George Buchanon

The *Wheeling Daily Register* tucked local news items into the first column on its third page on April 13, 1864. There was the "mysterious disappearance and suicide" of Mrs. William Sipe of Clay Street, the indictments of the federal grand jury in Wheeling, the death of D. Hull in a coal bank in nearby Bridgeport, Ohio, and the report of the death of a young woman who had lost both legs in an accident on the Cleveland and Pittsburg Railroad in Fairview, Ohio. Notice of the death of George Buchanon appeared in the middle of the column. Buchanon had died three days earlier as a hostage of the State of West Virginia (see appendix for a timeline of events). The *Daily Register*, a Democratic newspaper, provided a check and balance to the *Wheeling Daily Intelligencer*, a Republican newspaper that published material decidedly favorable to the administration of Gov. Arthur I. Boreman. In its report of Buchanon's death, the *Daily Register* noted solemnly, "*Some* person has incurred a fearful weight of responsibility in this matter, which should rest heavily upon his soul." The newspaper promised to "endeavor to trace it up."[1]

It proved difficult for the *Wheeling Daily Register* to follow up on Buchanon's death. Its owners dealt with their own troubles. Maj. Gen. David Hunter, commander of the Department of West Virginia, ordered the arrest of Lewis Baker, the publisher—and future president of the West Virginia Senate—and O. S. Long, the editor, in July 1864. The general resented an article that criticized his campaign in the Shenandoah Valley. Baker and Long themselves spent seven weeks in the Atheneum, while a soldier stood guard over their closed newspaper office.[2]

An effort to trace George Buchanon's story proves difficult, even without the ire of a Union general as a distraction. Buchanon existed as one of many West Virginians who went about their lives in the nineteenth century in relative anonymity. Few records document his life, but he contributed to the history of his state and region as a representative person. His struggles, his resistance to the changing status quo, his imprisonment, and his death all bring forward the experiences of common individuals who became victims of the Civil War generally and of the State of West Virginia and its hostage policy specifically.

George Buchanon's roots held to the lands of Marshall County, West Virginia, just south of Ohio County and Wheeling. His home community, Dallas—also known as West Union and Haneytown—hugged the corner of Marshall and Ohio Counties and the state of Pennsylvania. Many people with the same last name—sometimes spelled Buchanan—lived there. A small hamlet called Buchanan Hill lay to the southwest. The people of Dallas strongly asserted their political identity as Virginians before 1863, and as West Virginians afterward, but the culture and economy of the community easily melded with those of Washington County, Pennsylvania, just to the east. Certainly, the geography was indistinct from one state to the other as the upper branches of Wheeling Creek formed deep and narrow valleys and sharp ridges where the towns and roads characteristically clung. This gave the region—both in Virginia and Pennsylvania—a remote feel that accentuated its place on the edges of the respective counties.

Ohio and Marshall Counties in West Virginia's northern panhandle hugged the Ohio River between Ohio and Pennsylvania. Note Wheeling on the edge of Ohio County and George Buchanon's hometown, West Union or Dallas, in the northeastern corner of Marshall County (A. J. Johnson, *Johnson's Virginia, Delaware, Maryland & West Virginia.* [New York: Johnson and Ward, 1864] Map. https://www.loc.gov/item/lva0000096/)

George Buchanon and his wife, Mary, exemplified life at the edge. As in many other counties in West Virginia, the centers of society and the economy formed along the main transportation corridors. The county seats generally arose there. In the case of Marshall and Ohio Counties, Wheeling and Elizabethtown (later Moundsville) developed at the confluences of large creeks with the Ohio River. Major roads and railroads were constructed through creek valleys and over ridges to the next valley where necessary. Dallas lay between the transportation corridors and away from the county seats. The land was poor, and George and Mary Buchanon, like many others in the community, were poor farmers.

Others in the Buchanon family moved elsewhere. Another George Buchanon owned a prosperous farm at West Alexander, Pennsylvania, where good farmland lay along the National Road just across the state line. Still others moved closer to Wheeling, in the vicinity of Valley Grove, again along the National Road, not far northwest of Dallas. George and Mary Buchanon followed as the Civil War began. Regardless, ties to Dallas remained strong for the Buchanons and others who gravitated toward Wheeling.

Dallas was a community on the edge. Its people were caught in between as the Civil War heated and ignited, and they became volatile. The reputation of the community prompted the *Tribune* in nearby Washington, Pennsylvania, to remark that in Dallas, as throughout Virginia, "every petty postmaster and country squire is, *ex officio* inquisitor of the opinions of his neighbor." The newspaper added optimistically, "But Haineytown catches some of the healthy breezes of independence from our western boundary."[3] The divided people of Dallas included Unionists who had greater affinity to Wheeling and the upper Ohio River or to Pennsylvania and its commercial centers. The other side of the political spectrum in the community received its influence from Jacksonian Democracy, a strong influence in Marshall County and the nearby rural Pennsylvania counties south of Pittsburgh, which also stood on the edge of their commercial, political, and cultural universes. With the Civil War, that Democracy often erupted as Copperheadism in these areas. Opposition to the war or its administration came, not necessarily because of true support of the Confederacy, but because of resistance to the rapid changes that accompanied domination of national and state politics by the new Republican Party.

Among the residents and expatriates of Dallas, Rev. W. J. Alexander stepped forward as a leader among the Unionists. Alexander attended the convention that convened in Marshall County, as in many counties in northwestern Virginia, in the aftermath of the vote for secession in

Richmond in 1861. He also represented the county at the First Wheeling Convention that same spring. Alexander became known as the "patriotic pastor" as he did everything from rallying people to the cause of West Virginia statehood to gathering supplies for Soldiers' Aid Societies. He, too, lived in Dallas at the start of the war and moved to the Valley Grove area, but Alexander apparently commuted between the two communities. He maintained a presence in Dallas as the Presbyterian minister there.[4]

Resistance to the Lincoln, Pierpont, and Boreman administrations in the Dallas area surfaced in several ways. In the summer of 1863, an anti-draft movement began in Marshall County, and state independent scouts quickly rounded up the leaders and lodged them in the Atheneum.[5] Later in the fall, someone cut down a liberty pole while the Unionists were meeting in Dallas. The pro-Union men rousted all the known Copperheads from their homes and forced them to cut a new pole and erect it.[6]

Around the same time, George Buchanon gained a reputation for disloyalty to the Union and to West Virginia. Much of the reputation rested on hearsay. This caused Buchanon's arrest, and Rev. W. J. Alexander was a leading instigator. Buchanon became caught in the murky transition between the Restored Government of Virginia and the State of West Virginia, and little continuity in policy and records existed. This resulted in a state of limbo for Buchanon. Mystery shrouded the circumstances of his arrest. Even the date became a point of confusion.

In the fall of 1863, Gov. Arthur I. Boreman learned that Buchanon was held in the ranks of the Atheneum, but no record existed of the charges against him.[7] The governor did have affidavits that claimed Buchanon "bears the character of a disloyal man" and "that he denounced the Government and the Administration, said that Lincoln had violated the Constitution in declaring war and carrying it on, and in his emancipation Proclamation."[8] Boreman also received petitions from 139 people, including 18 Union soldiers, who insisted that Buchanon was indeed loyal. The governor later admitted that despite his uncertainty about Buchanon's case, he had become so annoyed by the petitions on the prisoner's behalf that he had decided to hold Buchanon as a hostage.[9]

While Buchanon waited in the Atheneum for word on his case, Secretary of War Edwin M. Stanton requested Brig. Gen. William W. Orme to tour Union prisoner of war camps. The general captured the state of the Atheneum in his report. He listed "twelve citizens held as hostages by the Governor's order." Buchanon was among them. Seven other citizens lived in the Atheneum "under military orders." In addition, the prison held thirty-two prisoners of war. In an understatement that belied coming criticisms of the place, Orme reported, "Those on hand are well fed and cared for." He wrote that the Atheneum had "abundant" supplies, and an "ample" garrison, that no recent deaths had occurred, and that only one inmate was sick.[10]

Meanwhile, a new commander took charge of the Atheneum. Prussian-born Capt. Ewald W. Over of the Sixth West Virginia Infantry had earned a recent reputation for rounding up spies and bushwhackers across northern West Virginia as brigade provost marshal at Clarksburg. In January 1864, as Over tried to get a handle on his new command, a petition arrived from residents of the Valley Grove and Dallas area, who sensed uncertainty over Buchanon's status. Reverend Alexander led the names. "The undersigned persons being Loyal Citizens & Neighbors of George Buchanan would represent to you that although it may be that no overt act of Treason can be proven against said George Buchanan, yet we know him to be a disloyal man; and believe that his return to his home would endanger the peace and harmony of the community," the petition read. "We would therefore earnestly ask of you that said Buchanan be transmitted across the Federal lines."[11] Over inquired of Joseph Darr, still assistant provost marshal general for West Virginia but promoted to lieutenant colonel, "Do you know of any other charges against Geo Buchanan, who was arrested by your order Oct 7th 1863 except those contained in a petition against him?" Over pushed the issue by adding that he intended to bring Buchanon's case to the attention of the department commander.[12]

The captain received no written reply from Darr, but the two apparently discussed the situation. Over became aware that Boreman played a role in Buchanon's captivity, and he approached the governor about the matter on the same day that he had written to Darr. "Is Geo Buchanan your prisoner and do you desire to have him held subject to your orders?" he asked.[13] Boreman confirmed that Buchanon was a state hostage.[14]

Over advised the governor that approval should be received from the US Army commissary general of prisoners to class Buchanon as a state prisoner rather than a federal one, a suggestion that revived issues raised in the George W. Thompson case. Captain Over contacted Col. William Hoffman, the commissary general. Over explained that since Buchanon had been listed among federal prisoners, he wished to cover all ends by seeking permission to transfer him to state jurisdiction.[15] Hoffman instructed Over that since Buchanon had not been arrested by the authority of the War Department, he was not a federal prisoner.[16] This answer seemingly contradicted Judge John J. Jackson Jr.'s opinion in 1863 that any person in the custody of federal troops in a federal prison enjoyed federal protection. Yet, it also implied, based on Hoffman's previous positions, that nobody except federal prisoners should be held in a federal prison, and the Atheneum was a federal prison. Still, Buchanon remained at the Atheneum.

In mid-February 1864, George Buchanon wrote to Captain Over. Buchanon pleaded his own case. He explained that he had been confined for nearly five months without knowing the charges against him. He requested to see Governor Boreman to discuss how he might help in gaining the release of the man for whom he supposedly was held as a hostage. Over forwarded the letter to the governor. Boreman replied to Over that he had no time to see Buchanon.[17]

Shortly afterward, Buchanon fell sick. The military hospital at the Atheneum was condemned on March 5 as unfit for the sick and wounded. It was overcrowded, and the army removed patients to St. Joseph's Hospital in North Wheeling.[18] The *Wheeling Daily Intelligencer* admitted that "certainly the accommodations for sick people at the Atheneum are not what they should be."[19] Nevertheless, the prison physician, Dr. John Frizzell, believed that Buchanon would recover in the prison with proper care and returned him to the Atheneum. Buchanon died there on April 10, 1864.[20]

Confusion stayed with Buchanon even after his death. Whereas, Buchanon had set the beginning of his confinement at late September or early October 1863, the *Wheeling Daily Intelligencer* reported that he had been arrested in August 1863. It repeated the hearsay that Buchanon had been arrested for "uttering treasonable language and advising forcible resistance to the draft." It noted that he left behind a wife and three children.[21]

George Buchanon had languished in prison and died in near anonymity. Common citizens often found themselves in this state in the midst of the government bureaucracy and the chaos of the Civil War. This certainly proved true for the hostages of the State of West Virginia. The tragedy of Buchanon's death deserved attention, but his death faded from the news and community memory. Death was all too common from the spring of 1864 until the end of the war and filled the news. The campaigns in Georgia and Virginia created a bloody record. The battles and raids in West Virginia brought plenty of death and heartache. Many people wished to know the fates of their loved ones, and many unanswered questions surrounded the deaths and disappearances of West Virginians.

Death stalked military and civilian prisoners alike in the Atheneum. With firsthand knowledge, the editor of the *Wheeling Daily Register* un-

The obscured grave of George Buchanon in Dallas Presbyterian Church Cemetery in Marshall County, West Virginia. (Photo by Carla Tustin, https://www.findagrave.com/memorial/94056792/george-buchanan/photo)

favorably compared the prison outpost to the larger Union prison camp at Johnson Island. "We know very well that, in some cases, prisoners in the Atheneum in this city fared even worse last summer [1864]."[22]

Accidents and sickness struck the prison guards and other members of Wheeling's military garrison and soldiers who were passing through the city. Disease and the rigors of confinement often placed prisoners and hostages in the post hospital at the Atheneum or in St. Joseph's Hospital. Gradually, health care and conditions improved in 1864. A commission of Wheeling citizens had advised the caretakers of the Atheneum on sanitation and had collected money and supplies to make improvements. An upgraded prison hospital took the place of the former one, which had received much criticism. Authorities expanded the prison to avert overcrowding—the second expansion in two years.[23] These changes prompted the *Wheeling Daily Register* to admit, "The military prison in this city has been, we are informed, much better and more humanely managed by the present officers in charge than by their predecessors."[24] After its editor toured the refurbished facility, the *Wheeling Daily Intelligencer* casually commented, "While we do not think the Atheneum particularly desirable as a residence, yet we believe those whose crimes have brought them within its walls have no grounds for complaint."[25]

Whether hostages and other prisoners entered the Atheneum before or after the improvements, life inside had its rituals and its routines. Guards registered new arrivals at the Atheneum and logged their physical descriptions and measured their height. Before 1864, guards then ushered the new prisoners into the converted theater building without a chance to wash and without a change of clothes. Water was available on each floor after the refurbishment. They were subjected to a hazing at the hands of the older inmates. Someone cried "fresh fish," and the newcomers were seized, each wrapped in a blanket, and thrown into the air until all of their valuables fell from their pockets and other hiding places. The prisoners scooped up the items and claimed them as their own. Only dignitaries—political leaders and clergy—were spared. They tended to be housed separately. After the spring of 1864, Union and Confederate prisoners also were separated, and hostages were kept from soldiers. New prisoners often found acquaintances who taught them about prison life. There was the deadline—across which no prisoner could pass. Prisoners who had been unruly or who had tried to escape walked the floor in ball and chain. Bartering took place to pass the time as much as to supply necessities, and after expansion, a prison yard allowed well-behaved prisoners to have some fresh air and exercise.[26]

The year 1864 passed with other hostages moving in and out of the Atheneum. Hostages arrived for the people who were taken by the Confederates in Berkeley Springs. Members of their party went to Richmond to seek the release of the Morgan County people, and the governor released all of them when the Confederates relented. Those who were held for Sheriff Shaw were released. The hostages from Wayne County came and went after John Adams's body was found.

In the summer of 1864, a new class of inmates joined the prisoners of war, court-martialed and arrested Union soldiers, and hostages at the Atheneum. Fifty former slaves arrived under guard from the Lynchburg area, where Union forces had freed them from slavery but classified them as contraband of war. Authorities did not confine them in the Atheneum but housed them there. They soon joined the Union Army and "created a great deal of merriment among the people on the street and particularly among the soldiers" as they marched to their new duties.[27]

As 1865 dawned, the Confederates became desperate and began holding Union officers from West Virginia as hostages for pro-Confederate civilians in the hands of the West Virginia government. The state legislature in Wheeling responded by allowing the governor to free state prisoners to gain the release of the officers. The number of people held at the Atheneum dwindled, and few new prisoners arrived as the war came to a close.[28] Most were deserters from both armies. An advertisement for recruits for a company of the Sixth West Virginia Infantry, based at the Atheneum, promised "comfortable quarters, good rations and clothing." It added that the "duty is very light in comparison to what is required of soldiers in the field." No longer was assignment to the Atheneum reserved just for the Exempts—invalids and older men.[29] At the same time, the guards at the Atheneum became apathetic and careless. In January, an escape occurred, and guards accidentally shot a seventeen-year-old Wheeling resident while they were pursuing the escapees. On the same night, an officer from the Atheneum arrested local clothier Henry Hartman as he exited Washington Hall. The officer mistook the business owner for a deserter and took him to the Atheneum. He gained his freedom after much difficulty.[30]

The last official report from the Atheneum before Robert E. Lee's surrender showed a prison that was wrapping up its work. Dated April 3, 1865, the report listed one captain from a West Virginia regiment who was held for a military violation, nine prisoners of war, seventeen Confederate deserters, one refugee from Roanoke County, Virginia, and two citizen prisoners—Charles H. Weir of Putnam County, who was held for giving aid to the enemy, and George Kingkade of Fayette County, who was held on unknown charges. Sixty-two Confederate deserters and eight refugees were sent to the prison station at Gallipolis, Ohio, that day. The report mentioned no hostages or other state prisoners.[31]

Activity at the Atheneum did not immediately end with Lee's surrender. The prison still housed Confederate prisoners of war, court-martialed Union soldiers, and deserters and stragglers who had not been mustered out. The last four Confederate prisoners of war left the Atheneum on June 6, and the jailers tended Union soldiers at the Atheneum more than Confederates or Confederate sympathizers. Nineteen court-martialed Union soldiers escaped in May and proved more successful than the escapees in January. Guards recaptured only eleven, and those had made it all the way to Pennsylvania. In June, members of the Seventy-Fourth Pennsylvania Infantry became impatient that they could not get transportation home and commandeered a B&O passenger train at Grafton. Detachments from the military post at Wheeling headed them off and temporarily confined them in the Atheneum. Even the Atheneum guards themselves caused problems. Fights broke out among them as they restlessly waited to go home. The most activity at the Atheneum took place in the post hospital, where transient soldiers coming from the front and prisoner of war camps recovered from sicknesses and wounds before continuing along the B&O Railroad. Once the Confederacy surrendered, the Soldiers' Aid Society and other local relief organizations assumed more and more of the work of the hospital as the army stepped back.[32]

The end came for the Atheneum prison rather suddenly in the early fall of 1865. Maj. H. A. Myers, provost marshal for the District of West Virginia, arrived in Wheeling on September 26 with orders from the War Department to close the prison. He accomplished the task in one day. Union soldiers serving sentences for military offenses went to Cumberland. Those who had been charged but not convicted were sent to their units. The 193rd New York Volunteer Infantry, which garrisoned the prison and the city at that time, left for New Creek the following day. Only members of the Exempts remained to assist with final clerical duties and in the prison hospital. In an epilogue for the Atheneum, the *Wheeling Daily Intelligencer* wrote:

> The Atheneum will long be remembered as a military prison. Hundreds of prisoners, rebel and Union, have been during the war confined in it, and frequently loud and long were the wails that came up from our erring Southern brethren, about the "horrors of this Bastile," which were regarded as unfounded, as we believe the prison has always been conducted on correct principles.[33]

Thereafter, the owners of the Atheneum filed claims against the government for damages and put the building up for sale. By 1866, a Wheeling brewing firm had bought it for use as a malthouse.[34]

The year 1866 also ushered in a new era in West Virginia politics. "As the war came to a close, the coalition that had been necessary to create West Virginia weakened as new differences over proscriptions and disfranchisement overshadowed the need for unity in crisis," explained the essay, "Neither War nor Peace: West Virginia's Reconstruction Experience," in *Reconstructing Appalachia: The Civil War's Aftermath.*[35] Stalwarts within the Union Party coalition had implemented new and continuing proscriptions against former Confederates and secured a state constitutional amendment that comprehensively disenfranchised these men. Opponents questioned the need for restrictions against former Confederates and, since many of them had been Democrats or conservative Whigs before the war, they associated with the Democrats on the national level.

Boreman and his supporters insisted that former Confederates were far from benign. Indeed, while the end of the Civil War had brought a cessation of open hostilities, violence lingered, especially in areas where guerrilla warfare had been common during the war. These were places where opposition to the new state, especially to its rulers, continued. It should be no surprise that these also were counties from where hostages—persons of known disloyal sentiments—had been taken during the war. In their insistence, the incumbent leaders of West Virginia became more and more defensive of their positions of power, and at the same time aligned themselves with the Republican Party on national issues.

As the opposing sides coalesced in 1866, Boreman faced opposition for election as governor for the first time. The governor had won reelection unopposed in 1864. Two years later, he encountered fierce opposition from US Attorney Benjamin H. Smith of Charleston. Smith ran as the candidate of the Conservative Party, an interim vehicle for the opposition. "Despite overall Unionist victories in the election of 1866, the contest exposed voter dissatisfaction with the status quo," concluded the essay "Neither War nor Peace."[36]

Either because their previous political sympathies aligned with the Democrats or because their wartime experiences embittered them toward incumbent state officials, former hostages of West Virginia generally sympathized with the Conservative movement. They tended to lie low politically, but there were exceptions. Among them were former Randolph County hostage Alfred Hutton, Uriah Ashcraft and Thomas Ash of Doddridge County, and William McClaskey and Joseph N. B. Crim of Barbour County, whose names sprinkled the newspapers when they attended local, regional, and state organizing meetings and conventions.[37] In the case of McClaskey and Crim, their former hostage status put a target on their political backs when they returned to Wheeling in January 1868 for a state Conservative Party convention. An anonymous Republican detractor from their home county immediately assailed them in a letter—reminiscent of the ridicule heaped upon the men by Spencer Dayton during the war—to the *Wheeling Daily Intelligencer.* The correspondent described McClaskey as "one of the most unblushing rebels, who have been permitted to survive the war." The writer alleged that McClaskey had been indicted for perjury for falsely swearing a loyalty oath to the United States after the war. In a strange contrast between the civil rights policies of the Democrats/Conservatives and the Republicans/Union Party, the correspondent unveiled racial prejudice against McClaskey and another convention delegate, Isaac H. Strickler, much as Dayton had during the war. "What can be the real cause of opposition on the part of Strickler and McClaskey to 'negro equality,' may well be a matter for curious inquiry; since judging from their complexions and physiognomies, they will be elevated rather than depressed in the scale of society by the operation of that principle." The letter referred to Crim as a "prominent rebel" who was "arrested as a hostage for Union men torn from their homes by rebels, and he served a term in prison, in the city now honored by his presence."[38]

During the year 1866, George Buchanon's family acted on their own bitterness toward the person whom they held responsible for his captivity and death. While Boreman fended off a challenge to his position as the state's chief executive, Buchanon's heirs took Arthur I. Boreman to court. George Buchanon's son-in-law, James Robinson, filed suit against Boreman in Ohio County Circuit Court in 1866. Robinson also served as the administrator of Buchanon's estate. The suit sought $5,000 in damages allowed under state law for death caused "by the wrongful act or default of another."[39]

The governor scrambled to recall Buchanon as he built his defense. This included an exchange of letters with Captain Over and Colonel Darr. The former provost marshal, now a federal tax collector in Ohio, insisted that Governor Pierpont had ordered Buchanon's arrest in 1862 for failure to obey an order calling the state militia into federal service. No written order from Pierpont—or indeed any mention of charges against Buchanon at any time—can be found among the papers that Boreman assembled for his defense. The papers do include a scribble, dated May 1, 1863, from Darr himself, ordering, "Arrest and bring to this city George Buchanon on the Clay Road." A local home guard captain had led soldiers from Wheeling's military outpost in making the arrest.[40] Darr's account did nothing to clarify the historical record of Buchanon's arrest.

For his part, Ewald Over rehearsed the series of events following his assumption of command over the Atheneum. This included his inquiry to Boreman about Buchanon's status, Boreman's reply that Buchanon was a hostage, and Over's suggestion that Colonel Hoffman, the commissary general of prisoners, be consulted.[41]

Over apparently forgot the details of his correspondence with the commissary general. He told Boreman in March 1867, "I am not certain however, whether I ever received any answer."[42] The governor seized upon this statement and crafted a possible defense on the notion that the US Army had never released George Buchanon to state custody. Therefore, according to Boreman's delusion, Buchanon had not been under the governor's authority when he had died. To seal this contention, the governor convinced Over to swear in a deposition that he "never received an answer or order" from Hoffman.[43]

Governor Boreman also prepared a moral strategy designed to appeal to the patriotism of the court. He gathered testimony from William C. Richman of Raleigh County and Thomas Hill and Ducket Gatrell, who will be remembered from Doddridge County. Buchanon had been designated as a hostage for these men, and they provided written affirmations of their tragic arrests, sufferings in prison, and harrowing escapes. Boreman drew every bit of sympathy that he could. He told Richman that the lawsuit had come about because of the governor's efforts to gain the man's freedom.[44]

Ewald Over advised Boreman of a third possible defense. The former captain pointed out that Buchanon's arrest was legally justified under not only the hostage law but the law that allowed the arrest of suspicious persons at the time. Further, the state constitution validated holding people without trial under such laws. It allowed for the suspension of habeas corpus during the rebellion.[45]

While Boreman surveyed the points of his defense, he also assembled his legal team. It consisted of three of the most eminent attorneys of the Ohio Valley. George H. Lee had recently ended a fourteen-year tenure on the Virginia Supreme Court of Appeals (he had remained on the court in its pro-Union iteration following secession of the Richmond government). Lee had studied law under the venerable Henry St. George Tucker and had served as commonwealth attorney in Harrison County, as a member of the Virginia House of Delegates, and as a US district attorney. Benjamin Stanton, from the same hometown in Jefferson County, Ohio, as Secretary of War Edwin M. Stanton, had served as a county prosecutor in Bellefontaine, Ohio, as an Ohio state senator, as a congressman from Ohio, and as lieutenant governor of Ohio during two years of the Civil War. He and his law partner, C. W. B. Allison, had relocated to Wheeling following the war. In 1867, Stanton was a candidate for the West Virginia House of Delegates on the Union Party ticket. Allison, a native of Pennsylvania, partnered with Stanton in Bellefontaine, and at the start of the Civil War, Allison received a commission as a colonel in the Eighty-Fifth Ohio Volunteer Infantry. He commanded Camp Chase in 1862 and 1863. After leaving the army, he served in the Ohio House of Representatives.[46]

Together, Boreman's lawyers settled on a defense based on the third point he had outlined. Their case stressed the governor's duty to promote peace and order in the state through measures such as the hostage law.[47]

Meanwhile, Buchanon's family acquired impressive legal counsel of their own. James S. Wheat, a native of Washington, DC, was an early city leader in Wheeling and had been active in Virginia's pro-Union government as a member of the Second Wheeling Convention and as the state's attorney general. Zachariah Jacob had been an attorney in Wheeling since the 1820s and was described as "the foremost lawyer of the section."[48]

The plaintiff, defendant, and their attorneys appeared in Ohio County Circuit Court on October 14, 1867. Everyone involved was very familiar with the judge, Elbert H. Caldwell. An early attorney in Marshall County, Caldwell had served as commonwealth attorney and as a member of the Virginia House of Delegates before the war. Otherwise, the attorneys in the courtroom that day, including Boreman, enjoyed more notoriety than Caldwell. The matters of the day proved procedural, and the newspapers overlooked—or ignored—the event. Questions and complications caused the judge to continue the case until the May term in 1868.[49]

As the parties prepared for the court date in 1868, the Union Party–dominated state legislature made its sentiments known. It appropriated $600 toward Boreman's legal costs.[50]

May arrived, and the impeachment of Andrew Johnson dominated the news. The circuit court convened in the case on the 12th with scant mention in the back pages of the newspapers and once again no mention of the

ST VIRGINIA HOUSE,

CAMERON, W. VA.,

H. WHITE, Proprietor.

is house has recently undergone com- repairs, has been furnished, and is

Convenient a Stopping Place

he traveling public as any other in the ocl6

INAUGURATION OF THE erman Turn-Halle!

Market Street.

tober 14th, 15th and 16th, 1868.

E CALL THE ATTENTION OF OUR friends and the public generally to the guration of our Halle. The festivities mplete programme of which has been lished) will take place in the following r:

FIRST DAY.

esday, Oct. 14—GRAND CONCERT AND GYMNASTIC EXHIBITION, by the Turnverein and the singing Societies Harmony and Maennerchor.

SECOND DAY.

nday, Oct. 15—FAIR AND FESTIVAL, arranged and presided over by the lady friends of the Society.

THIRD DAY.

ay, Oct. 16—PIC NIC ON THE FAIR-GROUND, (weather permitting,) and in the evening, to conclude the festivities, GRAND BALL AT THE TURN HALLE. 13-5td THE COMMITTEE.

BURNING OF THE ATHENEUM.

One Hundred Thousand Dollars Worth of Property Destroyed.

One of the most destructive fires which ever occurred in our city, took place on Saturday morning between the hours of one and three o'clock, involving the destruction of over *one hundred thousand dollars* worth of property the main part of which was one of the largest buildings of the city, the Atheneum building, of late owned and occupied by Messrs Butterfield & Co., and Messrs Dodson & Bros. About one o'clock flames were discovered in the dry-house or kiln attached to the main building, and an alarm was given which brought the fire companies to the spot. The fire had however secured to strong a hold and the dry house was speedily consumed. The danger to the main building was then thought to be over, and many persons who had come to the ground on the first alarm returned to their homes. It appears, however, that the fire, unknown to those who were watching it, had caught in the barge board on the main building, and had rapidly communicated the flames to the roof. When this was discovered it was found that the steam fire engine, owing to its location on the north side of the building, could not play upon the burning part, while the hose of the other companies was not long enough to reach it. Very speedily the flames, which had effected a lodgement in the south-east cornice of the building, burned through a large girder which ran the whole length

BASE BALL.—The second game of the match game between the Columbias and Baltics, was played on Saturday afternoon. We understand that the Columbias had been promised a new uniform if they succeeded in defeating the Baltics, and on this account we are really sorry to be compelled to record their vanquishment. They played well and pluckily, yet not well enough to gain the victory. The Baltics are well pleased with the new organization of their nine, who did better play in the estimation of their friends than at any previous game of the season.

The Uniteds were on the ground in a bran new uniform, which is bright and dashing, and will show to good advantage in the field. We append the score of the game:

COLUMBIA. BALTIC.

SUMMARY.

Umpires—Messrs. Norton and Harbrook.

As the lawsuit by George Buchanon's family against Governor Boreman stagnated, the Atheneum came to an unceremonious end as a fire destroyed it in October 1868, and the *Wheeling Daily Intelligencer* relegated the news to its back page. (*Wheeling Daily Intelligencer*, October 12, 1868)

case surrounding George Buchanon's fate. In a show of equity, Caldwell agreed to include the plaintiff's costs in any award that might result from a decision in his favor. Little else occurred. The judge continued the case until December 1868.[51]

Between May and December events overshadowed the lawsuit. The plaintiff's team suffered a setback in June when Zachariah Jacob died, but the political battles seemed more important than the legal battle in the summer and fall anyway. Andrew Johnson's impeachment, the presidential election, and state elections made 1868 a watershed year. Historian John E. Stealey III observed that the year's events "aroused a deep anxiety among loyal West Virginia Republicans" in an "upside-down world" where they "struggled to secure the fruits of military victory by supporting congressional reconstruction on the national level and state measures of proscription."[52] One of West Virginia's US senators, Peter G. Van Winkle, became a political casualty of the impeachment when he voted to acquit President Johnson, and Governor Boreman emerged as the top contender to replace Van Winkle. The rejection of Van Winkle symbolized a growing rift within the Republican Party in West Virginia. Clear radical and moderate wings of the party grew, and the moderates increasingly found common ground with the party now known as Conservative Democrats and with disenfranchised former Confederates, especially on economic issues. Boreman loosened his ties to the governor's office as he built support for his bid for the senate.

Arthur I. Boreman's elevation to the senate hinged on the outcome of legislative races in the state election in October 1868. As the election approached, the Athenaeum building burned in the early morning hours of October 10 "in one of the most destructive fires which ever occurred" in Wheeling.[53] This singular event pushed the hostage saga further into the past, even as the lawsuit shuffled through the judicial process.

Less than two weeks later, state senate president William E. Stevenson carried the Republican banner to the governorship, and the Republicans kept control of the state legislature. A local election had greater implications for the Buchanon lawsuit, however. Judge Caldwell experienced trouble with his reelection in October because of the split in the Republican Party. James Paull, a Democrat and protégé of Zachariah Jacob, challenged the Republican Caldwell. Paull claimed support from Conservative Democrats and many Republicans, including key Republicans in the Wheeling legal community. It initially appeared that Caldwell had narrowly won, but the Ohio County Board of Supervisors disputed the election and asked the governor to judge the election according to state law.

Caldwell argued that the county governing board had no jurisdiction in the election, but Governor Boreman disagreed and oversaw an extensive recount in November and December.[54]

The recount continued as Judge Caldwell's court convened in December. The defense had reoriented its arguments in the seven months since the last court appearance in the Buchanon case. Boreman's attorneys convinced Judge Caldwell that the matter was one of federal concern. They argued that Buchanon had been in federal custody at the time of his death. Besides, they pointed out, the statute of limitations had expired on the state law upon which Robinson had based his suit. The judge agreed that the case should be heard in federal court.[55] The governor decided the election in favor of Caldwell later in December.[56]

Nearly three more years passed before any movement took place in the lawsuit. Meanwhile, the Conservative Democrats gained momentum as boosters for West Virginia's economy under the leadership of industrialists Johnson N. Camden and Henry G. Davis. Through increasing interest in economic cooperation and lessened concern over political participation by ex-Confederates, a coalition of moderate Republicans and Conservative Democrats rose in power. Conservative Democrat and B&O Railroad attorney John J. Jacob was elected governor in 1870 at the expense of William E. Stevenson, the incumbent. Conservative Democrats also took over the state legislature with moderate Republicans holding key leadership roles. Political proscriptions against former Confederates fell away, and a movement to rewrite the state constitution arose in 1871. "After the October 1870 and the known accretion to their numbers, the Democratic/Conservative phalanx now possessed the means to test the limits of its power to reconstruct West Virginia government as it pleased," Dr. Stealey wrote. "After so many years of powerlessness, for them not to do otherwise would seem a denial of the experience of their harsh, if self-inflicted, exile."[57]

Perhaps "phalanx" is too strong a word. The coalition that gained control of West Virginia politics after 1870 was by no means a Conservative Democrat monolith, and its force was limited. Certainly, the family of George Buchanon belonged to the class that had experienced "powerlessness," but the ascent of the Conservative Democrats gave Buchanon's survivors little redress. The Buchanon case went before Judge John J. Jackson Jr. in August 1871. Jackson served as federal district judge in West Virginia but also sat as temporary associate judge on the US Circuit Court for the Fourth Circuit under Hugh L. Bond. Jackson convened court in Parkersburg on August 7 and heard the case. The judge listened to Boreman's contentions and supporting testimony that Buchanon simply was a federal prisoner. He had been arrested, they insisted, for his refusal to answer the call of the militia into federal service. Therefore, when he died, Buchanon was a federal prisoner. Considering his decision in the George W. Thompson case in 1863, it took little to convince Jackson. To him, a prisoner in a federal facility under control of federal soldiers was a federal prisoner. Boreman and his attorneys knew this.[58]

Judge Jackson worked under a handicap. He was not privy to the complete facts in the case. He did not know that no clear charges had ever been filed against Buchanon. Neither did he know that Boreman had specifically decided to hold Buchanon as a hostage out of annoyance. Had he known these points, he might have considered Buchanon's civil rights. Jackson certainly was known as a guardian of individual rights, regardless of political leanings. While the Fourteenth Amendment and Civil Rights Acts had not existed at the time of Buchanon's imprisonment and death, postwar court decisions such as *Ex parte Milligan* affirmed what Jackson himself had decided during the war. Prisoners were entitled to court hearings when courts were open and functioning. This was especially true for federal prisoners, a designation that both Jackson and Boreman assigned to Buchanon (at least in 1871). Further, the US Constitution, in article one, section ten, prohibited bills of attainder, whether in war or peace, at both the federal and state levels (West Virginia's constitution also forbade bills of attainder). This prohibition protected individuals from being grouped together by law and punished without court action. The designation of hostages based upon political sentiments rather than seditious or subversive actions had the effect of assigning people to preconceived groups. In practice, hostages were often labeled disloyal because of their votes on the Virginia secession ordinance in 1861, but viva voce voting took place in antebellum Virginia. The recorded, public vote of a person in a tense environment during a legally constituted election could hardly be judged as a disloyal act or even as a reflection of true sentiment.

It was not that Judge Jackson found no fault with the state practice of taking hostages. He had made that clear in the Thompson case. The judge acted upon the case brought before him. In legal terms, however, the hostage law of pro-Union Virginia and West Virginia barely withstood scrutiny. With all of the righteous rhetoric about preserving the Union and protecting loyal citizens, the hostage law had poor legal grounding. Both a federal judge and the War Department concluded that through the law, the state had assumed war-making powers that belonged to the national government. Indeed, the goals of preserving the Union and protecting loyal citizens was better accomplished by the federal government. Insofar as its police powers were concerned, the state could have exercised its authority in more efficient ways, and sometimes did. The hostage law was a hastily drafted measure that resulted from emotion more than sound legal and practical reasoning. It smacked of vengeance more than logic.

The operation of the hostage law had social and political consequences as well as legal ones. The element of vengeance made it an effective tool for personal vendettas. The law invited local charges of disloyalty, which could easily be fabricated. It also resulted in a pattern of retribution for the arrests of hostages. This undermined any effectiveness of the law in preserving the Union and protecting pro-Union citizens. It also further weakened the legal integrity of the hostage law.

Still, by 1871, the issues of the hostage law no longer pressed. The war was over. Many of the legal points were moot, and the consequences to individuals and communities faded or merged into the massed effects of the Civil War. New political considerations and new alliances came into being. This realignment produced a new state constitution in 1872 that John Stealey concluded brought "no return to the glorious revolutionary era of accomplishment and reformation."[59]

While some accomplishments and reformation took place during the Civil War and Reconstruction eras, West Virginia foundered in insecurity from both real threats and ones born in paranoia, and the state government paid little attention to other issues besides the economy. Both before and after the Civil War, opportunistic politicians often used wartime injuries and slights for partisan gain rather than as issues of true justice. Indeed, politics of the two legal teams in the Buchanon case cannot be overlooked—Boreman, Lee, Stanton, and Allison on the Republican side and Wheat and Jacob on the Democratic side—as the motives and timing of the suit are considered. Robinson and his Democratic attorneys filed it in a year when Boreman faced his first challenge for the governor's office, and it continued through an era when Republican fortunes declined and Democratic power rose in West Virginia. At the culmination of the suit, a Democrat-led coalition dominated state politics, but Radical Republicans held sway at the national level, and Sen. Arthur I. Boreman enjoyed their association.

The politics of West Virginia's Reconstruction Era even affected Judge Jackson. Radical Republicans accused Jackson of collusion with the Democrats, though he himself avoided open politics. Although Abraham Lincoln had appointed Jackson to the federal bench, West Virginia Republicans never forgave him for rulings that moderated the power of the state during the Civil War, including the ruling in the George W. Thompson hostage case, but they especially castigated him for his view that the Force Act of May 1870 protected the right of ex-Confederates to vote as well as the right of African Americans to vote. As a result, Radical newspapers treated Jackson's rulings with sarcasm. When the *Morgantown Post* questioned one of Jackson's decisions, the *Wheeling Daily Intelligencer* had an answer. "The *Post* ought to have discovered by this time that law is a matter of secondary consequence with that eminent functionary," it slurred. "Indeed it has sometimes been said of him, that like necessity, he knows no law."[60] If they could not attribute the judge's opinions to incompetence, the Radical Republicans at least tried to explain them as partisan. Early in 1871, they speculated that he might be a possible Democratic nominee for the US Senate.[61]

By 1871, however, the wartime injuries and slights meant less and less. Moderate ex-Confederates and moderate ex-Unionists cooperated on many political and economic issues that seemed more important. Even Arthur I. Boreman's views toward ex-Confederates had moderated. The former governor served as the chair of the Select Committee on the Removal of Political Disabilities in the US Senate beginning in 1871, and he sponsored the amnesty of several individual West Virginia Confederates. The most noteworthy was former US minister to France Charles J. Faulkner, of Berkeley County, who had been arrested very early in the Civil War for diplomatic work on behalf of the Confederacy. Boreman's position on a general amnesty for former Confederates thawed, and he supported a bill for that purpose in early 1872. Illinois Senator Lyman Trumbull took note of Boreman's position. "I was much gratified this morning when the Senator from West Virginia [Mr. Boreman] rose to call the attention of the Senate to the amnesty bill, and gave reasons why it ought to be passed," Trumbull remarked. "I was congratulating myself that the day of illiberality, of hate, was passing away, and that even the Senator from West Virginia, who had perhaps as persistently opposed amnesty as anybody else, rose in his place . . . in favor of amnesty."[62]

The trend toward moderation on wartime issues—the passing away of "illiberality" and "hate"—brought political realignments and accommodations on both the national and state levels, and in the end, after the taking of political sides in the case, after Boreman's exertions to delay and bury the suit, it faded in importance with neither the state nor the federal courts really addressing the issue of a man's death as a hostage of the State of West Virginia. Instead of the injuries of war, most state leaders occupied themselves with leaving the war behind and addressing railroads and economic development, resolving West Virginia's share of Virginia's antebellum debt, and land speculation. Former Unionists and former Confederates alike were concerned about these things, and on some points many of them agreed. The writing of a new state constitution in 1872 signified not so much a "counter-revolution" as John Stealey described it but the completion of a revolution that more permanently defined the state and pushed into the past the questions of war and statehood. A new normal came into existence in which West Virginians emerged as players in the national parties in contests over civil rights, the tariff, money policy, Native American relations, foreign affairs, and charges of corruption in Washington. Historian Ken Fones-Wolf observed that as the nineteenth century progressed, "In many ways the state remained a borderland, but one less and less captivated by its divided sectional identity and southern political and cultural institutions."[63]

EPILOGUE

# The Endgame

West Virginia's Civil War hostages experienced many of the adjustments and much of the anxiety that followed the state's people after the war. In that sense, the borderland nature of the state during the war haunted its people. Each day, West Virginians encountered people and places that reminded them of the four years of violence, fear, heartache, and sacrifice. Perhaps the farmer across the fence had been a comrade in arms. Maybe the storekeeper who sold coffee to your family had been in the enemy army. The woman who taught your children might have informed guerrillas of your family's store of cornmeal. The preacher might have sworn that you had "disloyal sentiments" and caused your captivity as a hostage. Families and communities passed along oral history and tradition about their wartime experiences, but written history of the war was cautious. County histories and obituaries and other occasional newspaper articles—often highlighting prominent businesspeople and politicians—were written, but usually as modest outgrowths of the oral history and tradition. Veteran Appalachian historian John C. Inscoe noted a dearth of writing about the Civil War in the region in the late nineteenth century. Misunderstood or misconstrued accounts provided the only relief in the barren field. "Only four or five decades removed from the conflict, and at a time when an obsession with 'the late unpleasantness' manifested itself in the ideological and ceremonial trappings of the Lost Cause throughout much of . . . the former Confederacy, the war's legacy became increasingly simplistic, vague, and detached from historical context in the masterworks of this age of Appalachian discovery," Inscoe wrote.[1]

One explanation for this drought is the reticence of Appalachians, including West Virginians, to frankly share highly personal experiences with writers with whom they had a fleeting and formally polite relationship. Invading armies and insurgents on both sides had violated the homes and hamlets of West Virginia during the Civil War, and subsequent invasions of land speculators, corporate officials, and hosts of migrant and immigrant laborers in the postwar era of extractive industrialization had revived a sense of caution toward people from outside the community or region. Sometimes storytelling passed along folklore about the war to strangers, but this practice at the same time entertained unsuspecting strangers with exaggerated history, preserved privacy by withholding truly personal feelings about the war, and exuded a bravado that subtly warned outsiders against taking advantage of the storyteller and his or her family.

The historical legacy of hostages was much more complicated. For one thing, few people understood or even knew of the legal distinctions between being a hostage and being a political prisoner. Even during the war, military officers, political leaders, and hostages themselves confused the differences. Families might remember that their loved one had been arrested or captured by the Union Army but might not have realized it was at the request or under the authority of the state government. So, oral history and tradition, county histories, and obituaries might mention a person's captivity but not his status as hostage.

For another thing, a hostage was a passive victim. Ideology makes heroes of political prisoners. A soldier, including a prisoner of war, is remembered for his bravery, and the woman at home is honored for her fortitude and courage in the face of armed intrusions, but hostages were swooped up because they were weak and vulnerable and confined for values that others ascribed to them. The only honor that might come to them was if they played a role in rescuing others by helping to negotiate exchanges. For these reasons, people might have downplayed or hidden their experiences as hostages.

Age presented another complication. Most hostages were beyond military age. This added to their vulnerability. It also made their histories less significant in the postbellum years. Those who became hostages enjoyed a level of local prominence before the war. They tended to hold elected or appointive office and were substantial farmers and businesspeople. Their selection as hostages meant that they had not stayed unnoticed. Yet, in many cases, this prominence faded after the war as they became older and new leaders replaced them in the community. Thus, the histories of the hostages went less noticed after the war.

While hostages were locally known, they were not generally prominent outside of their counties. Yes, they were chosen because their captivity might pressure the Confederates to release political prisoners, and they may have held enough influence to negotiate exchanges. Nevertheless, because these men were not influential outside of their communities, little history of them and their war records went into print. Their written histories consisted largely of courthouse records and occasional mention by local correspondents in the scattered newspapers and the numerous county histories of the late nineteenth century. The latter was more likely if the family bought a subscription and the rights to a family profile.

In writing about nearby Pennsylvania, Robert M. Sandow noted, "Wartime actions led to contested memories and legacies of the conflict among the bitterly—sometimes violently—divided communities of the Pennsylvania mountains, linking attitudes and developments from the antebellum age to the fractious period of Reconstruction."[2] The same can be said about West Virginia. Certainly, the Civil War affected perceptions of antebellum history by redefining alliances and animosities because of personal tragedy and suffering, but we also have seen that the antebellum period defined many of the personal and community relationships of the war.

Likewise, new influences determined postwar associations and antagonisms. "In the late nineteenth century, historians have shown, Americans in general began to downplay the sectional divisions of the war and focus on mutually ennobling memories of sacrifice and valor on both sides," noted Jonathan Dean Sarris.[3] They also downplayed differences and focused on mutually beneficial financial concerns. After the war, a new wave of economic development, spurred by railroad expansion and an increased awareness of the state's resources, swept West Virginia. Mountain lands, which had provided only average farms and investment havens for antebellum speculators, quickly became desirable as reserves of timber and coal. This took place in the same period in which the centers of market agriculture shifted farther west, and many West Virginia farmers transitioned to work in extractive industries, along with laborers from other states and countries. With the state freed from the uninviting stagnation of Virginia's slave-plantation economic and political institutions, capitalists and their agents—many of them former Union or Confederate officers who had discovered the economic possibilities in the state during their service there—exerted control over land, resources, and the labor force. Altina Waller's seminal work *Feud* and Ron Lewis's more recent *The Industrialist and the Mountaineer* nicely captured this dynamic between West Virginia's postwar industrial era, the Civil War, and the antebellum period and its impact on individuals, families, and communities. Both pointed to the shadow of the Civil War in determining political, social, and economic leadership and alignments. Yet, Waller and Lewis demonstrated that the industrial revolution after the Civil War shifted the alignments. Not only did Waller and Lewis explore the effects of industrialization and other events in leadership and the people who formed around the leaders, but they emphasized the role of geography and topography in these alliances. While events changed perceptions and loyalties, geography and topography were constants. They directed or at least influenced the rate and amount of change in the attitudes of people toward their communities, state, and nation. This included the attitudes of former hostages and attitudes toward them.

Despite the cloudiness of West Virginia's historical memory of its hostages, there is no doubt that these people left a legacy—a legacy formed by the same factors that obscured their history. Some glimmers emerge in the historical record and provide examples. Some, like Sylvester Stump and John Woofter of Gilmer County, were among those who enjoyed local notoriety but whose names are seldom found in written history. Stump, a teenager during his captivity, escaped the restraints of antebellum and wartime politics and society and readily grew with the postwar realities of West Virginia. Stump became a farmer and storekeeper and occasionally contracted labor for the timber and oil and gas industries. After the turn of the century, he operated a gasoline boat on the Little Kanawha River to haul goods for his store and freight for residents and industries in his community. He claimed a place in the pages of history as a postmaster of the community of Stumptown during the Grover Cleveland and Woodrow Wilson presidencies because of his Democratic patronage. Stump left a scattered history as an entrepreneur and political opportunist in West Virginia's late nineteenth- and early twentieth-century industrial era, but no mention of his time as a hostage during the Civil War exists in later years. The only allusion to the wartime past was his record as a Democrat in a region that had been largely pro Confederate during the war and that lingered in conservatism afterward.[4]

John Woofter was a generation older than Sylvester Stump, but he, too, successfully navigated the postwar years. Unlike Stump, he carried a personal history from the prewar years that had made him notable enough to be designated as a hostage. Instead of eschewing his antebellum reputation or clinging to it in futility, Woofter built upon it and used it to bridge the antebellum and postbellum periods and surmount the gulf of war. Born in 1816, James Woofter had become a farmer, but he also entered the ministry and became widely known in that field. By 1855, Woofter served on the state mission board for the Baptist Church. Following the Civil War, Woofter avoided the political strife of the Reconstruction and Bourbon years and instead preferred the continuity that the ministry provided. Known as "Uncle John," he was a popular circuit-riding preacher in Gilmer and Lewis Counties and left a legacy of performing numerous marriages in the region. Woofter, like Stump, was unknown in the written record as a hostage or victim of the Civil War.[5]

In Barbour County, Joseph N. B. Crim also managed to leverage his antebellum position to his benefit after the war. Unlike Woofter, however, Crim embraced politics and his wartime loyalties. The people of his community knew his status as a political prisoner during the war, though they may not have made the distinction that he was a hostage. He was active in the Conservative movement during Reconstruction and served in West Virginia's Constitutional Convention in 1872. Instead of allowing his politics to limit his economic and social opportunities, Crim, like many during the era, used common connections to network with Democrats and Republicans alike in the new economy of post–Civil War West Virginia. He was involved in railroad expansion and the associated development of natural resources in his region, and by the mid-1880s, was a founder and president of Tygarts Valley Bank in Philippi, a venture that brought together ardent Democrats and Republicans alike.[6] Although Barbour County Civil War historian John W. Shaffer nicely covered the war and Reconstruction in the county, he neglected to mention Crim. Still, Shaffer pointed to trends in Barbour County after the war that explained part of the changing attitudes and loyalties of West Virginians as whole, including the state's former hostages. Shaffer pointed to violent animosity toward returning enemies just after the end of the war, changing interests, out-migration and changing demographics, and finally a realization among former enemies that they were part of a dwindling minority of people who had experienced the Civil War, though from different perspectives. This series of transitions affected the way people dealt with effects of the war in their later years.[7]

The most prominent of West Virginia's Civil War hostages, George W. Thompson, experienced a rebirth of sorts in a different way after the war.

His political battles during the war and his notoriety as a state and federal prisoner and hostage greatly damaged Thompson's reputation, and he never recovered. He attempted to influence Reconstruction politics by writing to newspapers under a nom de plume, and he attempted some writings in religious philosophy. Unfortunately for Thompson, society wanted more direct, practical language from its leaders, and West Virginia no longer appreciated Thompson's style. The antebellum judge did retain his personal wealth and played a role in railroad and housing development in the Wheeling area. His legacy underwent revision primarily because of the work of his sons, however. His namesake, George W., became president and general manager of Ohio River Railroad, which linked Wheeling with Huntington. William P. Thompson emerged from the Civil War as an associate of his brother-in-law in the oil industry and became president of Camden Consolidated Oil Company, a subsidiary of Standard Oil Company. He eventually relocated to Cleveland as secretary and then as a vice president of Standard Oil. Later, he became head of the lead trust. Judge Thompson benefited from his sons' and his son-in-law's influence. At the time of his death in 1888, even his old nemesis, the *Wheeling Intelligencer*, praised him and noted that he had been imprisoned during the Civil War because he had "conscientiously" objected to taking the oath to the pro-Union government of Virginia.[8]

Another former hostage failed to make the transition from antebellum to postbellum times. Addison McLaughlin (Adison McLoughlin) had been a prominent landowner, legislator, and entrepreneur before the war. After the war, he struggled to keep his former influence. While nobody in West Virginia escaped the Civil War unscathed, McLaughlin's decline came not so much because of the war but because of changing economics and his inability to adjust. He had put his efforts into the booming salt industry in prewar western Virginia, but salt production shifted westward after the war, and coal and timber replaced it in importance in West Virginia. McLaughlin's failure to adjust came partly because of his rooting in former days of glory, but others in his generation adjusted. His failings came more from a conservatism in business practices that did not account for a more aggressive, corporate business model that brought national interests into competition for West Virginia land and resources.

McLaughlin made some early efforts to combat opportunism following the Civil War. In one instance, which was directly connected to the war, he called for the removal of a member of the board of voter registration in Lewis County. Radical Republicans had established such boards during Reconstruction to keep ex-Confederates from voting, but corrupt members in many counties used them to personal, not just party, political advantage. McLaughlin, who had not been openly aligned during the war, accused the board member of ostensibly removing political opponents from the voter lists when he himself was "one of the most rampant rebels in the country."[9]

Mostly, however, McLaughlin stumbled in the new environment after the war. Although he owned vast amounts of land in the Elk and Little Kanawha Rivers regions, debt strangled him and his partners, including former Virginia lieutenant governor and Confederate general William L. Jackson. Land investors and their agents—local lawyers and banks—gained control of the debts and forced the sale of over twenty-seven hundred acres of land to pay a debt of $403.[10] When McLaughlin died in 1872, the accolades that followed belied his lack of power at the time of his death. His estate foundered in his debts, and lawsuits picked away at his property.[11]

The cases of Stump, Woofter, Crim, Thompson, and McLaughlin give a sampling of the lives of West Virginia's hostages after the Civil War. They reveal fascinating aspects about the lives of these people, but the samplings show nothing striking about the relationship between the men's experiences as hostages and their postwar lives. As noted, evidence is scant about the personal lives of former hostages, but it seems that West Virginia's hostages were not unique in the ways in which they lived life after the hostilities were over. The Civil War impacted all West Virginians, and indeed all Americans. The burdens of death, physical and mental debility and disability, loss of loved ones, loss of property from sufferings on the battlefields, on the home front, and in the prisons were common among the people of the state and nation. Society shared them, often in silent understanding.

That is not to say that West Virginia's hostage law and its operation were not relevant following the war. They are still relevant. As history progresses, the experiences of West Virginia, its governor, and his hostages provide lessons in law and practicality, in power and its excesses. They teach about the dangers of personal violence and intimidation, not only to the victims, their families, and their communities, but to the instigators. Civil rights and civil liberties come under threat. Fine lines are crossed between the security of the state and the freedom of peoples to think and express themselves short of endangering their governments. Beyond these issues involving legitimate governments, additional problems arise when governments of questionable legitimacy are involved. West Virginia's hostage experience also contributed to the understanding of the role of state government versus the national government in the United States. Within the body of political and legal precedent that added to the notion of federal supremacy during the Civil War, the edicts of the War Department and the rulings of John J. Jackson Jr.'s court about the state practice of hostage-taking limited state powers in wartime, not just as they relate to hostages but as a whole. They also accelerated the demise of hostage-taking by the United States in general as the American military reflected inwardly upon the validity and usefulness of the practice.

In the endgame, the value of pawns was limited. Their play proved risky and distracting from the true aim of the game.

APPENDIX

# A Chronology of Hostages and Hostage-Taking in Civil War Western Virginia and West Virginia

The following timeline places hostage-taking in context with the broader history of secession and the Civil War in western Virginia and West Virginia. It includes events in the hostage saga (in italics) as well as pivotal political and military events and smaller, more localized military and paramilitary actions directly related to hostage-taking and the settings in which it took place.

## 1860

November 6—Abraham Lincoln elected president.
November 12—First antisecession convention in Virginia held in Preston County.
November 15—Gov. John Letcher called general assembly into session in response to secession crisis.

## 1861

January 1—John J. Jackson and Arthur I. Boreman addressed large Union meeting in Parkersburg.
January 5—Mass "Workingmen's Union Meeting" held in Wheeling.
January 7—Virginia General Assembly convened in answer to governor's call.
January 14—Virginia General Assembly called for state convention.
February 4—Voters elected delegates to state convention.
February 4—George W. Summers of Kanawha County attended Peace Conference in Washington.
February 13—State Convention assembled in Richmond.
March 4—Waitman T. Willey spoke against secession at Richmond Convention.

March 19—Convention's Committee on Federal Relations called for compromise and federal restraint.

April 4—Richmond Convention voted against secession, 45–85, but remained in session.

April 12—Fort Sumter was fired upon.

April 15—President Lincoln called for volunteers from the states.

April 16—Former governor Henry A. Wise convened a Southern rights conference in Richmond.

April 16—Virginia troops seized federal arsenal at Harpers Ferry and Gosport Naval Yard at Norfolk.

April 17—Richmond Convention voted 88–55 in favor of secession.

April 19—Governor Letcher appointed Robert E. Lee to command Virginia's armed forces.

April 20—Pro-Union delegates to Richmond Convention met and decided to leave convention.

April 22—Call from meeting in Clarksburg for statewide pro-Union convention in Wheeling.

April 22—Francis H. Pierpont challenges secessionists at meeting in Morgantown.

April 24—Virginia entered into treaty with Confederate States of America.

April 26—Former governor Joseph Johnson led Southern rights meeting in Clarksburg.

May 1—Governor Letcher called out state militia.

May 1—Union troops crossed Ohio River into Virginia.

May 4—Confederate forces dispatched to Grafton.

May 13—First Wheeling Convention met.

May 23—Statewide referendum favored secession; majority of western counties opposed.

May 30—Union troops occupied Fairmont and Grafton after Confederates withdrew from Grafton to Philippi.

June 3—Col. Benjamin F. Kelley routed Confederates at Philippi.

June 11—Second Wheeling Convention convened.

June 19—Second Wheeling Convention reorganized government of Virginia in favor of Union.

July 1—Pro-Union general assembly convened in extraordinary session.

July 6—Confederate general Henry A. Wise occupied Charleston.

July 8—Union troops overran Confederates under Robert S. Garnett at Laurel Hill in Barbour County.

July 9—Union general Jacob D. Cox invaded Kanawha Valley.

July 11—Forces under George B. McClellan flanked Confederates at Rich Mountain in Randolph County.

July 25—Confederates abandoned Charleston.

*July 29—Pro-Union leader Thomas A. Roberts arrested by Confederates in Roane County.*

August 12—Confederates under Robert E. Lee failed to solidify position at Cheat Mountain in Randolph and Pocahontas Counties.

August 20—Second Wheeling Convention authorized election on creation of new state from western Virginia.

September 10—Battle of Carnifex Ferry; William S. Rosecrans forced Confederate withdrawal from Kanawha Valley to Greenbrier County.

September 22—Confederates moved forward to Sewell Mountain on Fayette-Greenbrier County line.

October 20—Confederates withdrew from Sewell Mountain.

October 24—Voters approved creation of new state and elected delegates to constitutional convention.

November 26—State constitutional convention met in Wheeling.

## 1862

January 1—Stonewall Jackson moved against B&O Railroad and Potomac region.

April 3—Voters approved West Virginia Constitution.

May 12—Gen. George Crook's Union forces occupied Lewisburg.

May 13—Virginia (US) General Assembly approved creation of West Virginia.

May 23—Union troops in Lewisburg repelled attack from Gen. Henry Heth.

May 27—State elections ended the provisional status of the Restored Government of Virginia.

*May 30—Major Joseph Darr, provost marshal at Wheeling, ordered arrest of George W. Thompson and seven others.*

July 14—US Senate passed the West Virginia Statehood Bill, 23–17.

*August—State legislator James H. Trout arrested by Confederates in Hampshire County.*

*August—Pro-Confederate horse-theft ring heightened partisan tensions in Doddridge County.*

*August 8—Confederate government began efforts to exchange George W. Thompson for a Union sutler in its custody.*

August 24—Confederate general Albert G. Jenkins started a raid from Monroe County toward Ohio River.

September 1—Confederate general W. W. Loring invaded Kanawha Valley.

*September 23—George W. Thompson released from Camp Chase.*

*October 3—Judge Advocate Levi C. Turner ordered Provost Marshal Joseph Darr not to harass George W. Thompson.*

October 8—As Union forces massed at Clarksburg and Point Pleasant, Loring pulled back to Lewisburg.

October 16—Gen. John Echols relieved Loring of command and pressed back toward Charleston.

October 29—Union forced Echols out of Charleston.

December 10—US House of Representatives approved the statehood bill, 96–55.

December 31—President Lincoln signed the statehood bill.

## 1863

*January 4—Barbour County sheriff James Trahern captured by Confederates.*

*January 13—Governor Pierpont called for passage of hostage law.*

*February 3—Hostage bill passed Virginia (US) House of Delegates.*

*February 4—Hostage bill passed state senate and enacted into law.*

February 12—State constitutional convention reconvened to provide for gradual end of slavery as stipulated by Congress in its approval of statehood.

March 20—Confederate general Albert G. Jenkins left Dublin on expedition through Kanawha Valley toward Point Pleasant.

March 26—Voters approved gradual emancipation in state constitution.

March 28—Jenkins's force engaged Union troops at Hurricane Bridge in Putnam County and eventually bypassed them.

April 20—President Lincoln issued proclamation declaring that West Virginia statehood would occur in sixty days.

April 20—Brig. Gen. John D. Imboden left Augusta County on his prong of the Jones-Imboden Raid.

April 21—Brig. Gen. William E. Jones started from near Harrisonburg on his leg of the Jones-Imboden Raid.

*April 24—Confederate scouts captured Randolph Countians George Bradley, James McCall, and William S. Phares.*

April 24—Imboden captured Beverly.

April 26—Jones attacked Rowlesburg in Preston County.

April 27—Morgantown surrendered to Jones.

*April 28—George W. Thompson arrested and placed in Atheneum.*

April 29—Jones destroyed railroad bridge in Fairmont.

April 29—Imboden occupied Buckhannon.

*May 1—Maj. Joseph Darr ordered arrest of George Buchanon in Ohio County.*

May 2—Jones occupied Philippi.

May 6—Union Party convention in Parkersburg nominated Judge Arthur I. Boreman of Parkersburg for governor of West Virginia.

May 6—Jones left Weston and moved toward Northwestern Railroad.

May 9—Jones's forces targeted oil fields on Little Kanawha River.

*May 14—Confederate troops swooped down on the home of Union captain Nimrod H. Hyer in Braxton County and took George D. Mollohan and four others captive.*

May 14—Jones and Imboden joined forces at Summersville as they headed back to Shenandoah Valley.

May 19—Confederates under Brig. Gen. John McCausland shelled Fayetteville but failed to take the town.

May 28—Arthur I. Boreman was elected governor of West Virginia without opposition on the ballot.

May 28—Berkeley and Jefferson Counties voted to join West Virginia.

June 7—Confederates destroyed rail bridges in Hampshire County preliminary to Gettysburg Campaign.

*June 17—Attorney Nathaniel Richardson petitioned federal court for release of George W. Thompson as hostage.*

*June 19—Federal Judge John J. Jackson Jr. began hearing on petition in Thompson case.*

June 20—West Virginia became a state, and Boreman was inaugurated as governor.

*June 21—Judge Jackson issued writ of habeas corpus for George W. Thompson.*

*June 27—Habeas corpus hearing held in Thompson case.*

June 29—Gen. William L. Jackson led twelve hundred Confederates toward Tygarts Valley.

*June 29—Federal court ordered release of George W. Thompson and ordered his exile from the state.*

July 2—W. W. Averell's men repulsed Jackson at Beverly in Randolph County.

*July 2—Barbour County militia colonel William Price fell into Confederate hands near Beverly.*

July 4—Averell pursued Jackson and routed his force at Huttonsville in Randolph County.

July 18—Confederate John Morgan entered state near Ravenswood on his raid across Indiana and Ohio.

*August 3—Belmont County, Ohio, sheriff arrested Francis H. Pierpont for false imprisonment of George W. Thompson.*

August 5—W. W. Averell moved through Hardy County on raid into Greenbrier Valley.

August 19—Union destroyed saltpeter works at Franklin.

August 22—Averell defeated Confederates at Huntersville in Pocahontas County during protracted raid.

August 26—Union force killed three bushwhackers near Sutton.

August 26–27—Battle of White Sulphur Springs, Greenbrier County, ended in draw, and Averell withdrew to Beverly.

August 27—Union troops killed four guerrillas near Glenville.

August 27—Union troops pushed back guerrilla attack on Elk River.

September 4—Union detachment lost skirmish between Moorefield and Petersburg.

September 11—McNeill's Rangers surprised infiltrating Union battalion near Moorefield and took 138 prisoners.

*September 11—Confederate cavalry raided Troy, Gilmer County, and took four civilians and two soldiers captive.*

September 20—Confederates surprised Union outpost on Shavers Mountain, Randolph County, and killed four.

*September 21—Fifteen hostages for Gilmer County captives arrived at Atheneum by order of Governor Boreman.*

*September 23—Governor Boreman ordered Alfred Hutton, Adam See, Andrew M. Wamsley, and Samuel L. Wamsley taken as hostages for George Bradley and William S. Phares in Randolph County.*

*September 23—Gilmer County hostage Abraham Bush offered to cross Confederate lines to negotiate release of Adam Gluck and Henry Messenger, who had been captured at Troy.*

September 25—Confederates ambushed and captured thirty of Averell's men on Cheat River east of Beverly.

*September 28—Alfred Yoakum filed affidavit in Hardy County asking for hostages for his son, Michael, whom McNeill's Rangers had taken away.*

*October 2—Concerted lobbying began to gain release of Gilmer County hostages.*

*October 9—Hostages from Randolph County arrived at Atheneum; Governor Boreman allowed Hutton and Andrew Wamsley to go to Richmond to seek release of Bradley and Phares.*

October 13–14—Union garrison at Bulltown in Braxton County staved off forces under Brig. Gen. William L. Jackson.

*October 27—Braxton County prisoner George D. Mollohan appealed to Governor Boreman from Castle Thunder to exchange him for a prisoner being held in Camp Chase.*

*October 27—Governor Boreman ordered the taking of John Johnson, John Brown, William McClaskey, and William Hill as hostages for John M. Corley in Barbour County.*

*October 30—Gilmer County residents Adam and Peter Heckert had returned from Confederate captivity.*

November 1—General Averell led twenty-five hundred men into Pocahontas County in coordination with Union force moving out of Charleston.

*November 2—A rise in pro-Confederate violence in Doddridge County led to a series of affidavits identifying culprits to state officials.*

*November 3—Randolph County hostage Alfred Hutton reported to Governor Boreman on negotiations in Richmond, noted release of George Bradley; Boreman freed Adam See and Andrew Wamsley.*

November 5—Averell defeated Confederates at Hillsboro, Pocahontas County.

*November 5—Union commanders in the Potomac region began a monthlong correspondence over propriety of Governor Boreman asking army to arrest state hostages.*

November 6—Echols lost control of Greenbrier Valley to Averell in the Battle of Droop Mountain in Pocahontas County.

*November 10—Hostage Andrew M. Wamsley arrived in Randolph County with George Bradley after Bradley's release by the Confederates.*

November 12—Union again destroyed saltpeter works at Franklin.

*November 12—Barbour Countians called for seizure of hostages for William Price.*

November 15—Imboden sent company into Barbour County to disrupt wagon traffic.

November 16—McNeill attacked Union wagon train at Burlington, Hampshire County.

*November 19—Charges against Francis H. Pierpont dropped in Belmont County, Ohio.*

*November 19—George D. Mollohan's son, Harrison, a Union soldier, filed an affidavit to allow hostages to be taken for his father.*

*November 19—Lorenzo D. Dolbeare, J. N. B. Crim, Hiram Smith, John P. Thompson, and William McClaskey taken as hostages for William Price in Barbour County.*

*November 24—Governor Boreman ordered Braxton County residents Adison McLoughlin and John Laurence to be taken as hostages for George D. Mollohan.*

*November 28—Governor Boreman directed second order for arrest of hostages for Michael Yoakum to a state independent scout captain in Pendleton County.*

*November 28—Hostages requested for Samuel M. Day and John Greenawalt, who were taken by Confederates in Pendleton County; Joel Siples, Andrew W. Dyer, and Robert Phares were held.*

*November 30—A flurry of appeals from Barbour County sought release of hostage John P. Thompson for health reasons.*

*December 5—John Laurence arrived in Wheeling as a hostage for George D. Mollohan.*

December 8—Averell left New Creek on raid against Salem, Virginia.

December 11—William L. Jackson suffered defeat at Marlins Bottom, Pocahontas County.

December 16—Averell launched daring raid to destroy Virginia and Tennessee Railroad in southwestern Virginia.

*December 22—Governor Boreman released Barbour County hostages J. N. B. Crim and Hiram Smith.*

*December 27—Doddridge County Justice of the Peace Jacob Yeater called for hostages to be taken in retaliation for pro-Confederate terrorism in the county.*

## 1864

January 2—Gen. Fitzhugh Lee invaded the South Branch Valley.

January 3—Lee besieged Petersburg.

*January 4—A second petition from Doddridge County called for taking hostages in response to pro-Confederate activity.*

January 6—Fitzhugh Lee captured Romney.

January 6—McNeill captured Springfield, Hampshire County.

*January 20—Robert E. Lee ordered Imboden to release Hardy County Unionist Michael Yoakum from captivity.*

*January 20—In his annual message to the legislature, Governor Boreman called for use of the hostage law as a preemptive rather than punitive measure.*

*January 21—Petition calling for exile of George Buchanon prompted army investigation into his status as a captive in the Atheneum.*

*January 25—Putnam County sheriff William H. Shaw arrived in Libby Prison.*

*January 29—Nine hostages for Sheriff Shaw arrived in Wheeling from Putnam County.*

*January 30—Braxton County hostage John Laurence returned from Richmond to Wheeling with freed captive George D. Mollohan.*

January 30—Confederates captured a large wagon train in Hampshire County.

January 31—Union troops pulled back from Petersburg toward New Creek.

February 1—Jubal Early attacked Petersburg.

February 2—Confederates destroyed railroad bridges on North Branch of Potomac.

February 11—Confederates captured Gen. E. P. Scammon aboard steamer on Kanawha River in Putnam County.

February 11—Confederates derailed B&O train on Berkeley-Jefferson County line and robbed passengers.

*February 12—Union soldiers from Gilmer County called upon governor to take additional hostages for Adam Gluck and Henry Messenger, who remained in Libby Prison.*

*February 15—George Buchanon pleaded to commander of Atheneum to know the reason for his captivity and for chance to work toward his release.*

*February 16—Governor Boreman ordered five hostages taken for Thomas Hill and Ducket Gatrell, who were taken by Confederates from Doddridge County.*

*February 25—Lt. Jesse F. Snodgrass arrested two hostages for Hill and Gatrell.*

March 3—Union once again destroyed rebuilt saltpeter works at Franklin.

March 3—Union patrol lost seven men and thirteen horses in attack near Petersburg.

*March 5—US Army condemned prison hospital at Atheneum.*

*March 16—Hostages Alexander Handley, John Handley, and Jesse Timms traveled to Richmond to seek release of Sheriff Shaw of Putnam County.*

March 16–18—Union cavalry carefully probed Wayne and Cabell Counties in aftermath of capture of Confederate colonel Milton Ferguson and thirty-nine of his men.

*March 17—Wayne County Unionist John Adams taken by Confederates, prompting Governor Boreman to order three hostages held for him. Adams was later found dead.*

*March 19—Confederate troopers took West Virginia legislators Aaron Bechtol and Joseph S. Wheat captive along with Robert Finn and Thomas Shives in Berkeley Springs.*

*March 19—Doubts arose over disloyalty of Doddridge County hostage William M Bonnell.*

March 20—Union home guards killed three guerrillas at Sinks of Gandy, Randolph County.

*March 25—Governor Boreman asked Berkeley Springs Postmaster Simeon S. Buzzerd for recommendations for hostages for the four men taken from the town.*

*March 26—Petitioners called for release of Doddridge County hostage Thomas Swagger.*

*April 10—Hostage George Buchanon died from illness in Atheneum.*

*April 16—Sheriff Shaw released from prison in Richmond.*

*April 16 Five hostages sent to Wheeling for Unionists captured in Berkeley Springs.*

*April 21—Sheriff Shaw reported to officials in Wheeling, and Boreman ordered the release of his hostages.*

*April 21—Governor Boreman allowed hostages Robert Y. Conrad and A. Stephen Dandridge to travel to Richmond to negotiate release of Bechtol, Wheat, and their comrades.*

*April 23—Philip Williams, A. H. H. Boyd, and Nathan White, hostages for Berkeley Springs captives, asked Boreman for parole but were denied.*

May 2—Union general George Crook launched a raid from Charleston through Fayette, Raleigh, Wyoming, and Mercer Counties against saltworks at Saltville, Virginia.

*May 2—Confederate War Department ordered release of Bechtol, Wheat, Finn, and Shives.*

May 3—Confederates captured and burned fort at Bulltown.

May 4—McNeill captured Piedmont in Hampshire County and took 104 prisoners.

May 8—Confederates failed to take Union outpost at Halltown, Jefferson County.

May 9—General Crook fought a battle at Cloyds Mountain near Salem, Virginia, against Confederate general Albert G. Jenkins; Jenkins was killed.

May 10—Imboden defeated Ringgold Cavalry at Lost River Gap, Hardy County.

May 11—Imboden occupied Romney.

May 15—Union expedition in Elk River region captured thirty-six guerrillas.

*May 17—Conrad and Dandridge reported to Boreman on the release of the Berkeley County prisoners from Confederate custody.*

May 24—Mosby's Rangers lost skirmish near Charles Town.

June 6—Union company defeated Confederates at Moorefield.

June 17—Gen. David Hunter moved into Potomac region in attempt to head off Early's northern excursion.

June 19—McNeill's Rangers suffered heavy losses in attack on Union scouts in Pendleton County.

June 26—McNeill defeated a superior Union force at Springfield, Hampshire County.

*June 26—Berkeley Springs prisoners left Richmond under military escort.*

*July Gilmer County resident Henry Messenger died in Andersonville.*

July 3—Part of Early's army overcame Union opposition at Leetown, Jefferson County, as it pushed toward Chambersburg, Pennsylvania.

July 4—Imboden failed to take blockhouse and bridge on South Branch in Hampshire County.

July 4—McNeill burned railroad bridge over Patterson Creek, Hampshire County.

July 4—Union repulsed attack on North Branch Bridge, Hampshire County.

July 4–8—Confederates failed to capture Harpers Ferry after a four-day siege.

July 6—Imboden burned rail station at Sir Johns Run, Morgan County.

July 6—Union forces drove Imboden away from Big Capon Bridge, Morgan County.

*July 9—Governor Boreman released hostages for Bechtol, Wheat, Finn, and Shives.*

*July 10—Union leaders in Wayne and Cabell Counties petitioned for release of hostages taken for John Adams.*

July 14—McNeill recaptured Romney for Confederates.

July 25—Confederates defeated Gen. George Crook at Bunker Hill, Berkeley County.

July 25—Early's forces took Martinsburg.

August 2—Confederate general Bradley T. Johnson captured Green Spring, Hampshire County during Confederate withdrawal from Chambersburg, Pennsylvania.

August 2—McNeill destroyed rail culverts between New Creek in Hampshire County and Cumberland, Maryland.

August 2—General Early cut suspension bridge over South Branch near Springfield.

August 4—Generals Johnson and McCausland failed to take New Creek from Union.

August 7—General Averell intercepted Gen. John McCausland at Moorefield.

August 22—Gen. Philip Sheridan defeated Confederates at Halltown.

August 29—Sheridan defeated part of Early's force at Charles Town.

September 1—Averell withdrew from Early at Martinsburg.

September 2—Confederate cavalry defeated Averell at Bunker Hill.

September 18—Sheridan occupied Martinsburg.

September 19—Sheridan defeated Early at Winchester.

September 22—Col. Vincent A. "Clawhammer" Witcher left Lewisburg on a raid to gather horses for the Confederacy.

September 24—Big Sandy Rangers raided pro-Union town of Ceredo, Wayne County.

*October—Gilmer County resident Adam Gluck died in Andersonville.*

October 26—A newly established Union outpost at Winfield resisted a fierce Confederate attack.

October 27—Voters reelected Arthur I. Boreman as governor without opposition.

November 1—McNeill's Rangers took thirty prisoners at Green Spring, Hampshire County.

November 7—Union defeated McNeill's men at Moorefield.

November 8—West Virginians chose Abraham Lincoln for president over George B. McClellan, 23,152–10,438.

November 10—Capt. John H. McNeill died from wounds near Harrisonburg, Virginia; his son, Jesse, succeeded him in command.

November 27–28—Union failed to dislodge Confederates under Gen. Thomas L. Rosser from Moorefield.

November 28—Rosser overwhelmed Union garrison at New Creek and took civilian prisoners, prompting calls for hostages.

November 28—Confederates lost at Piedmont.

## 1865

*January 8—Atheneum guards accidentally shot a Wheeling teenager and mistakenly arrested a business owner while pursuing escapees.*

*January 10—McNeill's Rangers targeted West Virginia state scouts in their homes in Hardy County and killed two men, including Michael Yoakum.*

January 11—Union scouting party probed from New Creek into Pendleton County.

January 15—Union force defeated McNeill at Petersburg.

February 3—State legislature abolished slavery in West Virginia.

February 21—Confederate guerrillas captured Union generals George Crook and Benjamin F. Kelley in Cumberland, Maryland.

February 25—Legislature passed test oath for voters to ensure loyalty to state and Union.

*March 1—Samuel M. Day of Pendleton County was released from Confederate prison in Salisbury. North Carolina, and died later in month in hospital in Baltimore.*

March 15—Union company defeated guerrillas south of Moorefield.

March 22—Union defeated McNeill on Patterson Creek in Hampshire County.

March 30—McNeill derailed and robbed train on Patterson Creek.

May 8—McNeill surrendered at Romney.

*June 6—Last Confederate prisoners left Atheneum.*

*September 26—US Army closed Atheneum military prison.*

1866

May 24—Voters approved constitutional amendment to disenfranchise ex-Confederates.

October 25—Governor Boreman won reelection against US Attorney Benjamin H. Smith.

1867

*March 9—Former Atheneum commander E. W. Over gave affidavit in lawsuit of George Buchanon estate against Arthur I. Boreman.*

*October 14—Ohio County Circuit Court began hearing Buchanon suit, which dragged on due to procedural issues.*

1868

*May 12—Ohio County Circuit Court continued Buchanon case until December term.*

*October 10—Atheneum building destroyed by fire.*

October 22—Senate president William E. Stevenson elected governor over oil baron Johnson N. Camden.

*October 22—Reelection of Ohio County Circuit Judge Elbert H. Caldwell disputed; Governor Boreman had charge of resolving dispute.*

November 3—Ulysses S. Grant won state in presidential race.

*December 3—Ohio County Circuit Court convened and ruled that statute of limitation had expired in Buchanon case.*

## 1869

February 27—Arthur I. Boreman became US senator; state senate president Daniel D. T. Farnsworth assumed governorship until Stevenson took office on March 4.

## 1870

January 18—Governor Stevenson urged removal of restrictions on ex-Confederates.

February 7—Legislature abolished test oath for attorneys and teachers.

April 1—State capital switched from Wheeling to Charleston.

October 27—Governor Stevenson lost reelection to Democrat John J. Jacob.

## 1871

March 6—Supreme Court sustained 1863 transfer of Berkeley and Jefferson Counties from Virginia to West Virginia, essentially ratifying constitutionality of state's creation.

April 17—Voters ratified the Flick Amendment to state constitution, which removed restrictions on ex-Confederates and sustained the right of African American men to vote.

*August 7—Federal Judge John J. Jackson Jr. dismissed Buchanon lawsuit for lack of jurisdiction.*

August 24—Voters called for constitutional convention.

## 1872

January 16—Democrats and former Confederates dominated constitutional convention as it convened.

August 22—Voters ratified new West Virginia constitution.

October 8—Running as an independent, Gov. John J. Jacob won reelection against Democrat Johnson N. Camden with Republican support.

November 5—West Virginia favored Ulysses S. Grant in his reelection bid.

# Notes

## INTRODUCTION

1. "Death of a Prisoner," *Wheeling Daily Intelligencer,* Apr. 12, 1864.
2. "Pleasant Hill," CWSAC Battle Summaries.
3. Herrmann and Palmieri, "A Haunting Figure," 135–36.
4. Yang, "Hostages in Chinese History," 507.
5. Moscovich, "Obsidibus Traditis," 122–23; Moscovich, "Hostage Regulations in the Treaty of Zama," 417–18.
6. Hammer and Salvin, "The Taking of Hostages in Theory and Practice," 21–23.
7. Hening, *The Statutes at Large,* 1:396.
8. Hening, *The Statutes at Large,* 2:193.
9. US Congress, "Treaty with the Six Nations: 1784."
10. Igler, "Captive-Taking and Conventions of Encounters on the Northwest Coast, 1789–1810," 7–8.
11. US Dept. of War, "General Orders No. 100: The Lieber Code."
12. Neely Jr., *The Fate of Liberty,* 153.
13. Garrison, *Civil War Hostages,* 47.
14. "Death of a Prisoner," *Wheeling Daily Register,* Apr. 13, 1864.

## 1. THE ROOTS OF DIVISION AND ANIMOSITY IN VIRGINIA AND WEST VIRGINIA, 1787–1861

1. McPherson, *Battle Cry of Freedom,* 293–97.
2. McPherson, *Battle Cry of Freedom,* 285–89; Randall and Donald, *Civil War and Reconstruction,* 232–33.
3. McPherson, *Battle Cry of Freedom,* 290–93.
4. "Gov. Andrew Johnson, of Tennessee, and the Guerillas," *Wheeling Daily Intelligencer,* May 19, 1862.
5. Ambler, *Sectionalism in Virginia,* 3.
6. Ambler, *Sectionalism in Virginia,* 3.

7. Sarris, *A Separate Civil War*, 7.
8. Gooden, "The Completion of a Revolution," xi–xiii.
9. Davis and Robertson, *Virginia at War*, vii.
10. *Leesburg (VA) Genius of Liberty*, Aug 2–9, 1825.
11. Virginia, *Proceedings and Debates of the Virginia State Convention of 1829–30*, 882, 903.
12. Ambler, *Sectionalism in Virginia*, 165.
13. "Convention," *Richmond Enquirer*, July 22, 1845.
14. Callahan, *Semi-Centennial History of West Virginia*, 134.
15. Ambler, *Sectionalism in Virginia*, 187.
16. *Encyclopedia Virginia*, s.v. "The Virginia Slavery Debate of 1831–1832."
17. Ambler, *Sectionalism in Virginia*, 192.
18. "To the People of Western Virginia," *Richmond Whig*, Dec. 1, 1831.
19. Ambler, *Sectionalism in Virginia*, 199.
20. Green, *Constitutional Development in the South Atlantic States*, 287–88.
21. Ruffner, *Address to the People of West Virginia*, 5 and 40.
22. Chandler, *Representation in Virginia*, 51–60.
23. Chandler, *Representation in Virginia*, 51–60.
24. Virginia, General Assembly, House of Delegates, *Journal of the House of Delegates, 1852*, 11 and 13.
25. "Democratic Convention: Second Day," *Richmond Daily Dispatch*, Dec. 6, 1854.
26. Heinemann, Kolp, Parent, and Shade, *Old Dominion, New Commonwealth*, 212.
27. *Richmond Daily Dispatch*, Dec. 10, 1855.
28. Bean, "John Letcher and the Slavery Issue," 27 and 35.
29. "Frank H. Peirpoint, Esq.," *Pruntytown (VA) Family Visitor*, Mar. 31, 1860.
30. "The Union and Frank Pierpoint's Speech," *Wheeling Daily Intelligencer*, May 24, 1860.
31. *Wheeling Daily Intelligencer*, July 27 and Dec. 29, 1860; Atkinson and Gibbens, *Prominent Men of West Virginia*, 509.
32. *Richmond Enquirer*, Jan. 24, 1860*; Staunton (VA) Spectator*, Feb. 28 and Mar. 13, 1860; *Alexandria (VA) Gazette*, May 4, 1860.
33. *Alexandria (VA) Gazette*, Jan. 9 and 15, 1860; *Richmond Daily Dispatch*, Jan. 14, 15 and 18, 1860.
34. Freehling and Simpson, *Showdown in Virginia*, x–xi.
35. Williams, *West Virginia*, 57–58.
36. Williams, *West Virginia*, 46–47.
37. Majewski, "The Political Impact of Great Commercial Cities," 2, 4, 14, and 20.
38. Majewski, "The Political Impact of Great Commercial Cities," 17.
39. "Editorial Correspondence," *Pruntytown (VA) Family Visitor*, Apr. 13, 1860.
40. Crawford, *Ashe County's Civil War*, 8–9.
41. Stewart, "Introduction," 2–3.
42. Hornbeck, *Upshur Brothers of the Blue and the Gray*, 16.
43. Crawford, *Ashe County's Civil War*, 13.
44. Peirce, *The Border South States*, 152.
45. Paludan, *Victims*, 56–57.
46. Groce, *Mountain Rebels*, 66–67.
47. Crawford, *Ashe County's Civil War*, 13–14.

## 2. PRO-UNION VIRGINIA AND THE MOVE TOWARD HOSTAGE-TAKING, 1861–63

1. "Our Wheeling Correspondence," *New York Herald*, June 18, 1861.
2. "Dust," *Wheeling Daily Intelligencer*, June 17, 1861.
3. Gooden, "The Completion of a Revolution," 11–12.
4. "The Wheeling Convention," *Harper's Weekly*, July 6, 1861, 418.
5. Gooden, "The Completion of a Revolution," 12.
6. Lewis, *How West Virginia Was Made*, 140.
7. Ambler, *Francis H. Pierpont*, 78.
8. *Wheeling Daily Intelligencer*, Jan. 15 and 18, Mar. 23, and Apr. 18, 1861.
9. "Another Grand Rally in Monongalia," *Wheeling Daily Intelligencer*, Apr. 29, 1861.
10. *Wheeling Daily Intelligencer*, May 6, 1861.
11. *Wheeling Daily Intelligencer*, May 6, 1861.
12. *Wheeling Daily Intelligencer*, May 13, 15, and 18, 1861.
13. Lewis, *How West Virginia Was Made*, 145; "Virginia Convention," *Wheeling Daily Intelligencer*, June 21, 1861.
14. Lewis, *How West Virginia Was Made*, 134.
15. Lewis, *How West Virginia Was Made*, 135, 156.
16. Groce, *Mountain Rebels*, 113.
17. Gooden, "The Completion of a Revolution," 13–15.
18. Gooden, "The Completion of a Revolution," 15–17.
19. "More Money Wanted," *Richmond Enquirer*, Oct. 3, 1861.
20. Francis H. Pierpont Papers, West Virginia Dept. of Archives and History.
21. "Gov. Peirpoint's Message to the Senate and House of Delegates," *Wheeling Daily Intelligencer*, July 3, 1861.
22. Gooden, "The Completion of a Revolution," 38.
23. Bishop, *History of Roane County*, 103–5.
24. Bishop, *History of Roane County*, 642; *Wheeling Daily Intelligencer*, Nov. 2 and 4, 1861, and Jan. 13, 1863.
25. Bishop, *History of Roane County*, 642; *Wheeling Daily Intelligencer*, Nov. 2 and 4, 1861, and Jan. 13, 1863.
26. US Dept. of War, *War of the Rebellion*, ser. 2, 4:848, 855, 876; 5:216–17, 6:317–19; "Escape of Dr. Rucker," *Richmond Daily Dispatch*, Oct. 20, 1863.
27. *Wheeling Daily Intelligencer*, Jan. 13, 1863.
28. "An Extraordinary Letter," *Point Pleasant (VA) Weekly Register*, Mar. 27, 1862.
29. US Dept. of War, *War of the Rebellion*, ser. 2, 2:246–47, 258.
30. US Dept. of War, *War of the Rebellion*, ser. 2, 270.
31. US Dept. of War, *War of the Rebellion*, ser. 2, 3:427; *Wheeling Daily Intelligencer*, Mar. 29, May 23, June 17, and Dec. 30, 1862; *Point Pleasant (VA) Weekly Register*, May 29, June 19, 1862, and Jan. 31, 1863.
32. Blair, *With Malice toward Some*, 100, 104–5.
33. *Hillsborough (OH) Highland News*, June 4, 1857; *Wheeling Daily Intelligencer*, Dec. 5, 1861.
34. US Dept. of War, *War of the Rebellion*, ser. 2, 4:422.
35. US Dept. of War, *War of the Rebellion*, ser. 2, 2:260, 3:644.
36. US Dept. of War, *War of the Rebellion*, ser. 2, 4:196, 641.
37. Blair, *With Malice toward Some*, 106.

38. Blair, *With Malice toward Some,* 4:254.

39. *Wheeling Daily Intelligencer,* Jan. 13, 1863; Maxwell and Swisher, *History of Hampshire County,* 144–45.

40. "Shall the Union Men Be Protected?" *Wheeling Daily Intelligencer,* May 23, 1862.

41. *Wheeling Daily Intelligencer,* Dec. 4, 1862.

42. Virginia (US), General Assembly, House of Delegates, *Journal of the House of Delegates, 1862,* 13.

43. *Wheeling Daily Intelligencer,* Jan. 24, 1863, 1; Maxwell, *History of Barbour County,* 267.

44. Atkinson and Gibbens, *Prominent Men of West Virginia,* 161; Wiley, *History of Preston County,* 440, 442.

45. "Virginia Legislature," *Wheeling Daily Intelligencer,* Jan. 13, 1863; Virginia (US), General Assembly, House of Delegates, *Journal of the House of Delegates;* Atkinson and Gibbens, *Prominent Men of West Virginia,* 959.

46. Atkinson and Gibbens, *Prominent Men of West Virginia,* 314–15; Hornbeck, *Upshur Brothers of the Blue and the Gray,* 16.

47. Virginia (US), General Assembly, House of Delegates, *Journal of the House of Delegates,* 101.

48. Virginia (US), General Assembly, House of Delegates, *Journal of the House of Delegates,* 101.

49. Virginia (US), General Assembly, House of Delegates, *Journal of the House of Delegates,* 101.

50. *Wheeling Daily Intelligencer,* Jan. 15, 1863; Atkinson and Gibbens, *Prominent Men of West Virginia,* 392.

51. "Virginia Legislature," *Wheeling Daily Intelligencer,* Feb. 2, 1863; Atkinson and Gibbens, *Prominent Men of West Virginia,* 370.

52. "Virginia Legislature," *Wheeling Daily Intelligencer,* Feb. 2, 1863; Virginia (US), General Assembly, House of Delegates, *Journal of the House of Delegates,* 177; Atkinson and Gibbens, *Prominent Men of West Virginia,* 332.

53. "Virginia Legislature," *Wheeling Daily Intelligencer,* Feb. 2, 1863; Atkinson and Gibbens, *Prominent Men of West Virginia,* 327.

54. "Virginia Legislature," *Wheeling Daily Intelligencer,* Feb. 2, 1863; Atkinson and Gibbens, *Prominent Men of West Virginia,* 52; Maxwell, *History of Tucker County,* 342–43.

55. "Virginia Legislature," *Wheeling Daily Intelligencer,* Feb. 2, 1863.

56. "Virginia Legislature," *Wheeling Daily Intelligencer,* Feb. 2, 1863.

57. Virginia (US), General Assembly, House of Delegates, *Journal of the House of Delegates,* 189; Wiley, *History of Monongalia County,* 144, 166, 580; *Wheeling Daily Intelligencer,* May 7, 1862, 2.

58. Virginia (US), General Assembly, *Journal of the Senate, . . . 1862,* 121, 126; Ambler, Atwood and Mathews, *Debates and Proceedings of the First Constitutional Convention of West Virginia,* 1:26.

59. Virginia (US), *Acts of the General Assembly of the State of Virginia,* chap. 66.

60. Virginia (US), *Acts of the General Assembly of the State of Virginia,* chap. 67, no. 15; *Wheeling Daily Intelligencer,* Jan. 29 and Feb. 5–6, 1863.

61. Ersland, *Civil War Provost Marshal Records,* 4.

62. *Alexandria (VA) Gazette,* Feb. 24, 1863.

63. Davis, *Bits of Gossip,* 116–17.

## 3. JUDGE GEORGE W. THOMPSON, GOVERNOR PIERPONT, AND THE FIRST HOSTAGE CASE

1. *Wheeling Daily Intelligencer*, Jan. 1, 1861.

2. "The Workingmen's Union Meeting at the Atheneum on Saturday Night," *Wheeling Daily Intelligencer*, Jan. 7, 1861; *The West Virginia Encyclopedia*, s.v. "Atheneum Prison."

3. W. I. Boreman to F. H. Pierpont, Apr. 25, 1861, Francis H. Pierpont Papers, West Virginia and Regional History Center.

4. Maxwell, *History of Randolph County*, 147; *Wheeling Daily Intelligencer*, May 8 and 20, 1861.

5. *Wheeling Daily Intelligencer*, May 17, 1861.

6. Hall, *Rending of Virginia*, 229–30.

7. Maxwell, *History of Randolph County*, 147–48; "Proclamation of Judge Thompson," *Wheeling Daily Intelligencer*, May 28, 1861.

8. "Judge Thompson's Pronunciamento," *Wheeling Daily Intelligencer*, May 28, 1861.

9. *Wheeling Daily Intelligencer*, June 18, 1861; *Richmond Enquirer*, Aug. 6, 1861.

10. *Richmond Enquirer*, Aug. 6, 1861.

11. "Judge Thompson's Pronunciamento," *Wheeling Daily Intelligencer*, July 8, 1861.

12. "Some Observations on the Above Production," *Wheeling Daily Intelligencer*, July 8, 1861.

13. "Judge Thompson," *Wheeling Daily Intelligencer*, July 2, 1863.

14. George W. Thompson to Col. James Washburn, Mar. 3, 1865, image 611, United States, "United States Union Provost Marshals' File of Papers Relating to Individual Civilians."

15. *Wheeling Daily Intelligencer*, July 10, 1861; Lewis, *How West Virginia Was Made*, 154, 202, 298.

16. "Judge Thompson in the Lower Counties," *Wheeling Daily Intelligencer*, Aug. 1, 1861.

17. "Federal Court," *Wheeling Daily Intelligencer*, Sept. 16, 1861.

18. "Our Correspondence," *Richmond Daily Dispatch*, Sept. 12, 1861.

19. Atkinson and Gibbens, *Prominent Men of West Virginia*, 782; Stutler, *West Virginia in the Civil War*, 136–40; US Dept. of War, *War of the Rebellion*, ser. 1, 5:460–63.

20. *Richmond Daily Dispatch*, Jan. 15, 1862.

21. *Wheeling Daily Intelligencer*, May 31 and June 2, 1862; *Alexandria (VA) Gazette*, June 5, 1862.

22. *Wheeling Daily Intelligencer*, June 2, 5, and 6, 1862.

23. "Political Martyrs in and about Wheeling, and Especially the Ex-Judge," *Wheeling Daily Intelligencer*, June 11, 1862.

24. Summers, *Johnson Newlon Camden*, 84, 87, 90, 104–5, and 112.

25. George W. Thompson to Col. James Washburn, Mar. 3, 1865.

26. "Local Matters," *Richmond Daily Dispatch*, Aug. 8, 1862.

27. United States, "United States Records of Confederate Prisoners of War."

28. *Wheeling Daily Intelligencer*, Sept. 25, 1862, and July 1, 1863.

29. L. C. Turner to Jos. Darr, Sept. 29, 1862, image 596, United States, "United States Union Provost Marshals' File of Papers Relating to Individual Civilians."

30. George W. Thompson, Wheeling, to Col. James Washburn, Mar. 3, 1865.

31. L. C. Turner to Jos. Darr Jr., Oct. 3, 1862, image 84, United States, "United States Union Provost Marshals' File of Papers Relating to Individual Civilians."
32. "Judge Thompson's Return," *Wheeling Daily Intelligencer,* Sept. 26, 1862.
33. *Wheeling Daily Intelligencer,* Feb. 7 and 14, 1863.
34. "A Correspondence," *Alexandria (VA) Gazette,* Feb. 3, 1863.
35. US Dept. of War, *War of the Rebellion,* ser. 1, 21:1102.
36. Woodward, "Arthur Ingraham Boreman," 54–55.
37. US Dept. of War, *War of the Rebellion,* ser. 1, 25:652, 660–61.
38. Wingerter, *History of Greater Wheeling and Vicinity,* 213.
39. *Wheeling Daily Intelligencer,* Apr. 28, 29, 30 and May 1, 4, 14, 1863.
40. Lawrence, *Border and Bastille,* 164.
41. Blair, *With Malice toward Some,* 114.
42. *Wheeling Daily Intelligencer,* July 1, 1863.
43. US Dept. of War, *War of the Rebellion,* ser. 2, 5:545.
44. US Dept. of War, *War of the Rebellion,* ser. 2, 5:548.
45. L. C. Turner to Joseph Darr Jr., May 4, 1863, image 59, United States, "United States Union Provost Marshals' File of Papers Relating to Individual Civilians."
46. Blair, *With Malice toward Some,* 101.
47. Blair, *With Malice toward Some,* 100–101.
48. George W. Thompson, Wheeling, to Col. James Washburn, Mar. 3, 1865.
49. *Wheeling Daily Intelligencer,* June 18 and July 1, 1863.
50. "United States District Court," *Wheeling Daily Intelligencer,* June 19, 1863.
51. "Federal Court," *Wheeling Daily Intelligencer,* June 20, 1863.
52. "Federal Court," *Wheeling Daily Intelligencer,* June 24, 1863.
53. "Federal Court," *Wheeling Daily Intelligencer,* June 29, 1863.
54. "Federal Court," *Wheeling Daily Intelligencer,* June 29, 1863.
55. "Federal Court," *Wheeling Daily Intelligencer,* June 29, 1863.
56. "Federal Court," *Wheeling Daily Intelligencer,* June 29, 1863.
57. "Federal Court," *Wheeling Daily Intelligencer,* June 29, 1863.
58. "Federal Court," *Wheeling Daily Intelligencer,* June 29, 1863.
59. "Federal Court," *Wheeling Daily Intelligencer,* June 30, 1863.
60. Atkinson and Gibbens, *Prominent Men of West Virginia,* 165.
61. "The Habeas Corpus Writ in the Case of Judge Thompson—Decision of Judge Jackson—The Alternative Presented to the Prisoner," *Wheeling Daily Intelligencer,* July 1, 1863.
62. "The Habeas Corpus Writ in the Case of Judge Thompson—Decision of Judge Jackson—The Alternative Presented to the Prisoner," *Wheeling Daily Intelligencer,* July 1, 1863.
63. "The Habeas Corpus Writ in the Case of Judge Thompson—Decision of Judge Jackson—The Alternative Presented to the Prisoner," *Wheeling Daily Intelligencer,* July 1, 1863.
64. "The Habeas Corpus Writ in the Case of Judge Thompson—Decision of Judge Jackson—The Alternative Presented to the Prisoner," *Wheeling Daily Intelligencer,* July 1, 1863.
65. "Review of Judge Jackson's Opinion in the Case of Geo. W. Thompson," *Wheeling Daily Intelligencer,* July 16, 1863.
66. "Review of Judge Jackson's Opinion in the Case of Geo. W. Thompson," *Wheeling Daily Intelligencer,* July 16, 1863.
67. "Review of Judge Jackson's Opinion in the Case of Geo. W. Thompson," *Wheeling Daily Intelligencer,* July 16, 1863.

68. "Review of Judge Jackson's Opinion in the Case of Geo. W. Thompson," *Wheeling Daily Intelligencer*, July 16, 1863.

69. "Gov. Peirpoint Arrested," *Wheeling Daily Intelligencer*, Aug. 5, 1863.

70. "Gov. Peirpoint Arrested," *Wheeling Daily Intelligencer*, Aug. 5, 1863.

71. *Morgantown (WV) Monitor*, Aug. 22, 1863.

72. "Arrest of Gov. Pierpont," *Columbus Ohio Statesman*, Aug. 8, 1863.

73. *Wheeling Daily Intelligencer*, Nov. 4 and 19, 1863; Louis H. Pelouze to commander at Wheeling, July 16, 1864, image 586, United States, "United States Union Provost Marshals' File of Papers Relating to Individual Civilians"; George W. Thompson, Wheeling, to Col. James Washburn, Mar. 3, 1865.

74. US Dept. of War, *War of the Rebellion*, ser. 2, 6:160–61.

## 4. THE NEW STATE AND HOSTAGE-TAKING AFTER THE JONES-IMBODEN RAID OF 1863

1. *Wheeling Daily Intelligencer*, May 9 and 11, 1863.

2. Lewis, *The Industrialist and the Mountaineer*, 43.

3. *Wheeling Daily Intelligencer*, May 9, 1863.

4. *Wheeling Daily Intelligencer*, May 26, 1863.

5. *Wheeling Daily Intelligencer*, May 9, 1863.

6. Maxwell, *History of Randolph County*, 156–58; Wiley, *History of Preston County*, 169–70.

7. Maxwell, *History of Randolph County*, 156–58.

8. US Dept. of War, *War of the Rebellion*, ser. 1, 25:98–105, 113–15, 134, 142; Wiley, *History of Monongalia County*, 150; Wiley, *History of Preston County*, 171–73.

9. Thacker, *French Harding Civil War Memoirs*, 89–90, 94.

10. Thacker, *French Harding Civil War Memoirs*, 89.

11. United States, "United States Census, 1860," images 1–130 of 130.

12. Thacker, *French Harding Civil War Memoirs*, 90.

13. Diary and Letters of Rutherford B. Hayes.

14. *Wheeling Daily Intelligencer*, Feb. 24, 1863.

15. US Dept. of War, *War of the Rebellion*, ser. 1, 25:103–4, 478.

16. Mollohan, *By the Banks of the Holly*, 348.

17. *Wheeling Daily Intelligencer*, July 2, 1862.

18. Sutton, *History of Braxton County*, 195; United States, "United States Census, 1860."

19. Sutton, *History of Braxton County*, 194–200.

20. Sutton, *History of Braxton County*, 134, 137, 178–84; United States, "United States Census, 1850"; United States, "United States Census, 1860."

21. George D. Mollohan to Arthur I. Boreman, Oct. 27, 1863, Arthur I. Boreman Papers.

22. US Dept. of War, *War of the Rebellion*, ser. 3, 3:224–25.

23. *Wheeling Daily Intelligencer*, June 13, 1863.

24. *Wheeling Daily Intelligencer*, June 22, 1863.

25. *Wheeling Daily Intelligencer*, June 22, 1863.

26. Wittenberg, Sargus, and Barrick, *Seceding from Secession*, 186.

27. "West Virginia Legislature," *Wheeling Daily Intelligencer*, June 24, 1863.

28. "West Virginia Legislature," *Wheeling Daily Intelligencer*, June 24, 1863.

29. "West Virginia Legislature," *Wheeling Daily Intelligencer*, June 24, 1863.

30. US Dept. of War, *War of the Rebellion,* ser. 1, 27:300.
31. US Dept. of War, *War of the Rebellion,* ser. 1, 25:502, 527.
32. US Dept. of War, *War of the Rebellion,* ser. 1, 27:300, 576; *Wheeling Daily Intelligencer,* June 26, 1863.
33. Warrant for the Seizure of Andrew M. Wamsley and Adam See as Hostages, Sept. 23, 1863, Arthur I. Boreman Papers.
34. Warrant for the Seizure of Andrew M. Wamsley and Adam See as Hostages, Sept. 23, 1863, Arthur I. Boreman Papers.
35. Cranmer, *History of Wheeling City and Ohio County,* 716.
36. Warrant for the Seizure of Andrew M. Wamsley and Adam See as Hostages, Sept. 23, 1863, Arthur I. Boreman Papers; Warrant for the Seizure of Alfred Hutton and Samuel Wamsley as Hostages, n.d., Arthur I. Boreman Papers.
37. *Wheeling Daily Register,* Oct. 10, 1863.
38. United States, "United States Census, 1860"; Bosworth, *History of Randolph County,* 71, 75.
39. Hutton, "Roster of Confederate Veterans from Randolph County," 83.
40. United States, "United States Census, 1870"; Maxwell, *History of Randolph County,* 475.
41. United States, "United States Census, 1860."
42. Maxwell, *History of Randolph County,* 394–98; Hutton, "Roster of Confederate Veterans from Randolph County," 76, 80.
43. United States, "United States Union Provost Marshal Files of Individual Civilians," image 1305, https://www.familysearch.org/ark:/61903/3:1:939X-FQ1Y-5?i=1304&wc=M6Y2-1WL%3A162306601&cc=1834304.
44. , https://www.familysearch.org/ark:/61903/3:1:939X-FQ1Y-G?i=1300&wc=M6Y2-1WL%3A162306601&cc=1834304
45. Thacker, *French Harding Civil War Memoirs,* 126, 183.
46. United States, "United States Census, 1860."
47. Bosworth, *History of Randolph County West Virginia,* 75.
48. Louis A. Myers to N. Wilkinson, Oct. 1, 1863, Arthur I. Boreman Papers.
49. *Wheeling Daily Intelligencer,* Nov. 2, 1863.
50. Alfred Hutton to Gov. A. I. Boreman, Nov. 3, 1863, Arthur I. Boreman Papers.
51. A. M. Wamsley to Gov. A. I. Boreman, Nov. 11, 1863, Arthur I. Boreman Papers.
52. A. M. Wamsley to Gov. A. I. Boreman, Nov. 11, 1863, Arthur I. Boreman Papers.
53. A. M. Wamsley to Gov. A. I. Boreman, Nov. 11, 1863, Arthur I. Boreman Papers.
54. George D. Mollohan to Arthur I. Boreman, Oct. 27, 1863, Arthur I. Boreman Papers.
55. *Wheeling Daily Intelligencer,* Apr. 28, 1862; Sutton, *History of Braxton County,* 203.
56. "A Returned Hostage," *Wheeling Daily Intelligencer,* Jan. 30, 1864.
57. Arthur I. Boreman to Col. W. Hoffman, Nov. 9, 1863, Arthur I. Boreman Papers; Affidavit Attesting to Capture of George D. Mollohan, Nov. 19, 1863, Arthur I. Boreman Papers.
58. Sutton, *History of Braxton County,* 54–55, 88, 282, 294, 404.
59. S. A. Rollyson to His Excellency Arthur I. Borman, Nov. 19, 1863, Arthur I. Boreman Papers.
60. Warrant for the Seizure of John Laurence and Adison McLoughlin as Hostages, Nov. 24, 1863, Arthur I. Boreman Papers.
61. Warrant for the Seizure of John Laurence and Adison McLoughlin as Hostages, Nov. 24, 1863, Arthur I. Boreman Papers.

62. Warrant for the Seizure of John Laurence and Adison McLoughlin as Hostages, Nov. 24, 1863, Arthur I. Boreman Papers.
63. A. Moor to His Excellency A. I. Boreman, Dec. 6, 1863.
64. *Wheeling Daily Register,* Dec. 5, 1863.
65. Sutton, *History of Braxton County,* 404; *Charles Town Virginia Free Press,* May 14, 1840; *Staunton (VA) Spectator and General Advertiser,* Apr. 14, 1842; *Richmond Enquirer,* June 10, 1845.
66. *Wheeling Daily Intelligencer,* Dec. 5, 1863.
67. Parole of John Lorentz, Dec. 4, 1863, Arthur I. Boreman Papers.
68. "A Returned Hostage," *Wheeling Daily Intelligencer,* Jan. 30, 1864.

## 5. HOSTAGE POLITICS IN BARBOUR COUNTY IN 1863

1. Shaffer, "Loyalties in Conflict: Union and Confederate Sentiment in Barbour County."
2. "A New Company from Barbour—The State of Things in that County," *Wheeling Daily Intelligencer,* Sept. 4, 1862.
3. Dayton, *Samuel Woods and His Family,* 6–7, 10.
4. Sutherland, "Guerrilla Warfare, Democracy, and the Fate of the Confederacy," 260–62.
5. "The Circumstances Attending the Abduction of Sheriff Trahorn of Barbour County," *Wheeling Daily Intelligencer,* Jan. 24, 1863.
6. Maxwell, *History of Barbour County,* 242–46, 371–72.
7. *Wheeling Daily Intelligencer,* Jan. 24 and 31, 1863; "Correspondence Between Milroy and General Imboden—Threats and Counter-Threats," *Staunton Spectator,* Feb. 3, 1863; Maxwell, *History of Barbour County,* 267.
8. "The Circumstances Attending the Abduction of Sheriff Trahorn of Barbour County," *Wheeling Daily Intelligencer,* Jan. 24 and 31, 1863.
9. Shaffer, *Clash of Loyalties,* 93.
10. US Dept. of War, *War of the Rebellion,* ser. 1, 27: 806–13.
11. Spencer Dayton to Hon. A. I. Boreman, Nov. 12, 1863, Arthur I. Boreman Papers.
12. US Dept. of War, *War of the Rebellion,* ser. 2, 6:378.
13. Affidavit of Spencer Dayton, Nov. 12, 1863, Arthur I. Boreman Papers.
14. Spencer Dayton to Hon. A. I. Boreman; A. I. Boreman to F. Howes, Oct. 27, 1863, Arthur I. Boreman Papers; Maxwell, *History of Barbour County,* 229, 247.
15. United States, "United States Census, 1850"; United States, "United States Census, 1860"; United States, Internal Revenue Assessment Lists for West Virginia, 1862–1866.
16. Cone and Duroch, "Don't Shoot the Ambulance: Medicine in the Crossfire," 65–77.
17. US Dept. of War, *War of the Rebellion,* ser. 2, 5:212.
18. Arthur I. Boreman Papers.
19. Arthur I. Boreman Papers.
20. Arthur I. Boreman Papers.
21. Arthur I. Boreman Papers.
22. Arthur I. Boreman Papers.
23. Maxwell, *History of Barbour County,* 210, 227, 230, 245, 280, 315.
24. Arthur I. Boreman Papers.
25. Maxwell, *History of Barbour County,* 441.

26. Maxwell, *History of Barbour County,* 301–5.
27. Arthur I. Boreman Papers.
28. Arthur I. Boreman Papers.
29. Arthur I. Boreman Papers.
30. Shaffer, *Union and Confederate Soldiers and Sympathizers of Barbour County,* 68.
31. Arthur I. Boreman Papers.
32. Arthur I. Boreman Papers.
33. Shaffer, *Union and Confederate Soldiers and Sympathizers of Barbour County,* 68; United States, "United States Census, 1870."
34. US IRS Tax Assessment Lists, 1862–1918 for LD Dolbeare..
35. United States, IRS Tax Assessment Lists, 1862–1918, District 1 Annual Lists May 1864.
36. Memorandum from Spencer Dayton to Arthur I. Boreman, n.d., Arthur I. Boreman Papers.
37. Memorandum from Spencer Dayton to Arthur I. Boreman, n.d., Arthur I. Boreman Papers.
38. Memorandum from Spencer Dayton to Arthur I. Boreman, n.d., Arthur I. Boreman Papers.
39. Maxwell, *History of Barbour County,* 310–11.
40. Gaskins, "An Introduction to the Guineas," 234–36.
41. Dayton, *Samuel Woods and His Family,* 6–7.

## 6. GUERRILLAS AND RETRIBUTION IN GILMER AND DODDRIDGE COUNTIES, 1863–64

1. "The Oil Region," *Wheeling Daily Intelligencer,* Dec. 9, 1864.
2. Stutler, *West Virginia in the Civil War,* 141.
3. Knotts and Stevens, *Calhoun County in the Civil War.*
4. US Dept. of War, *War of the Rebellion,* ser. 1, 27:886.
5. "Guerrilla Raid," *Wheeling Daily Register,* Sept. 14, 1863.
6. *Point Pleasant Daily Register,* Sept. 24, 1863; *Wheeling Daily Intelligencer,* Apr. 4, 1863; FamilySearch.org, passim.
7. Affidavit of David Heckert, Sept. 16, 1863, Arthur I. Boreman Papers; Order for Arrest of Hostages for Adam Heckert, Peter Heckert, Henry Messenger and Adam Gluck, Sept. 17, 1863, Arthur I. Boreman Papers; *Point Pleasant Daily Register,* Sept. 24, 1863; *Wheeling Daily Register,* Sept. 22, 1863.
8. Bond of Abraham Bush and George F. Bush, Sept. 23, 1863, Adjutant General's Papers, WV.
9. C. S. Lewis, Clarksburg, to Nathan Goff, Esq., Oct. 2, 1863, Arthur I. Boreman Papers; Atkinson and Gibbens, *Prominent Men of West Virginia,* 74, 390; Haymond, *History of Harrison County,* 379.
10. L. Haymond, Clarksburg, to N. Goff, Oct. 2, 1863, Arthur I. Boreman Papers.
11. John Irwin, Clarksburg, WV, to D. Haymond, Oct. 2, 1863, Arthur I. Boreman Papers; Atkinson and Gibbens, *Prominent Men of West Virginia,* 55.
12. John Bennett to F. P. Pierpoint, Oct. 26, 1863, Adjutant General's Papers; A. I. Boreman to Capt. W. L. Thorp, Dec. 9, 1863, United States, "United States Union Provost Marshal Files of Individual Citizens."

13. *Wheeling Daily Intelligencer,* Oct. 30, Dec. 9, 1863; George K. Cox to A. I. Boreman, July 21, 1863, Adjutant General's Papers; Letter of George K. Cox, Dec. 15, 1863, Adjutant General's Papers.

14. *Wheeling Daily Intelligencer,* Oct. 30, 1863.

15. G. H. McQuain, William W. Yerkey, John Woofter, John Wolf, Joseph M. Wood, George F. Bush, Edgar M. Wolf, and William Wright to A. I. Boreman, Jan. 13, 1864, Arthur I. Boreman Papers.

16. Larkin Peirpoint to Jos. Darr, Nov. 19, 1862, United States, "United States Union Provost Marshal Files of Individual Citizens."

17. T. M. Harris, to Major Darr, Nov. 19, 1862, United States, "United States Union Provost Marshal Files of Individual Citizens."

18. Larkin Peirpoint to Jos. Darr, Nov. 19, 1862, United States, "United States Union Provost Marshal Files of Individual Citizens."

19. Petition to A. I. Boreman, Feb. 12, 1864, Arthur I. Boreman Papers.

20. J. C. Gluck to A. I. Boreman, Feb. 13, 1864, Arthur I. Boreman Papers; Atkinson and Gibbens, *Prominent Men of West Virginia,* 949.

21. *A List of Federal Prisoners Buried at Andersonville,* 72.

22. *Wheeling Daily Intelligencer,* Nov. 10, 1863.

23. *Wheeling Daily Intelligencer,* Apr. 15, 1862.

24. United States, Civil War Prisoner of War Records, 1861–1865. e

25. Affidavit of Matilda Williams, Nov. 2, 1863, Arthur I. Boreman Papers.

26. United States Civil War Soldiers Index, 1861–1865..

27. McKinney, "Women's Role in Civil War North Carolina," 38.

28. Affidavit of Matilda Williams.

29. United State Civil War Soldiers Index, 1861–1865.

30. Affidavit of Martha E. Kile, Nov. 2, 1863, Arthur I. Boreman Papers.

31. Affidavit of Nancy Ann Kile, Nov. 2, 1863, Arthur I. Boreman Papers.

32. Affidavit of Ruth Bates, Nov. 2, 1863, Arthur I. Boreman Papers.

33. Affidavit of Belinda Booher, Nov. 2, 1863, Arthur I. Boreman Papers.

34. Affidavit of Elisa Ann Coffman, Nov. 2, 1863, Arthur I. Boreman Papers.

35. Affidavit of Susannah Coffman, Nov. 1863, Arthur I. Boreman Papers.

36. Affidavit of Sary Jane Shields, Nov. 2, 1863, Arthur. I. Boreman Papers.

37. Affidavit of Thomas Shields, Nov. 2, 1863, Arthur I. Boreman Papers.

38. Waller, *Feud,* 86.

39. Jacob Yeater to Jesse F. Snodgrass, Nov. 10, 1863, Arthur I. Boreman Papers.

40. "Ratification Meeting in the Fourth Ward," *Wheeling Daily Intelligencer,* Jan. 22, 1864.

41. Jacob Yeater to Lt. J. F. Snodgrass, Jan. 21, 1864, Arthur I. Boreman Papers.

42. Petition from Loyal Citizens of Doddridge County to His Excellency A. I. Borman, Dec. 27, 1863, Arthur I. Boreman Papers.

43. Jacob Yeater to Lt. J. F. Snodgrass, Jan. 21, 1864, Arthur I. Boreman Papers.

44. Petition from Citizens of Doddridge and Adjoining Counties to His Excellency Gov. A. I. Boreman, Jan. 4, 1864, Arthur I. Boreman Papers.

45. Waller, *Feud.*

46. Waller, *Feud.*

47. Affidavit of Jesse F. Snodgrass, Feb. 16, 1864, Arthur I. Boreman Papers.

48. "From Libby Prison," *Wheeling Daily Intelligencer,* Nov. 23, 1863.

49. US Dept. of War, *Official Record of the War of the Rebellion,* ser. 2, 6:918.

50. "From Libby Prison," *Wheeling Daily Intelligencer,* Nov. 23, 1863.

51. "From Libby Prison," *Wheeling Daily Intelligencer,* Nov. 23, 1863.

52. Order to Seize Hostages for Thomas Hill and Ducket Gatrell, Feb. 16, 1864, Arthur I. Boreman Papers.

53. *Cooper's Clarksburg (VA) Register,* July 20, 1853.

54. *Cooper's Clarksburg (VA) Register,* Apr. 2, Sept. 10–17, 1858.

55. Order to Seize Hostages for Thomas Hill and Ducket Gatrell, Feb. 16, 1864, Arthur I. Boreman Papers.

56. Jacob Yeater to Lt. J. F. Snodgrass, Mar. 19, 1864, Arthur I. Boreman Papers.

57. Affidavit of Andrew J. Bates and Vincent A. Glover, Mar. 19, 1864, Arthur I. Boreman Papers.

58. Petition from Doddridge County, West Virginia, to His Excellency A. I. Borman, Mar. 26, 1864, Arthur I Boreman Papers.

59. Affidavit of Jacob Yeater, Joshua Allen, and Stephen J. Allen, Mar. 19, 1864, Arthur I. Boreman Papers.

60. Jacob Yeater to His Excelence [*sic*] A. I. Boreman, Mar. 28, 1864, Arthur I. Boreman Papers.

61. Jacob Yeater to J. F. Snodgrass, Mar. 28, 1864, Arthur I. Boreman Papers.

62. Certificates of Mary Beverline, Dorcas Prunty, Sarah Loughry, and Elizabeth Allen, Apr. 20, 1864, Arthur I. Boreman Papers.

63. C. J. Stuart, Floyd Neely, and B. H. Maulsby to His Excellency Gov. Boreman, Arthur I. Boreman Papers.

64. US Dept. of War, *War of the Rebellion,* ser. 2, 6:918.

65. United States, Union Provost Marshals' Papers, 1861–1867.

## 7. REBEL RANGERS, UNION SCOUTS, AND HOSTAGES ON THE SOUTH BRANCH

1. "The Highlands of Virginia," *Washington Evening Star,* May 14, 1856.

2. *South Branch Intelligencer* (Romney, VA), Feb. 1, 1861.

3. *South Branch Intelligencer* (Romney, VA), Feb. 1, 1861.

4. "History of the Fifth Va.," *Knapsack* (Gauley Bridge, VA), Sept. 10, 1863.

5. "From the Mountain Department," *Wheeling Daily Intelligencer,* May 21, 1862.

6. "Guerilla Organizations," *Wheeling Daily Intelligencer,* May 20, 1862.

7. Bright, "McNeill's Rangers," 338–87; *Glasgow (MO) Weekly Times,* Oct. 19, 1854; *History of Daviess County,* 676.

8. US Dept. of War, *War of the Rebellion,* ser. 1, 21:1086.

9. US Dept. of War, *War of the Rebellion,* ser. 1, 25:656.

10. "Another Train Captured," *Wheeling Daily Intelligencer,* Feb. 20, 1863.

11. US Dept. of War, *War of the Rebellion,* ser. 1, 29:105–6.

12. US Dept. of War, *War of the Rebellion,* ser. 1, 29:105–6.

13. J. Thoburn, to Lt. M. J. Russell, Nov. 5, 1863, Arthur I. Boreman Papers.

14. Hardy County Militia Files, West Virginia, Office of Adjutant General, Adjutant General's Papers, passim.

15. Affidavit of Alfred Yoakum, Sept. 28, 1863, Warrant for Arrest of Hostages for Michael Yoakum, Oct. 1, 1863, Arthur I. Boreman Papers.

16. Family Search, www.familysearch.org., passim.

17. Warrant for Arrest of Hostages for Michael Yoakum, Oct. 1, 1863, Arthur I. Boreman Papers.

18. J. Thoburn to Lt. M. J. Russell, Nov. 5, 1863, Arthur I. Boreman Papers.
19. Jas. A. Mulligan to Dept. Headquarters, Nov. 6, 1863, Arthur I. Boreman Papers.
20. Jas. A. Mulligan to Dept. Headquarters, Nov. 6, 1863, Arthur I. Boreman Papers.
21. T. Melvin to Col. Mulligan, Nov. 21, 1863, Arthur I. Boreman Papers.
22. J. Thoburn to Lt. M. J. Russell, Dec. 1, 1863, Arthur I. Boreman Papers.
23. J. Thoburn to Lt. M. J. Russell, Nov. 5, 1863, Arthur I. Boreman Papers.
24. T. Melvin to Colonel Mulligan, Dec. 4, 1863, Arthur I. Boreman Papers.
25. Family Search, www.familysearch.org., passim.
26. Family Search, www.familysearch.org., passim.
27. A. I. Boreman to Capt. E. C. Harper, Nov. 28, 1863, West Virginia, Office of Adjutant General, Adjutant General's Papers.
28. E. C. Harper to Governor Boreman, Jan. 16, 1864, West Virginia, Office of Adjutant General, Adjutant General's Papers.
29. Statement of William C. Van Meter, Dec. 15, 1863, Arthur I. Boreman Papers.
30. J. Thoburn to Lt. M. J. Russell, Nov. 5, 1863, Arthur I. Boreman Papers.
31. J. Thoburn to Lt. M. J. Russell, Nov. 5, 1863, Arthur I. Boreman Papers.
32. US Dept. of War, *War of the Rebellion,* ser. 2, 6:862.
33. Ambler, Atwood, and Mathews, *Debates and Proceedings of the First Constitutional Convention of West Virginia,* 1:70.
34. "A Narrow Escape," *Wheeling Daily Intelligencer,* May 27, 1863.
35. "Hunting Down a Union Man," *Wheeling Daily Intelligencer,* June 1, 1863.
36. *Wheeling Daily Intelligencer,* "From Pendleton County, June 6, 1863.
37. *Wheeling Daily Intelligencer,* May 27 and Aug. 20, 1863.
38. F. P. Pierpoint to Capt. E. C. Harper, Nov. 28, 1863, West Virginia, Office of Adjutant General, Adjutant General's Papers (this letter is misfiled in militia correspondence for Gilmer County). .
39. Affidavits from Pendleton County, Arthur I. Boreman Papers; United States, "United States Census, 1860."
40. Morton, *History of Pendleton County,* 127, 364.
41. "More About the Late New Creek Raid," *Wheeling Daily Intelligencer,* Dec. 7, 1864.
42. James Carskadon, New Creek, to Gov. A. I. Boreman, Nov. 30, 1864, Arthur I. Boreman Papers.
43. Atkinson and Gibbens, *Prominent Men of West Virginia,* 64, 434.
44. Affidavit of James Carskadon, Dec. 8, 1864, Arthur I. Boreman Papers.
45. Affidavit of James Carskadon, Dec. 8, 1864, Arthur I. Boreman Papers.
46. Tho. P. Adams to A. I. Boreman, Dec. 8, 1864, Arthur I. Boreman Papers.
47. *Wheeling Daily Intelligencer,* 1863–64, passim; Atkinson and Gibbens, *Prominent Men of West Virginia,* 399.
48. Affidavit of Geo. W. Tuxworth and John Hughes, Dec. 8, 1864, Arthur I. Boreman Papers.
49. Affidavit of Geo. W. Tuxworth and John Hughes, Dec. 8, 1864, Arthur I. Boreman Papers.
50. James Rohrbaugh to F. P. Pierpoint, Jan. 15, 1865, West Virginia, Office of Adjutant General, Adjutant General's Papers. 1
51. "Capture of Swamp Dragons," *Richmond Enquirer,* Jan. 24, 1865.
52. Bright, "McNeill's Rangers," 338–87.
53. United States, Compiled Service Records of Volunteer Union Soldiers.
54. "Poetical," *South Branch Intelligencer* (Romney, WV), Jan. 19, 1866.

## 8. THE PLIGHT OF SOUTHWESTERN WEST VIRGINIA IN 1864

1. "Governor's Message," *Wheeling Daily Register*, Jan. 21, 1864.
2. "Rebel Raid," *Wheeling Daily Register*, Jan. 12, 1864.
3. US Dept. of War, *War of the Rebellion*, ser. 1, 33:111.
4. "Guerrillas," *Wheeling Daily Intelligencer*, Jan. 29, 1864.
5. "Governor's Message," *Wheeling Daily Register*, Jan. 21, 1864.
6. "Governor's Message," *Wheeling Daily Register*, Jan. 21, 1864.
7. Petition from Joseph C. Gary and Other Putnam County Residents, 1864, Arthur I. Boreman Papers; "Arrival of Hostages," *Wheeling Daily Intelligencer*, Feb. 1, 1864.
8. *Alexandria (Virginia) Gazette*, Apr. 26, 1864.
9. "Arrival of Hostages," *Wheeling Daily Intelligencer*, Feb. 1, 1864.
10. Petition from Joseph C. Gary and Other Putnam County Residents, Arthur I. Boreman Papers.
11. Petition of John W. English and Others, Point Pleasant, WV, Mar. 9, 1864, Arthur I. Boreman Papers.
12. Petition of John W. English and Others, Point Pleasant, WV, Mar. 9, 1864, Arthur I. Boreman Papers; "Arrivals at the Libby," *Richmond Daily Dispatch*, Jan. 26, 1864.
13. US Dept. of War, *War of the Rebellion*, ser. 2, 6:875.
14. US Dept. of War, *War of the Rebellion*, 6:895–96.
15. Petition of John W. English and Others, Point Pleasant, WV, Mar. 9, 1864, Arthur I. Boreman Papers.
16. US Dept. of War, *War of the Rebellion*, 6:1048.
17. "The Legislature," *Staunton (VA) Spectator*, Mar. 15, 1864.
18. *Abingdon Virginian*, Jan. 22, 1864.
19. *Staunton Spectator*, Mar. 1, 1864.
20. "Address of the General Assembly to the Soldiers of Virginia," *Staunton Spectator*, Mar. 22, 1864.
21. "Confederate States Congress," *Richmond Whig*, Jan. 4, 1864.
22. US Dept. of War, *War of the Rebellion*, ser. 2, 6:810.
23. Warrant for Hostages for A. J. Stephenson, Nov. 28, 1863, Arthur I. Boreman Papers.
24. *Alexandria (VA) Gazette*, Mar. 19, 1864.
25. "Released," *Point Pleasant (WV) Weekly Register*, Apr. 21, 1864.
26. "The Hostage Business," *Wheeling Daily Register*, Apr. 23, 1864.
27. US Dept. of War, *War of the Rebellion*, ser. 1, 33:250–51.
28. "8 Virginia Cavalry, Confederate, Wayne Co. WV," http://files.usgwarchives.net/wv/wayne/military/8.txt.
29. Perkins, "Guerrilla Chieftain 'Rebel Bill' Smith, CSA."
30. John Adams, Find a Grave, https://www.findagrave.com/memorial/72397753/john-adams.
31. *Wheeling Daily Intelligencer*, Nov. 3, 1857.
32. Letter of John Adams, Ceredo, WV, Oct. 5, 1863, Wayne County Militia Files, West Virginia, Office of Adjutant General, Adjutant General's Papers.
33. Wayne County Militia Files, West Virginia, Office of Adjutant General, Adjutant General's Papers.
34. Petition of Benjamin R. Haley and Others, July 10, 1864, Arthur I. Boreman Papers.

35. “Released,” *Wheeling Daily Intelligencer*, July 29, 1864; B. D. McGinnis to Arthur I. Boreman, July 12, 1864, Arthur I. Boreman Papers.

36. Family Search, https://www.familysearch.org/search/record/results?q.givenName=John%20N.&q.surname=Smith&q.residencePlace=Wayne%20County%2C%20Virginia&f.recordCountry=United%20States&f.recordSubcountry=United%20States%2CVirginia&m.defaultFacets=on&m.queryRequireDefault=on&m.facetNestCollectionInCategory=on&count=20&offset=0.

37. Family Search, https://www.familysearch.org/search/record/results?q.givenName=William&q.surname=Stewart&q.residencePlace=Wayne%20County%2C%20Virginia&f.recordCountry=United%20States&f.recordSubcountry=United%20States%2CVirginia&count=20&offset=0&m.defaultFacets=on&m.queryRequireDefault=on&m.facetNestCollectionInCategory=on.

38. Results for Erbin Walker, Ancestry.com, https://www.ancestrylibrary.com/search/?name=Erbin_Walker&event=_wayne-west+virginia-usa_3103&pg=2&birth=1800.

39. Petition of Benjamin R. Haley and Others, July 10, 1864, Arthur I. Boreman Papers.

40. B. D. McGinnis to Arthur I. Boreman, July 12, 1864, Arthur I. Boreman Papers.

41. Petition of Cassander Spurlock and Others, Arthur I. Boreman Papers.

42. “Released,” *Wheeling Daily Intelligencer*, July 29, 1864.

43. “A Raid,” *Wheeling Daily Intelligencer*, Sept. 24, 1864.

44. *Wheeling Daily Intelligencer*, Nov. 12, 1864.

45. “Governor’s Message,” *Wheeling Daily Register*, Jan. 18, 1865.

46. “Giving Themselves Up,” *Wheeling Daily Intelligencer*, Jan. 18, 1865.

47. *Point Pleasant Weekly Register*, Mar. 2, 1865.

48. *Point Pleasant Weekly Register*, Mar. 2, 1865.

49. “Letter from Wayne County,” *Charleston West Virginia Journal*, Apr. 5, 1865.

## 9. THE UNION LEAGUE RAID IN BERKELEY SPRINGS IN 1864

1. *Annapolis Maryland Gazette*, June 19, 1784.

2. “Virginia Illustrated: Adventures of Porte Crayon and His Cousins,” 318.

3. “The Campaign in Morgan County,” *Richmond Daily Whig*, Oct. 13, 1860.

4. *Wheeling Daily Intelligencer*, Dec. 3, 1863.

5. *Wheeling Daily Intelligencer*, July 21, 1863.

6. Atkinson and Gibbens, *Prominent Men of West Virginia*, 103.

7. *Wheeling Daily Intelligencer*, Jan. 23, 1864; *Wheeling Daily Register*, Jan. 27, 1864.

8. Taylor, *The Most Complete Political Machine Ever Known*, 135.

9. *Wheeling Daily Intelligencer*, Apr. 23, May 5, 1863.

10. *Wheeling Daily Intelligencer*, Dec. 7, 1863, Sept. 17, 1864.

11. *Wheeling Daily Intelligencer*, Mar. 21 and 26, 1864.

12. US Dept. of War, *War of the Rebellion*, ser. 1, 33:701–3.

13. Lewis Allen to Hon. Arthur I. Boreman, Mar. 23, 1864, Arthur I. Boreman Papers.

14. “‘A Union League’ Broken Up,” *Richmond Enquirer*, Mar. 29, 1864.

15. O’Ferrall, *Forty Years of Active Service*, 89–90.

16. O’Ferrall, *Forty Years of Active Service*, 90.

17. O’Ferrall, *Forty Years of Active Service*, 91–92.

18. O'Ferrall, *Forty Years of Active Service*, 91.
19. *Wheeling Daily Intelligencer*, Mar. 24 and 26, 1864.
20. O'Ferrall, *Forty Years of Active Service*, 91.
21. US Dept. of War, *War of the Rebellion*, ser. 2, 6:1119–20.
22. US Dept. of War, *War of the Rebellion*, ser. 2, 6:1119–20.
23. US Dept. of War, *War of the Rebellion*, ser. 2, 6:1119–20.
24. S. S. Buzzerd to Arthur I. Boreman, Mar. 25, 1864, Arthur I. Boreman Papers.
25. Lewis Allen to Arthur I. Boreman, Mar. 23, 1864, Arthur I. Boreman Papers.
26. S. S. Buzzerd to Arthur I. Boreman, Mar. 25, 1864, Arthur I. Boreman Papers.
27. Family Search, https://www.familysearch.org/search/record/results?q.givenName=Adam%20Stephen&q.surname=Dandridge&q.birthLikePlace=Jefferson%20County%2C%20Virginia&q.birthLikeDate.from=1810&q.birthLikeDate.to=1820&f.recordCountry=United%20States&f.recordSubcountry=United%20States%2CVirginia&m.defaultFacets=on&m.queryRequireDefault=on&m.facetNestCollectionInCategory=on&count=20&offset=0.
28. Family Search, https://www.familysearch.org/search/record/results?q.givenName=Nathan&q.surname=White&q.birthLikePlace=Jefferson%2County%2C%20Virginia&q.birthLikeDate.from=1810&q.birthLikeDate.to=1820&frecordCountry=United%20States&f.recordSubcountry=United%20States%2CVirginia&count=20&offset=0&m.defaultFacets=on&m.queryRequireDefault=on&m.facetNestCollectionInCategory=on; Find a Grave, https://www.findagrave.com/memorial/40920696/nathan-smith-white.
29. *Richmond Daily Dispatch*, May 31, 1856; *Staunton Spectator*, Feb. 17, 1863; *Alexandria (VA) Gazette*, Dec. 26, 1865.
30. *Martinsburg (VA) Gazette*, Aug. 15, 1844, Dec. 21, 1848; *Richmond Daily Dispatch*, Aug. 10, 1853; *Alexandria (VA) Gazette*, Oct. 5, 1860.
31. Cartmell, *Shenandoah Valley Pioneers and Their Descendants*, 502.
32. S. S. Buzzerd to Arthur I. Boreman, Mar. 25, 1864, Arthur I. Boreman Papers.
33. Jones, *Southern Historical Society Papers*.
34. S. S. Buzzerd to Arthur I. Boreman, Mar. 25, 1864, Arthur I. Boreman Papers.
35. US Dept. of War, *War of the Rebellion*, ser. 2, 7:6–8.
36. US Dept. of War, *War of the Rebellion*, ser. 2, 7:6–8.
37. Affidavit of S. S. Buzzerd, Mar. 29, 1864, Arthur I. Boreman Papers.
38. A. I. Boreman to Military Authorities U.S. in the Department of West Virginia, Mar. 29, 1864, Arthur I. Boreman Papers.
39. Lt. Col. W. C. Starr to Arthur I. Boreman, Apr. 16, 1864, Arthur I. Boreman Papers.
40. Lt. Col. W. C. Starr to Arthur I. Boreman, Apr. 23, 1864, Arthur I. Boreman Papers.
41. D. H. Strother to A. I. Boreman, Apr. 16, 1864, Arthur I. Boreman Papers.
42. Paroles of Robert Y. Conrad and A. Stephen Dandridge, Apr. 21, 1864, Arthur I. Boreman Papers.
43. P. Williams, A. H. H. Boyd, N. S. White to Arthur I. Boreman, Apr. 23, 1864, Arthur I. Boreman Papers.
44. P. Williams, A. H. H. Boyd, N. S. White to Arthur I. Boreman, Apr. 30, 1864, Arthur I. Boreman Papers.
45. US Dept. of War, *War of the Rebellion*, ser. 2, 7:70–71.
46. O'Ferrall, *Forty Years of Active Service*, 181–83.
47. US Dept. of War, *War of the Rebellion*, ser. 2, 7:70–71.
48. US Dept. of War, *War of the Rebellion*, ser. 2, 7:70–71.

49. US Dept. of War, *War of the Rebellion,* ser. 2, 7:70–71.
50. US Dept. of War, *War of the Rebellion,* ser. 2, 7:70–71.
51. A. S. Dandridge to Governor Boreman, May 26, 1864, Arthur I. Boreman Papers.
52. Enclosures in Robert Y. Conrad to Arthur I. Boreman, May 17, 1864, Arthur I. Boreman Papers.
53. *Wheeling Daily Intelligencer,* June 1, 1864.
54. Robert Y. Conrad to Arthur I. Boreman, May 17, 1864, and A. S. Dandridge to Arthur I. Boreman, May 17, 1864, Arthur I. Boreman Papers.
55. Robert Y. Conrad to Arthur I. Boreman, May 17, 1864, and A. S. Dandridge to Arthur I. Boreman, May 17, 1864, Arthur I. Boreman Papers.
56. Enclosures in Robert Y. Conrad to Arthur I. Boreman, May 17, 1864, Arthur I. Boreman Papers.
57. Robert Y. Conrad to Arthur I. Boreman, May 17, 1864, Arthur I. Boreman Papers.
58. Robert Y. Conrad to Arthur I. Boreman, May 17, 1864, Arthur I. Boreman Papers.
59. A. S. Dandridge to Governor Boreman, May 26, 1864, Arthur I. Boreman Papers.
60. Ro. Ould to A. S. Dandridge, June 9, 1864, Arthur I. Boreman Papers.
61. "The West Virginia Patriots," *The Soldier's Journal* (Alexandria, VA), July 6, 1864.
62. *Wheeling Daily Intelligencer,* July 16, 1864.
63. *Wheeling Daily Intelligencer,* July 16, 1864.
64. Release Order, July 9, 1864, Arthur I. Boreman Papers.
65. "Released," *Wheeling Daily Intelligencer,* July 12, 1864; E. R. S. Canby to Franz Sigel, Apr. 30, 1864, Arthur I. Boreman Papers.
66. "The War News," *Richmond Daily Dispatch,* Nov. 16, 1864.
67. "Frederick County," *Richmond Daily Whig,* June 6, 1865.
68. "Virginia Election," *Alexandria (VA) Gazette,* Oct. 19, 1865; *Richmond Daily Whig,* Dec. 4, 1865.
69. "Death of Dr. Boyd," *Staunton Spectator and General Advertiser,* Dec. 26, 1865.
70. Cartmell, *Shenandoah Valley Pioneers and Their Descendants,* 503.

## 10. Governor Boreman and George Buchanon

1. "Death of a Prisoner," *Wheeling Daily Register,* Apr. 13, 1864.
2. *Wheeling Daily Register,* Sept. 22, 1864.
3. *Potter Journal* (Coudersport, PA), Feb. 16, 1860.
4. *Wheeling Daily Intelligencer,* May 3, 1861, Aug. 18, 1862, Feb. 4, Mar. 4, 1863.
5. *Wheeling Daily Intelligencer,* Aug. 22, 1863.
6. *Wheeling Daily Intelligencer,* Oct. 30, 1863.
7. A. I. Boreman to Capt. E. W. Over, Jan. 29, 1864, Arthur I. Boreman Papers.
8. Affidavits Against George Buchanon, 1863, Arthur I. Boreman Papers.
9. A. I. Boreman to Capt. E. W. Over, Jan. 29, 1864, Arthur I. Boreman Papers.
10. US Dept. of War, *War of the Rebellion,* ser. 2, 6:662–64.
11. Petition of W. J. Alexander and Others to Col. Darr, and Capt. Stone, United States, "United States Union Provost Marshal Files of Individual Civilians, 1861–1866."
12. E. W. Over to Lt. Col. Jos. Darr Jr., Jan. 21, 1864, United States, "United States Union Provost Marshal Files of Individual Civilians, 1861–1866."
13. E. W. Over, Jan. 21, 1864, United States, "United States Union Provost Marshal Files of Individual Civilians, 1861–1866."
14. A. I. Boreman to Capt. E. W. Over, Jan. 29, 1864, Arthur I. Boreman Papers.
15. E. W. Over to Col. William Hoffman, Jan. 30, 1864, Arthur I. Boreman Papers.

16. W. Hoffman to Capt. E. Over, Feb. 6, 1864, Arthur I. Boreman Papers.
17. George Buchanon to Capt. Over, Feb. 15, 1864, Arthur I. Boreman Papers.
18. *Wheeling Daily Register,* Mar. 7, 1864.
19. *Wheeling Daily Intelligencer,* Mar. 31, 1864.
20. Darel Peck to A. I. Boreman, Jan. 1870, Arthur I. Boreman Papers.
21. "Death of a Prisoner," *Wheeling Daily Intelligencer,* Apr. 12, 1864.
22. "Treatment of Prisoners," *Wheeling Daily Register,* Feb. 17, 1865.
23. *Wheeling Daily Register,* Mar. 29 and 31, Apr. 8, 1864.
24. "Treatment of Prisoners," *Wheeling Daily Register,* Feb. 17, 1865.
25. *Wheeling Daily Intelligencer,* Mar. 27, 1865.
26. "The Prisoners at the Atheneum," *Wheeling Daily Register,* Apr. 19, 1864; *Wheeling Daily Intelligencer,* Mar. 27, 1865.
27. *Wheeling Daily Intelligencer,* July 12, 1864.
28. *Wheeling Daily Register,* Jan. 27, 1865.
29. *Wheeling Daily Register,* Jan. 7, 1865.
30. *Wheeling Daily Register,* Jan. 9, 1865.
31. United States, "United States Union Provost Marshal Files of Two or More Civilians, 1861–1866."
32. *Wheeling Daily Intelligencer,* May 19 and 30, June 7 and 26–27, July 17, 1865.
33. "The Wheeling Atheneum Prison Discontinued," *Wheeling Daily Intelligencer,* Sept. 27, 1865.
34. *Wheeling Daily Intelligencer,* Oct. 17 and 25, 1865, Jan. 9, 1866.
35. Gooden, "Neither War nor Peace," 213.
36. Gooden, "Neither War nor Peace," 219.
37. *Wheeling Daily Register,* June 18, 1868, July 15, 1870.
38. *Wheeling Daily Register,* Jan. 11, 1868.
39. Buchanon Suit Files, Arthur I. Boreman Papers.
40. Buchanon Suit Files, Arthur I. Boreman Papers.
41. Buchanon Suit Files, Arthur I. Boreman Papers.
42. E. W. Over to Gov. Boreman, Mar. 9, 1867, Arthur I. Boreman Papers.
43. Deposition of E. W. Over, Arthur I. Boreman Papers.
44. Buchanon Suit Files, Arthur I. Boreman Papers.
45. Buchanon Suit Files, Arthur I. Boreman Papers.
46. Atkinson, *Bench and Bar of West Virginia,* 147–48; Newton, Sprankle, and Nichols, *History of the Panhandle,* 266.
47. Buchanon Suit Files, Arthur I. Boreman Papers.
48. Atkinson, *Bench and Bar of West Virginia,* 23–24, 119.
49. West Virginia, Law Trial Docket (1867–69), 74, 100, 126.
50. West Virginia, *Acts of the West Virginia Legislature of 1868,* chap. 185.
51. West Virginia, Law Trial Docket.
52. Stealey, *West Virginia's Civil War–Era Constitution,* 133.
53. *Wheeling Daily Intelligencer,* Oct. 12, 1868.
54. *Wheeling Daily Intelligencer,* Dec. 23, 1868.
55. West Virginia, Law Trial Docket.
56. *Wheeling Daily Intelligencer,* Dec. 23, 1868.
57. Stealey, *West Virginia's Civil War–Era Constitution.*
58. Buchanon Suit Files.
59. Stealey, *West Virginia's Civil War–Era Constitution.*
60. *Wheeling Daily Intelligencer,* May 13, 1871.

61. *Wheeling Daily Intelligencer*, Jan. 16, 1871.
62. US Congress, *Congressional Globe*, 42nd Cong., 2nd sess., 3189.
63. Fones-Wolf, "A House Redivided," 238.

## EPILOGUE

1. Inscoe, "A Northern Wedge Thrust into the Heart of the Confederacy," 323–24.
2. Sandow, "Grudges and Loyalties Die So Slowly," 269.
3. Sarris, *A Separate Civil War*, 172.
4. *Wheeling Register*, July 24, 1897; *Calhoun Chronicle* (Grantsville, WV), July 16, 1901, Sept. 19, 1911, Oct. 10, 1911.
5. *Cooper's Clarksburg (VA) Register*, July 11, 1855; *Weston (WV) Democrat*, Nov. 23, 1870, Dec. 15, 1873; *Wheeling Daily Register*, Aug. 31, 1871.
6. *Wheeling Daily Intelligencer*, Mar. 11, 1886.
7. Shaffer, *Clash of Loyalties*, 153–74.
8. *Wheeling Daily Intelligencer*, Feb. 25, 1888; Atkinson, *Prominent Men of West Virginia*, 824–27, 834–35, 848–50.
9. *Wheeling Daily Register*, Oct. 15, 1869.
10. *Weston (WV) Democrat*, Jan. 10, 1870.
11. *Weston (WV) Democrat*, June 17, 1872, Apr. 20–Aug. 3, 1874.

# Bibliography

## BOOKS


Ambler, Charles H. *Francis H. Pierpont: Union War Governor of Virginia and Father of West Virginia.* Chapel Hill: Univ. of North Carolina Press, 1937.

———. *Sectionalism in Virginia from 1776 to 1861.* Chicago: Univ. of Chicago Press, 1910.

Ambler, Charles H., Frances Haney Atwood, and William B. Mathews, eds. *Debates and Proceedings of the First Constitutional Convention of West Virginia (1861–1863).* Huntington, WV: Gentry Brothers, [1939].

Atkinson, George W., ed. *Bench and Bar of West Virginia.* Charleston: Virginian Law Book Co., 1919.

Atkinson, George W., and Alvaro F. Gibbens. *Prominent Men of West Virginia.* Wheeling, WV: W. L. Callin, 1890.

Bishop, William H. *History of Roane County West Virginia from the Time of Its Exploration to A.D. 1927.* Spencer, WV: By the author, 1927.

Blair, William A. *With Malice toward Some: Treason and Loyalty in the Civil War Era.* Chapel Hill: Univ. of North Carolina Press, 2014.

Bosworth, Dr. A. S. *A History of Randolph County West Virginia from Its Earliest Settlement to the Present.* Elkins, WV: By the author, 1916.

Callahan, James Morton. *Semi-Centennial History of West Virginia.* Charleston: Semi-Centennial Commission of West Virginia, 1913.

Cartmell, T. K. *Shenandoah Valley Pioneers and Their Descendants: A History of Frederick County, Virginia (Illustrated), from Its Formation in 1738 to 1908.* Winchester, VA: By the author, 1909.

Chandler, Julian A. C. *Representation in Virginia. The Johns Hopkins University Studies in Historical and Political Science,* 14th series, edited by Herbert Baxter Adams and John Martin Vincent. Baltimore: Johns Hopkins Univ. Press, 1896.

Cranmer, Hon. Gibson Lamb, ed. and comp. *History of Wheeling City and Ohio County, West Virginia and Representative Citizens.* Chicago: Biographical Publishing Co., 1902.

Crawford, Martin. *Ashe County's Civil War: Community and Society in the Appalachian South.* Charlottesville: Univ. Press of Virginia, 2001.

Davis, Rebecca Harding. *Bits of Gossip.* New York: Houghton, Mifflin & Co., 1904.

Davis, William C., and James I. Robertson, eds. *Virginia at War, 1861.* Lexington: Univ. Press of Kentucky, 2005.

Dayton, Ruth Woods. *Samuel Woods and His Family.* Charleston, WV: By the author, 1939.

Ersland, Jack Ersland. *Civil War Provost Marshal Records: A Snapshot in Time.* Kansas City: National Archives and Records Administration, n.d.

Freehling, William W., and Craig M. Simpson, eds. *Showdown in Virginia: The 1861 Convention and the Fate of the Union.* Charlottesville: Univ. of Virginia Press, 2010.

Garrison, Webb. *Civil War Hostages: Hostage Taking in the Civil War.* Shippensburg, PA: White Mane Books, 2000.

Green, Fletcher Melvin. *Constitutional Development in the South Atlantic States, 1776–1860: A Study.* Chapel Hill: Univ. of North Carolina Press, 1930.

Groce, W. Todd. *Mountain Rebels: East Tennessee Confederates and the Civil War, 1860–1870.* Knoxville: Univ. of Tennessee Press, 1999.

Hall, Granville Davisson. *The Rending of Virginia, a History.* Glencoe, IL: By the author, 1902.

Haymond, Henry. *History of Harrison County West Virginia, from the Earliest Days to the Present.* Morgantown, WV: Acme Publishing Co., 1910.

Heinemann, Ronald L., John G. Kolp, Anthony S. Parent Jr., and William G. Shade. *Old Dominion, New Commonwealth: A History of Virginia, 1607–2007.* Charlottesville: Univ. of Virginia Press, 2007.

*The History of Daviess County, Missouri.* Kansas City: Birdsall & Dean, 1882.

Hornbeck, Betty. *Upshur Brothers of the Blue and the Gray.* Parsons, WV: McClain Printing Co., 1967.

Knotts, Robert J., Jr., and Robert E. Stevens. *Calhoun County in the Civil War.* Grantsville, WV: Calhoun County Historical & Genealogical Society, 1982. http://www.wvgenweb.org/calhoun/calhouncwbk/moc.htm.

Lawrence, George A. *Border and Bastille.* New York: W. I. Pooley & Co., [1863].

Lewis, Ronald L. *The Industrialist and the Mountaineer: The Eastham-Thompson Feud and the Struggle for West Virginia's Timber Frontier.* Morgantown: West Virginia Univ. Press, 2017.

Lewis, Virgil A., ed. *How West Virginia Was Made: Proceedings of the First Convention of the People of Northwestern Virginia at Wheeling, May, 13, 14 and 15, 1861 and the Journal of the Second Convention of the People of Northwestern Virginia at Wheeling.* Charleston: News-Mail Co., 1909.

*A List of Federal Prisoners Buried at Andersonville.* New York: Tribune Assoc., 1866.

Maxwell, Hu. *The History of Barbour County, West Virginia, from Its Earliest Exploration and Settlement to the Present Time.* Morgantown, WV: Acme Publishing Co., 1899.

———. *The History of Randolph County, West Virginia, from Its Earliest Settlement to the Present.* Morgantown, WV: Acme Publishing Co., 1898; repr., Parsons, WV: McClain Printing Co., 1961.

———. *History of Tucker County, West Virginia, from the Earliest Explorations and Settlements to the Present Time.* Kingwood, WV: Preston Publishing Co., 1884.

Maxwell, Hu, and Howard Llewellyn Swisher. *History of Hampshire County, West Virginia, from Its Earliest Settlement to the Present.* Morgantown, WV: A. Brown Boughner, 1897.

McPherson, James M. McPherson. *Battle Cry of Freedom: The Civil War Era.* New York: Oxford Univ. Press, 1988.

Mollohan, B. Marie. *By the Banks of the Holly: Notes and Letters from the Desk of Bernard Mollohan.* New York: iUniverse, 2005.

Morton, Oren F. *A History of Pendleton County West Virginia.* Franklin, WV: By the author, 1910.

Neely, Mark E., Jr. *The Fate of Liberty: Abraham Lincoln and Civil Liberties.* New York: Oxford Univ. Press, 1991.

Newton, J. H., A. G. Sprankle, and G. G. Nichols. *History of the Panhandle: Being Historical Collections of the Counties of Ohio, Brooke, Marshall and Hancock, West Virginia.* Wheeling, WV: J. A. Caldwell, 1879.

O'Ferrall, Charles T. *Forty Years of Active Service.* Washington, DC: Neale Publishing Co., 1904.

Paludan, Phillip Shaw. *Victims: A True Story of the Civil War.* Knoxville: Univ. of Tennessee Press, 1981.

Peirce, Neal R. *The Border South States: People, Politics, and Power in the Five Border South States.* New York: W. W. Norton & Co., 1975.

Randall, J. G., and David Herbert Donald. *The Civil War and Reconstruction.* 2nd ed. Lexington, MA: D. C. Heath & Co., 1969.

Ruffner, Rev. Henry, D. D. *Address to the People of West Virginia Shewing That Slavery Is Injurious to the Public Welfare, and That It May Be Gradually Abolished, without Detriment to the Rights and Interests of Slaveholders.* Lexington, VA: R. C. Noel, 1847.

Sarris, Jonathan Dean. *A Separate Civil War: Communities in Conflict in the Mountain South.* Charlottesville: Univ. of Virginia Press, 2006.

Shaffer, John W. *Clash of Loyalties: A Border County in the Civil War.* West Virginia and Appalachia 3. Morgantown: West Virginia Univ. Press, 2003.

———. *Union and Confederate Soldiers and Sympathizers of Barbour County, West Virginia.* Baltimore: Genealogical Publishing Co., 2005.

Stealey, John E., III. *West Virginia's Civil War–Era Constitution: Loyal Revolution, Confederate Counter-Revolution, and the Convention of 1872.* Kent, OH: Kent State Univ. Press, 2013.

Stutler, Boyd B. *West Virginia in the Civil War.* 2nd ed. Charleston: Education Foundation, 1966.

Summers, Festus P. *Johnson Newlon Camden: A Study in Individualism.* New York: G. P. Putnam's Sons, 1937.

Sutton, John Davison. *History of Braxton County and Central West Virginia.* Sutton, WV: By the author, 1919.

Taylor, Paul. *The Most Complete Political Machine Ever Known: The North's Union Leagues in the American Civil War.* Kent, OH: Kent State Univ. Press, 2020.

Thacker, Victor L., ed. *French Harding Civil War Memoirs.* Parsons, WV: McClain Printing Co., 2000.

Waller, Altina L. *Feud: Hatfields, McCoys, and Social Change in Appalachia, 1860–1900.* Chapel Hill: Univ. of North Carolina Press, 1988.

Wiley, Samuel T. *History of Monongalia County, West Virginia, from Its First Settlements to the Present Time.* Kingwood, WV: Preston Publishing Co., 1883.

———. *History of Preston County (West Virginia).* Assisted by A. W. Frederick. Kingwood, WV: Journal Printing House, 1882; repr., Parsons, WV: McClain Printing Co., 1968.

Williams, John Alexander. *West Virginia: A Bicentennial History.* New York: W. W. Norton & Co. and Nashville: American Assoc. for State and Local History, 1976.
Wingerter, Charles A., ed. *History of Greater Wheeling and Vicinity: A Chronicle of Progress and a Narrative Account of the Industries, Institutions and People of the City and Tributary Territory.* 2 vols. New York: Lewis Publishing Co., 1912.
Wittenberg, Eric J., Edmund A. Sargus Jr., and Penny Barrick. *Seceding from Secession: The Civil War, Politics, and the Creation of West Virginia.* El Dorado Hills, CA: Savas Beatie, 2020.

## CHAPTERS IN BOOKS

Fones-Wolf, Ken. "A House Redivided: From Sectionalism to Political Economy in West Virginia." In *Reconstructing Appalachia: The Civil War's Aftermath,* edited by Andrew L. Slap, 237–68. Lexington: Univ. Press of Kentucky, 2010.
Gooden, Randall S. "Neither War nor Peace: West Virginia's Reconstruction Experience." In *Reconstructing Appalachia: The Civil War's Aftermath,* edited by Andrew L. Slap, 211–36. Lexington: Univ. Press of Kentucky, 2010.
Inscoe, John C. "A Northern Wedge Thrust into the Heart of the Confederacy: Explaining Civil War Loyalties in the Age of Appalachian Discovery, 1900–1921." In Slap, *Reconstructing Appalachia,* 323–48.
Sandow, Robert M. "Grudges and Loyalties Die So Slowly: Contested Memories of the Civil War in Pennsylvania's Appalachia." In Slap, *Reconstructing Appalachia,* 269–92.
Stewart, Bruce E. "Introduction." In *Blood in the Hills: A History of Violence in Appalachia,* edited by Bruce E. Stewart, 1–24. New Directions in Southern History Series. Lexington: Univ. Press of Kentucky, 2012.

## JOURNALS

Bean, W. G. "John Letcher and the Slavery Issue in Virginia's Gubernatorial Contest of 1858–1859." *The Journal of Southern History* 20, no. 1 (Feb. 1954): 22–49.
Bright, Simeon Miller. "McNeill's Rangers: A Study in Confederate Guerrilla Warfare." *West Virginia History* 12, no. 4 (July 1951): 338–87.
Cone, Jason, and Francoise Duroch. "Don't Shoot the Ambulance: Medicine in the Crossfire." *World Policy Journal* 30, no. 3 (Fall 2013): 65–77.
Gaskins, Avery F. "An Introduction to the Guineas: West Virginia's Melungeons." *Appalachian Journal* 1, no. 3 (Autumn 1973): 234–37.
Hammer, Ellen, and Marina Salvin. "The Taking of Hostages in Theory and Practice." *The American Journal of International Law* 38, no. 1 (Jan. 1944): 20–33.
Herrmann, Irene, and Daniel Palmieri. "A Haunting Figure: The Hostage through the Ages." *International Review of the Red Cross* 87, no. 857 (Mar. 2005): 135–45.
Igler, David. "Captive-Taking and Conventions of Encounters on the Northwest Coast, 1789–1810." *Southern California Quarterly* 91, no. 1 (Spring 2009): 3–25.
Majewski, John. "The Political Impact of Great Commercial Cities: State Investment in Antebellum Pennsylvania and Virginia." *The Journal of Interdisciplinary History* 28, no. 1 (Summer 1997): 1–26.
McKinney, Gordon B. "Women's Role in Civil War North Carolina." *The North Carolina Historical Review* 69, no. 1 (Jan. 1992): 37–56.

Moscovich, M. James. "Hostage Regulations in the Treaty of Zama." *Historia Zeitschrift fur Alte Geschichte* 23, no. 4 (4th qtr., 1974): 417–27.

———. "Obsidibus Traditis: Hostages in Caesar's De Bello Gallico." *The Classical Journal* 75, no. 2 (Dec. 1979–Jan. 1980): 122–28.

Sutherland, Daniel E. "Guerrilla Warfare, Democracy, and the Fate of the Confederacy." *The Journal of Southern History* 68, no. 2 (May 2002): 259–92.

Yang, Lien-Sheng. "Hostages in Chinese History." *Harvard Journal of Asiatic Studies* 15, no. 3–4 (Dec. 1952): 507–21.

## ELECTRONIC JOURNALS

Jones, Rev. J. William, ed. *Southern Historical Society Papers* 36 (1908). https://www.perseus.tufts.edu/hopper/text?doc=Perseus%3Atext%3A2001.05.0294%3Achapter%3D1.28.

Shaffer, John W. "Loyalties in Conflict: Union and Confederate Sentiment in Barbour County." *West Virginia History* 50 (1991). http://www.wvculture.org/history/journal_wvh/wvh50-7.html.

## MAGAZINES

Hutton, Henry C., comp. "Roster of Confederate Veterans from Randolph County." *Magazine of History and Biography by the Randolph County Historical Society*, Apr. 1961.

"Virginia Illustrated: Adventures of Porte Crayon and His Cousins." *Harper's New Monthly Magazine*, Aug. 1856.

"The Wheeling Convention," *Harper's Weekly*, July 6, 1861.

## ONLINE MAGAZINES

Perkins, Marlitta H. "Guerrilla Chieftain 'Rebel Bill' Smith, CSA." *Eastern Kentucky and the Civil War*. http://eakycivilwar.blogspot.com/2010/07/captain-rebel-bill-smith-csa.html.

## NEWSPAPERS

*Abingdon Virginian*
*Alexandria (VA) Gazette*
*Annapolis Maryland Gazette*
*Calhoun Chronicle* (Grantsville, WV)
*Charles Town Virginia Free Press*
*Charleston West Virginia Journal*
*Columbus Ohio Statesman*
*Cooper's Clarksburg (VA) Register*
*Glasgow (MO) Weekly Times*
*Hillsborough (OH) Highland News*

*Knapsack* (Gauley Bridge, WV)
*Leesburg (VA) Genius of Liberty*
*Martinsburg (VA) Gazette*
*Morgantown (WV) Monitor*
*New York Herald*
*Point Pleasant (VA) Weekly Register*
*Potter Journal* (Coudersport, PA)
*Pruntytown (VA) Family Visitor*
*Richmond Daily Dispatch*
*Richmond Enquirer*
*Richmond Whig*
*Richmond Whig and Commercial Journal*
*Soldier's Journal* (Alexandria, VA)
*South Branch Intelligencer* (Romney, VA–WV)
*Staunton (VA) Spectator*
*Staunton (VA) Spectator and General Advertiser*
*Washington Evening Star*
*Weston (WV) Democrat*
*Wheeling Daily Intelligencer*
*Wheeling Daily Register*
*Wheeling Register*

## THESES AND DISSERTATIONS

Gooden, Randall S. "The Completion of a Revolution: West Virginia from Statehood through Reconstruction." PhD diss., West Virginia University, 1995.

Woodward, Isaiah Alfonso. "Arthur Ingraham Boreman: A Biography." PhD diss., West Virginia University, 1970.

## MANUSCRIPT COLLECTIONS

Arthur I. Boreman Papers, West Virginia and Regional History Center, West Virginia Univ., Morgantown, WV

Diary and Letters of Rutherford B. Hayes, vol. 2, 1861–1865, Rutherford B. Hayes Presidential Library and Museums Digital Collection, Ohio Memory, https://www.ohiomemory.org/digital/collection/p16007coll67/id/2380/rec/2

Francis H. Pierpont Papers, West Virginia Dept. of Archives and History, Charleston, WV

Francis H. Pierpont Papers, West Virginia and Regional History Center, West Virginia Univ., Morgantown, WV

## REFERENCE WORKS

*Encyclopedia Virginia.* S.v. "The Virginia Slavery Debate of 1831–1832" (by Erik S. Root). Edited by Virginia Humanities in cooperation with Library of Virginia. https://www.encyclopediavirginia.org/Virginia_Slavery_Debate_of_1831-1832_The#start_entry.

*The West Virginia Encyclopedia.* S.v. "Atheneum Prison" (by Margaret Brennan). Edited by Ken Sullivan. Charleston: West Virginia Humanities Council, 1906.

## PUBLIC DOCUMENTS

Hening, William Waller, ed. *The Statutes at Large: Being a Collection of All the Laws of Virginia, from the First Session of the Legislature, in the Year 1619.* 13 vols. New York: By the editor, 1819–23.

US Congress. *Congressional Globe.* 46 vols. Washington: Blair & Rives, 1834–73.

US Dept. of War, comp. *The War of the Rebellion.* H. R. Doc. 284, 55th Cong., 3rd sess. Washington: Government Printing Office: 1899.

Virginia. General Assembly, House of Delegates. *Journal of the House of Delegates of the State of Virginia for the Session of 1852.* Richmond: William F. Ritchie, 1852.

———. *Proceedings and Debates of the Virginia State Convention of 1829–30.* Richmond: Ritchie & Cook, 1830.

Virginia (US). *Acts of the General Assembly of the State of Virginia Passed at the Extra Session Commenced December 4, 1862 in the 87th Year of the Commonwealth.* Wheeling: John F. M'Dermot, 1863.

———. General Assembly, House of Delegates. *Journal of the House of Delegates, of the Commonwealth of Virginia, Extra Session, Held in the City of Wheeling, on Thursday, December the 4th, 1862.* Wheeling: A. S. Trowbridge, 1862.

———. General Assembly. *Journal of the Senate of the Commonwealth of Virginia, Extra Session, Held in the City of Wheeling, on Thursday, December the 4th, 1862.* Wheeling: A. S. Trowbridge, 1862.

West Virginia. *Acts of the Legislature of West Virginia at Its Sixth Session Commencing January 21st, 1868.* Wheeling: John Frew, 1868.

———. County of Ohio. Circuit Court. Law Trial Docket (1867–1869). West Virginia and Regional History Center, West Virginia Univ., Morgantown, WV.

———. Office of Adjutant General. Adjutant General's Papers. West Virginia Dept. of Archives and History, Charleston, WV. http://www.wvculture.org/history/ag/militia/gilmer/gilmer15-06.html.

## PUBLIC DOCUMENTS ONLINE

### UNITED STATES

———. Civil War Prisoner of War Records, 1861–1865. Ancestry.com, https://www.ancestrylibrary.com/.

———. Compiled Service Records of Volunteer Union Soldiers Who Served in Organizations from the State of Virginia, National Archives and Records Administration. https://www.fold3.com/.

———. Internal Revenue Assessment Lists for West Virginia, 1862–1866. National Archives Microfilm Publication M795, 4 rolls. Records of the Internal Revenue Service, Record Group 58. The National Archives at Washington, DC. Ancestry.com, https://www.ancestrylibrary.com/.

———. "United States Census, 1850." Database with images. FamilySearch, https://familysearch.org/ark:/61903/3:1:33SQ-GBSN-93C?cc=1473181&wc=7QK5-TZ3%3A1589436503%2C1589422256%2C1589422206.

———. "United States Census, 1860." Database with images. FamilySearch, https://familysearch.org/.

———. "United States Census, 1870." Database with images. FamilySearch, https://familysearch.org//search/record/results?givenname=Adam&surname.=See&birth_place=Virginia&birth_year_from=1800&birth_year_to=1840&record_country=United%20States&record_subcountry=United%20States%2CWest%20Virginia.

———. Union Provost Marshals' Papers, 1861–1867. Ancestry.com, https://www.ancestrylibrary.com/.

———. "United States Records of Confederate Prisoners of War." RG 109 War Department Collection of Confederate Records. NARA Publication M598. National Archives and Records Administration, Washington, DC. https://www.familysearch.org/ark:/61903/3:1:33SQ-G5MK-JT4?i=239&wc=M8VN-C38%3A203215501%2C203253501&cc=1916234.

———. "United States Union Provost Marshal Files of Individual Civilians, 1861–1866." NARA Publication M345. National Archives and Records Administration, Washington, DC. https://www.familysearch.org/ark:/61903/3:1:939X-2R97-X8?i=497&wc=M6YL-KNL%3A162464801&cc=1834304.

———. "United States Union Provost Marshals' File of Papers Relating to Individual Civilians." https://www.familysearch.org/ark:/61903/3:1:939X-2T96-GF?i=610&wc=M6YL-2Z9%3A162470001&cc=18343043:1:939X-2T96-GF?i=610&wc=M6YL-2Z9%3A162470001&cc=1834304.

———. "United States Union Provost Marshal Files of Two or More Civilians, 1861–1866." NARA Publication M416. National Archives and Records Administration, Washington, DC. https://www.familysearch.org.

US Congress. Treaty with the Six Nations: 1784. The Avalon Project: Documents in Law, History and Diplomacy. Lilian Goldman Law Library, Yale Univ. Law School. https://avalon.law.yale.edu/18th_century/six1784.asp.

US Dept. of War. General Orders No. 100: The Lieber Code. The Avalon Project: Documents in Law, History and Diplomacy. Lillian Goldman Law Library, Yale Law School. http://avalon.law.yale.edu/19th_century/lieber.asp.

## DATABASES

Ancestry.com, https://www.ancestrylibrary.com/

CWSAC Battle Summaries, http://www.nps.gov/abpp/battles/

Family Search, https://www.familysearch.org/

Find a Grave, https://www.findagrave.com/

United States Civil War Soldiers Index, 1861–1865, Family Search, https://www.familysearch.org/

US IRS Tax Assessment Lists, 1862–1918 for LD Dolbeare. Ancestry.com, https://www.ancestrylibrary.com/

US School Catalogs, 1765–1935 for LD Dolbeare. Ancestry.com, https://www.ancestrylibrary.com/

USGW Archives. http://files.usgwarchives.net/

# Index